MANAGING BUDGETS AND FINANCES

A How-To-Do-It Manual
for Librarians and
Information Professionals

Arlita W. Hallam
Teresa R. Dalston

**HOW-TO-DO-IT MANUAL
FOR LIBRARIANS**

NUMBER 138

NEAL-SCHUMAN PUBLISHERS, INC.
New York, London

Published by Neal-Schuman Publishers, Inc.
100 William Street, Suite 2004
New York, NY 10038

Printed and bound in the United States of America

The paper used in this publication meets the minimum requirements of American National Standard for Information Sciences—Permanence of Paper for Printed Library Materials. ANSI Z39.48-1992. ∞

Library of Congress Cataloging-in-Publication Data

Hallam, Arlita.
    Managing budgets and finances : a how-to-do-it manual for librarians and information professionals / by Arlita W. Hallam and Teresa R. Dalston.
        p.   cm.— (How-to-do-it manuals for librarians ; no. 138)
    Includes bibliographical references and index.
    ISBN 1-55570-519-7
    1. Library finance—United States—Handbooks, manuals, etc.   I. Dalston, Teresa R., 1965–   II. Title.   III. How-to-do-it manuals for libraries ; no. 138.
    Z683.2.U6H355 2005
    0.25.1'1—dc22   2004024707

To my perfect husband, Don, and my wonderful library management students in the School of Library and Information Sciences at the University of North Texas.
Arlita Hallam

To my loving and patient parents, Daniel and Dorina.
Teri Dalston

CONTENTS

LIST OF FIGURES

PREFACE

There was a time, in the 1960s and 1970s, when budgeting was quite simple. In the "good old days," each line item of the library budget increased by 10 to 15 percent each year and the librarian figured out how to spend it. If there was a windfall, or an additional funding source (such as revenue sharing), then totally new projects could be planned and funded. Libraries circulated everything—art prints, sculpture, garden tools, calculators, and all kinds of equipment.

Then came the 1980s, with recessions and layoffs and budget cuts. Budgeting became a longer and more arduous process, and financial planning and forecasting became essential skills.

Today budgets are cut more frequently (sometimes even during the fiscal year) than they are increased. Budget time is not as much fun as it once was, when librarians thumbed through catalogs looking for new things to buy and new projects to implement. Now, we must forecast more closely, budget more frugally, plan better, stretch staffing and materials further, and still anticipate and meet increased demands for library and information center services.

Managing Budgets and Finances: A How-To-Do-It Manual for Librarians and Information Professionals serves today's practicing librarian, board member, financial manager, or information professional who needs to meet new demands—needs to learn a new budget format; decide whether to outsource a service; solicit an RFP, RFI, or RFQ; maintain a facility; handle a capital project; or seek alternative funding through foundations or grants. Because this book stems from our search for a textbook for our graduate course, Financial Management for Libraries and Information Agencies, it also meets the needs of students or professionals just beginning their careers in librarianship or information studies.

ORGANIZATION

Managing Budgets and Finances takes a thorough look at the budgeting process for libraries. It explains the core elements and provides the guidance that managers need to put it all together. Because budgeting is best learned by doing, helpful checklists, examples, scenarios, forms, and other hands-on materials are included throughout the text.

Part I, "Budgeting Basics for Libraries," examines the basic elements of library budgets—what they are, how they are created, and how they are managed. Since many libraries spend as much as two-thirds of the year working on their budget, it is important that managers understand these basics.

Chapter 1, "What Is a Budget?", explains where library money comes from, the various models by which it is allotted, and the key terms used in the process.

Chapter 2, "How Do Libraries Budget?", looks at the components of a library budget, planning and scheduling systems, and the steps toward finalization and adoption.

Chapter 3, "How Can a Library Monitor Its Budget?", outlines the day-to-day maintenance of the plan, the tracking of orders and bills, and adjusting to increases or decreases in funds.

Part II, "Special Topics in Financial Management for Libraries," guides readers through the additional considerations that affect library budgets. Libraries, like so many other institutions, experience multiple factors that can either help or hurt their operations. Chapters in Part II help inform and prepare managers for these elements.

Chapter 4, "Outsourcing," discusses one of the most controversial issues affecting libraries today. This chapter looks at both the positive and negative effects of outsourcing, its impact on finances, its strategic use in libraries, and the means by which managers determine whether to include it in their institutions.

Chapter 5, "Protecting Library Property," takes Ben Franklin's famous advice, "A penny saved is a penny earned," and applies it to libraries. Having spent their money on various resources and property, managers now need to look at how those products will be preserved, including the recovery of library materials, policies dealing with theft and mutilation, the proper selling or disposal of public property, the installation of security systems, insurance coverage, and planning for emergencies or disaster. This chapter also looks at the traditional fines and penalties charged for overdue materials as well as new revenue streams generated by fee-based services, and considers how they supplement budgets.

Chapter 6, "Capital Projects," provides guidance for managing major expenditures—new buildings, renovations, expansions—over several years. The process is followed from the initial needs assessment, through budgeting, and into the referenda or bond campaigns that award funds. This is a topic that some managers may only experience once in their careers—but it is an experience that requires special planning and guidance.

Chapter 7, "Contracts and RFPs," explores the planning, consideration, and selection of vendors, consultants, and other collaborators. This chapter shows how to analyze the proposal, compare bid responses, and award the contract.

Part III, "Alternative Library Funding," helps managers solicit outside funders and incorporate them into planning and budgeting.

Chapter 8, "Funding Sources," covers special scenarios, including library foundations and friends groups, trusts and wills, endowments, and gifts and donations. It also offers best practices for donor relations, gift accounting, and the use and recognition of volunteers.

Chapter 9, "Grants for Libraries," looks at one of the major sources from which libraries receive funding to provide services. This chapter lists grant-funding sources and outlines the steps to requesting, receiving, and administering a grant.

Readers will find practical tools and samples in the appendices of *Managing Budgets and Finances*, including an accounting manual outline, a library annual report form, a RFP for a building consultant, a lease agreement, and advice from a successful fundraiser on starting a major donor program.

Managing Budgets and Finances: A How-To-Do-It Manual for Librarians and Information Professionals is designed to be a straightforward, holistic look at budgeting. Upon completion of this book, you will have a basic understanding of, and will know how to perform, the following tasks:

- Create and manage a budget for a library or other information agency.
- Understand the fiscal aspects of managing a facility.
- Decide which services should be contracted or outsourced.
- Realize the stewardship responsibilities of public property management.
- Identify alternative funding sources.
- Prepare a grant proposal.
- Comprehend the financial issues of capital campaigns.

More to the point, it is our hope that librarians faced with their first budget challenges—as well as students looking to assume management positions—will walk away from reading this book with a greater knowledge of the importance, practice, and responsibility involved in library finance.

BUDGETING BASICS FOR LIBRARIES

1 WHAT IS A BUDGET?

OVERVIEW

A budget is a planning document in which you record your best guess of how to pay for the expenses that you anticipate for a given year—taking into consideration the amount and sources of available funds. In this chapter, you will review the key financial management concepts necessary to design a budget and set up the budgeting process. A well-defined budget process will address many fundamental budgeting tasks and establish the budget as a communication and planning tool.

Libraries use a variety of budget types, each with varying levels of control and complexity. This chapter provides an overview of the basic budgetary formats and examples of the following types of budgets: lump sum, formula, line-item, program, performance, PPBS (planning, programming, budgeting system), zero-based, and responsibility-centered budgets. Each type is suited to a particular situation, and you will learn the inherent strengths and weaknesses of each type.

The chapter concludes with a review of essential terms critical to understanding the budget process: Budgeting Lingo A–Z. Each discipline has its own language, and financial management is no exception. By the end of the chapter you will become familiar with the basic terminology of financial management, review a checklist of tasks in the budgeting process, study several fundamental financial management tools, and assemble the basic building blocks for planning your own library of financial procedures. These will enable you to gain a firm foundation on which to define your own budgetary process and to select the tools that best fit your library's needs.

A useful community needs assessment answers key questions.

- How well is the collection being used?
- Where are the gaps in the collection?
- Who uses the library?
- How can the library reach nonusers?
- How successful are library services?
- How can they be improved to reflect the community's needs?
- Are the space and physical building adequate for providing library services and meeting other community needs?
- Where does the user community stand demographically (e.g., socioeconomic status)? What does that mean for library programming?
- Are staffing patterns and library hours adequate?

For a more extensive discussion of how to conduct an analysis, see "Community Needs Assessment," www.lib.az.us/cdt/comm-needs.htm.

HOW DOES THE BUDGET PROCESS BEGIN?

The budget process begins with a community needs analysis to determine what products and services your institution wants or needs to provide to the community it serves. What services and programs does the community want the library to offer? How much do those services and programs cost? What lesser-used programs might be dropped in favor of those that are now in demand? What revenues are anticipated? How is the community changing?

The needs assessment will reveal whether the library is meeting the needs of the community's residents. It will also show needs that are not being met in the community and may even result in some partnerships for potential joint-service delivery.

DESIGNING A BUDGET AND A BUDGET PROCESS

Budgeting is the process of estimating the revenues that will be available for spending in a given fiscal year and then planning how to spend them. The completed budget records these estimates and serves as your guide during the year. The more accurate the estimate of revenues and costs, the less you will need to revise the budget during the process.

MAINTAINING AN ACCOUNTING PROCEDURES MANUAL

You can never underestimate the importance of financial accountability and the open communication of financial plans. This is why you should always maintain an accounting procedures manual that will record both financial management procedures and the reasoning behind the procedures. This manual extends the community-needs analysis by placing the findings into the context of your institution's mission, financial management goals, fiscal responsibilities, and established financial management practices. The accounting procedures manual provides continuity and makes it possible to codify duties efficiently. See Appendix A for a sample accounting procedures manual outline.

BUDGETARY SOURCES

Initially, you may be tempted to simply base your budget on last year's revenues and expenditures. Remember that many variables might cause those older budget figures to be inaccurate. Has your institution experienced:

- a raising or lowering of the tax base (value of property taxed for the support of the library)?
- building expenditures with increased costs for staffing, utilities, and so on?
- increased benefits to staff?
- changes in staffing and related costs?
- the additional cost of offering new services?
- increased or decreased grants and alternative income?
- a change in priorities that shifts the focus of the budget to meet new community needs?

BUDGET TYPES

Library managers are likely to encounter many types of budgets. This is a list of the most common types and what best characterizes each. Read the descriptions in the following sections to learn the differences between these methods and their advantages and disadvantages.

- lump sum—total only
- formula—prioritized standards
- line item—categorization
- program—library program centered
- performance—library functions centered
- PPBS (planning, programming, budgeting systems)—program + performance
- zero based—substantiate
- responsibility centered—department centered

Checklist: Steps to Budgeting

1. Identify the person who will coordinate the budgeting process and will train key staff in methods, definitions, and document formats; assign responsibilities; and communicate deadlines.
2. Analyze yearly operational objectives and service goals with the help of staff recommendations.
3. Align objectives and goals with long-term strategic plans, staffing requirements, and initial budget estimates.
4. Prioritize services and goals in order to construct budget details.
5. Determine the total financial resources necessary, and document assumptions and budget formulas.
6. Compile and distribute draft budget to staff and revise as required.
7. Begin the budget approval (notification of public hearing and negotiations) and/or revision process.
8. Secure budget approval and ensure revenues.
9. Keep meticulous records. (Good bookkeeping makes accurate accounting possible.)
10. Assess the environment and adapt the budget as necessary.
11. Revise budget and secure additional funds as required.

LUMP-SUM BUDGET

If you use lump-sum budgeting, your library receives a certain amount of funds from the funding source, and the board or librarian decides how to allocate the funds and develops a budget. Grants or endowments may be awarded as lump-sum gifts, and, as the recipient, the library decides how to allocate the funds. Usually grants require a budget as part of the application process and a financial report of how the funds were expended at the end of the grant.

Today's site-based school management and pilot programs frequently have lump-sum budgets. Even some university libraries are awarded lump-sum amounts and have authority over how those funds are spent.

Advantage of a Lump-Sum Budget

With a lump-sum budget, the library staff (or the board) has the flexibility to move funds where they are needed.

Disadvantage of a Lump-Sum Budget

Lump-sum budgets can lead to a lack of accountability and vision. Long-term strategic budgeting mandates "budgeting around a plan" rather than just "planning around a budget." In other words, you want a budget that follows a plan, not a plan the follows the budget.

FORMULA BUDGET

If you are in an academic setting, you may use a formula budget; that is where this type of budget is most frequently found. Library funds are allocated according to the number of undergraduate, master's, or doctoral students; the population of the community; the size of the materials budget; the average school attendance; or other formulas. Within the formula budget, another formula may allocate portions of the library budget to the departmental materials budgets of different departments or schools. These allocations are based on the percentage of the university's students that are in that department or school, or, for example, if you are in an elementary school, the percentage of the district's elementary students attending that school.

Advantages of a Formula Budget

Formula budgets respond to growth and reductions in number (of students, financial resources, populations, etc.), and the budget expenditures can generally be allocated with flexibility when the formula funding arrives.

Disadvantages of a Formula Budget

These same advantages can easily become disadvantages when use of a service in a formula-funded area decreases (even if the costs for providing that service have increased), or if the governing authorities decide to allocate the formula funding to a different area from that funded by the formula the prior year.

LINE-ITEM BUDGET

You might automatically picture a line-item budget when you hear the word *budget*. There is a line for each revenue or expenditure, and the separate amounts—revenues or expenditures—are each entered on a separate line. The format frequently follows the numbering system and account headings of the chart of accounts (the list of every item that the accounting system tracks; see "Budgeting Lingo A–Z" in this chapter). Usually you cannot move funds from one line to another without the approval of your governing authority. Consequently, you might have money left in one line item while you actually need it for another. So, for example, there may be money left in printing, but it can't be used for postage; or there is money in the book budget, but there are no funds left for processing supplies. One of the authors remembers flying to Chicago from Springfield, Illinois, to pick up state paychecks because her agency had no money in the postage account, but still had funds in the travel account. However, some governing authorities permit a variance of 10 percent or so in a line item as long as the bottom line of the budget does not change.

Advantages of a Line-Item Budget

It is easy to construct a line-item budget and follow it from year to year because it is merely based on the previous year's funding. Usually you can justify adding a percentage that represents the normal increase in expenses (increases in health care costs, utilities, the cost of journals, etc.) to each line.

Disadvantages of a Line-Item Budget

When you use a line-item budget, the governing authority can easily apply across-the-board cuts that may have no relationship to actual library programs, needs, or services (e.g., cutting the equipment budget by 10 percent may mean that you cannot afford the one piece of equipment that was to be purchased with that money). It is also difficult to add lines to the budget for new services or to change a line item. So, for example, you might have a line for microfilm, but not a line for databases. Furthermore, line-item budgets do not show the cost of individual library programs or services.

I always kept an information sheet (updated annually) for each branch in the library system and had it with me at budget hearings. Then, when someone suggested cutting a branch, I could quote that the branch was used X times last year by X people who checked out X materials, asked X reference questions, and attended X programs at an average cost of X cents per transaction . . . and that the total branch budget was X (X percent of the library's budget). Closing a branch was never worth the sacrifice to so many patrons for such a small amount of money. —Dr. Arlita Hallam

A zealous council member may push to cut the travel line, not realizing that the travel budget also includes the outreach librarian's visits to the nursing facility where the council member's mother lives.

The U.S. Office of Management and Budget Standard Form 424A (SF424A, or the Federal Budget Information Form) uses the line-item format found at www.whitehouse.gov/omb/grants/index.html. Figure 1-1 is an example of the SF424A form. This example is taken from instructions offered by the U.S. Department of Health and Human Services Administration on Aging (AOA) Office of Grants Management. Figure 1-2 illustrates a model line-item grants budget; the figure is taken from Daniel Barber's highly regarded book.

Most enlightened budget managers realize that in a library setting, a line-item budget does not tell them anything. When fiscal authorities are looking for something to cut, they look for the low-hanging fruit, such as travel, training, or equipment, without realizing the consequences of the cuts.

If you are a manager working with a mandated line-item budget reporting system, perhaps the best approach is to work on defining the line items as broadly as possible so that you have the greatest versatility in spending. Then supplement the budget with facts, statistical data, and other budget tools. The line-item budget does not tie costs to services; however, program budgets, zero-based budgets, and performance budgets do. These other budget forms enable financial managers and fiscal authorities to see the impact of closing a branch, discontinuing a program, or outsourcing a service because all costs are listed with that program.

By supplementing the required line-item budget with these more robust financial tools, you can provide some eye-opening information that will be useful for making important administrative decisions so that you are not forced into an uninformed decision, either on your own or at the behest of the governing authority. Even if a library's governing authority continues to use a line-item budget, it is a good idea to develop an internal program or performance-based budget for accurate cost accounting.

PROGRAM BUDGET

A program budget ties all costs to programs, so if a program is added or deleted all of the related costs are added or deleted. Program budgets are difficult to set up at first, but you will find that they are fairly easy to maintain as long as you track the cost categories. If the total expense is tied to the program (branch, bookmobile, DVD collection), then you will have all of the related expenses together when deciding to add or drop a program. When costs are split (for example, 25 percent of the cost of the children's librarian for outreach goes to day care centers, 10 percent of library administration costs are spread among ten programs, the delivery truck driver is also a custodian, or all full-time staff take turns covering Sunday hours),

AOA instructions for completing standard forms 424 and 424A.

Object Class Category	Federal Funds	Nonfederal Cash	Nonfederal In-Kind	TOTAL	Justification
Personnel	$40,000		$5,000	$45,000	Project Supervisor (name)=.3FTE @ $50,000/yr=$15,000 Project Director (name) = 1FTE @ $30,000 =$30,000
Fringe Benefits	$12,600	0	0	$12,600	Fringes on Supervisor and Director @ 28% of salary. FICA (7.65%) = $3,442 Health (12%) = $5,400 Dental (5%) = $2,250 Life (2%) = $ 900 Workers Comp Insurance (.75%) = $ 338 Unemployment Insurance (.6%) = $ 270
Travel	$3,000	0	$967	$3,967	Travel to Annual Grantee Meeting: Airfare: 1 RT×2 people×$750/RT = $1,500 Lodging: 3 nights×2 people×$100/night = $ 600 Per Diem: 4 days×2 people×$40/day = $ 320 Out-of-Town Project Site Visits Car mileage: 3 trips×2 people×350 miles/trip×$.365/mile = $767 Lodging: 3 trips×2 people×1 night/trip×$50/night = $300 Per Diem: 3 trips×2 people×2 days/trip×$40/day = $480
Equipment	0	0	0	0	No equipment requested
Supplies	$1,500		$2,000	$3,500	Laptop computer for use in client intakes = $1,340 Consumable supplies (paper, pens, etc.) $100/mo×12 months = $1,200 Copying $80/mo×12 months = $ 960

Contractual	$200,000	$50,000	0	$250,000	Contracts to A,B,C direct service providers (name providers)
					  adult day care contractor = $75,000
					  respite care contractor in home = $75,000
					  respite care contractor—NF = $50,000
					  personal care/companion provider = $50,000
					
					See detailed budget justification for each provider
					(and then provide it!)

Other	$10,000	$8,000	$19,800	$37,800	Local conference registration fee (name conference) =$ 200
					Printing brochures (50,000 @ $.05 ea) = $ 2,500
					Video production = $19,800
					Video reproduction = $ 3,500
					NF Respite Training Manual reproduction
					  $3/manual×2000 manuals = $ 6,000
					Postage $150/month×12 months = $ 1,800
					Caregiver Forum meeting room rentals
					  $200/day×12 forums = $ 2,400
					Respite Training Scholarships = $ 1,600

Indirect Charges	0	0	0	0	None
TOTAL	$265,700	$60,800	$27,767	$354,267	

Figure 1-1. Line-item Budget from Office of Grants Management

LINE ITEM	DONATED	REQUESTED	TOTAL
Executive director ($40,000 annual)	$10,000 (25%)	$30,000 (75%)	$40,000
Project coordinator(s) (2) ($25,000 per person)		$50,000	$50,000
Fiscal officer		$30,000	$30,000
Accountant (10 days @ $300)	$3,000		$3,000
Communications		$3,400	$3,400
Travel		$2,225	$2,225
Desktop consumables	$1,000	$1,000	$2,000
Outside services (printing, data analysis)	$2,000	$4,500	$6,500
SUBTOTAL	$16,000	$121,125	$137,125
Indirect costs (overhead)	$41,138	$13,712	$54,850
TOTAL	$57,138	$134,837	$191,975

Figure 1-2. Model Line-item Grant Budget

Source: This budget is an example of a line-item budget for a grant proposal presented in Daniel M. Barber. *Finding Funding: The Comprehensive Guide to Grant Writing,* 2nd Edition. Long Beach, CA: Bond Street Publishers, 2002.

it is harder to get a true cost or realize a savings when the program is deleted. In a program-budget scenario, it is important that you keep records of all program statistics documenting usage (program attendance, reference questions answered, circulation, Internet log-ons, etc.) to justify the library system's continuing to provide these programs.

Advantages of a Program Budget

Program budgets are closely tied to the mission, goals, and objectives of the library. Total costs for programs are kept together, so cost accounting is easier and nonproductive programs can be easily identified.

Disadvantages of a Program Budget

Everything must be quantified and tied to a program, so administrative and overhead costs are sometimes prorated throughout the organization. Programs that are not cost effective but are "good for the community" (such as branches in ethnic neighborhoods, preschool story times for migrant children, and deliveries to homebound patrons) may be vulnerable at budget-cutting time.

Classifying programs is unique to each library system. Figure 1-3 shows a sample program taxonomy from the State of Wisconsin's Department of Public Instruction.

In figure 1-4 you see an example of a program budget for a six-week summer accelerated-reader program. In this program, children read library books at or above their reading level; pass an accompanying test; and win one-, two-, and three-dollar achievement awards, hence the name *Earning by Learning*.

You can easily turn this *program budget* into a *performance budget* (see the next section) by adding the numbers of children participating at each level in order to do a cost analysis of the program.

PERFORMANCE BUDGET

With a performance-based budget, you tie the library's functions to various performance indicators. For example, the reference budget may include indicators such as the number of students who receive bibliographic instruction, number of telephone reference questions, accuracy of answers given, number of databases accessed, and so forth. You can divide the number of items cataloged by the number of catalogers, you can divide technical services costs by the number of items processed to obtain a per-unit cost, costs per circulation can be used to justify a self-check-out/self-check-in system, and so on.

You can convert a program budget to a performance budget fairly easily, as shown in figures 1-5a and 1-5b. Figure 1-5a shows a program budget for a teen library center that is to be established at the local shopping mall with floor space provided by the mall owners. Figure 1-5b shows this same program budget after it has been converted to a performance budget. The program budget lists the cost for each item (personnel and nonpersonnel) in the program, while the performance budget shows the calculated amount for each activity or function in the same program.

Advantage of a Performance Budget

A performance-based budget makes it very easy to track the cost of each library service and its efficiency.

Disadvantage of a Performance Budget

The performance budget has been criticized for emphasizing economy over service. It is important to be careful that the maintenance of statistics does not overshadow the reasons for tracking the performance.

One of the authors remembers costing interlibrary loan in the olden days and discovering that it cost $33 to borrow a book for a patron. We instituted a policy so that if we had to borrow the material twice, we bought it (if possible). It was too expensive to keep borrowing the same thing over and over.

We costed the preschool story time and discovered that it cost about $77 per year per child. No one wanted to drop it, but at least we knew the cost.

We decided to outsource the repair of audiovisual materials after discovering that our full-time MLS librarian, who was splicing tapes, could be more effectively used in the children's department where we needed more staff—and there was a local vendor who would splice tapes for $1 each.

The public library system annual plan includes a program budget that allocates all funding available to the public library system in the plan year by program category and funding source.

Program categories:

❏   Technology, reference, and interlibrary loan services

❏   Continuing education and consulting services

❏   Delivery services

❏   Library services to special users

❏   Library collection development

❏   Direct payments to member libraries for county nonresident access and for nonresident crossover access

❏   Direct payments for service provided across system borders

❏   Library services to youth

❏   Public information

❏   Administration

❏   Other program categories: *All system activities and costs must be included in a program category.* If a system provides activities that cannot be included in the previously listed program categories, the library system should establish additional program categories, for example, bookmobile services and books-by-mail programs.

The following classifications for program funding sources are used:

❏   2004 state aid to public library system funds

❏   Other state aid to public library system funds

❏   State and federal library program funds

❏   All other income: income from local and county sources, contract income, and all other sources

Figure 1-3. Sample Program Budget Taxonomy

Source: State of Wisconsin's Department of Public Instruction, http://www.dpi.state.wi.us/dltcl/pld/sysbudget.html.

Earning by Learning
An Accelerated Reader Program

Personnel

Position	Allotment
Reception clerk	$3,000.00
Test proctor	$4,000.00
Test assistant	$3,000.00
Bursar	$3,000.00
Total:	**$13,000.00**

Materials

Description	Allotment
0.5–3.0 (Reading level)	$2,000.00
3.1–6.0 (Reading level)	$2,200.00
6.1 and above (Reading level)	$1,800.00
Test disks (CD-ROMs)	$1,300.00
Copies (Notices and forms)	$200.00
Total:	**$ 7,500.00**

Awards

Category	Allotment
0.5–3.0 @ $1	$3,000.00
3.1–6.0 @ $2	$3,800.00
6.1 and above @ $3	$5,200.00
Total:	**$12,000.00**

Program total is $32,500.00.

Figure 1-4. Sample Program Budget

Source: G. Steven Clegg, School of Library and Information Sciences (SLIS) 5303, University of North Texas School of Library and Information Sciences.

Personnel Services Expenditures

Position	FTE	Annual Rate	Cost to Program
Branch manager	.5	$78,000	$39,100
Clerk	2.0	34,000	68,500
Page	1.0	32,000	32,300
Total	3.5	—	$139,900

Nonpersonnel Expenditures

Category	Cost to Program
Publicity	$31,200
Ongoing	101,400
Materials	61,400
Facilities—related	29,500
Equipment	6,500
Total	$230,000

Total Program Budget: $139,900 + $230,000 = **$369,900**

Figure 1-5a. Teen Library Center Budget as Program Budget

Indicator	Transactions	Cost per Transaction	Total
Circulation	71,000 items	$3.59	$255,200
Reference	5,325 questions	6.89	36,700
Programming	4,600 attendees	12.26	56,400
Cataloging	3,450 items	6.26	21,600
Total	—	—	**$369,900**

Figure 1-5b. Teen Library Center Budget as Performance Budget

Source: Gary Werchan, School of Library and Information Sciences (SLIS) 5303, University of North Texas School of Library and Information Sciences.

PLANNING, PROGRAMMING, BUDGETING SYSTEMS (PPBS)

The planning, programming, budgeting system (PPBS) is a combination of program and performance-based budgeting. The primary emphasis of PPBS is on planning. First you set goals and objectives, then you allocate resources so that you can reach those goals. You have to state the goals, objectives, and activities in measurable terms so that the agency can gauge the effect of adding monetary resources to each program. Cost-benefit analyses play an important role in PPBS.

Using the formula of session + full text divided by cost, the cost analysis in figure 1-6 indicates that the average cost of the Texshare databases at this university extension is $.67 per use. The cost per use decreases when the databases are used more often. It is interesting to note that some of the less costly databases actually can cost more per use if they do not get heavy usage. On the other hand, some of the databases with higher up-front costs can actually cost less per use.

Advantages of PPBS

PPBS provides the easiest budget format for cost analysis of a program or service. Individual staff performance can be analyzed for productivity and planning.

Disadvantages of PPBS

PPBS does not assess the quality of the service provided, nor does it assess the need for service. It only indicates the cost of providing the service. A particular staff member might answer more reference questions than anyone else, but you do not know if the answers are correct.

ZERO-BASED BUDGET

The zero-based budget is not based on the past year's budget, but rather on what is needed for the future. Each program begins with a zero, and you justify it as if it is a new program. The budget process begins with the goals and objectives for the coming budget year. Each program is packaged into "decision packages," which include all of the program costs, the benefits and consequences of implementing or not implementing the program, and the performance measures for each activity of the program. Figure 1-7 shows a decision package form.

The library ranks all of its decision packages and merges those rankings into the rankings of other departments, which have also ranked their own

Texshare database cost per use (estimated).

Rank	TexShare Database	Sessions	Full-Text Retrievals	Subscription	Cost per Use
	Twentieth Century English Poetry (Proquest)	92	236	$32,750.00	$355.98
	Salud Para Todos (EBSCO)	11	0	$2,000.00	$181.82
	Scribner Writers Series (Gale)	196	143	$13,512.00	$68.94
	Clinical Pharmacology (EBSCO)	66	68	$4,500.00	$68.18
	Twayne's Authors Series (GALE)	628	556	$39,843.00	$63.44
	HeritageQuest Online (Proquest)	386	18,933	$21,301.00	$55.18
	Texas Digital Sanborn Maps	696	67,936	$12,900.00	$18.53
	Biography & Genealogy Master Index (Gale)	1,351	1,277	$18,708.00	$13.85
	STATIRef	606		$6,672.00	$11.01
0	Archives USA (Proquest)	626	1,003	$5,520.00	$8.82
1	Literature Resource Center (Gale)	32,207	12,964	$227,976.00	$7.08
2	Inform Spanish (Gale)	230	107	$1,500.00	$6.52
3	Military Library FullTEXT (EBSCO)	588	146	$3,500.00	$5.95
4	elibrary Classic (Electric Library) (Bigchalk)	3,868	10,567	$22,750.00	$5.88
5	MasterFILE Premier (EBSCO)	6,854	9,117	$35,000.00	$5.11
6	Religion & Philosophy Collection (EBSCO)	1,480	399	$6,500.00	$4.39
7	Funk and Wagnalls New Encyclopedia (EBSCO)	833	885	$3,000.00	$3.60
8	Business & Company Resource Center (Gale)	39,469	16,681	$141,013.00	$3.57
9	Regional Business News (EBSCO)	1,105	651	$3,000.00	$2.71
0	Health and Wellness Resource Center (Gale)	26,260	8,180	$70,000.00	$2.67
1	Texas Almanac 2000–2001 Edition	547	292	$1,000.00	$1.83
2	World Almanac (OCLC)	573	0	$1,000.00	$1.75
3	Health Source: Consumer Edition (EBSCO)	1,721	1,536	$3,000.00	$1.74
4	Computer Source: Consumer Edition (EBSCO)	2,200	1,892	$3,000.00	$1.36
5	Ulrichsweb.com (Bowker)	2,377		$3,175.00	$1.34
6	Booksinprint.com (Bowker)	5,051	0	$6,495.00	$1.29
7	ProceedingsFirst (OCLC)	797	0	$1,000.00	$1.25
8	Alternative Health Watch (EBSCO)	2,400	3,762	$3,000.00	$1.25
9	What Do I Read Next? (Gale)	1,278	1,355	$1,500.00	$1.17

Figure 1-6. TexShare Database Cost Analysis

Rank	TexShare Database	Sessions	Full-Text Retrievals	Subscription	Cost per Use
0	InfoTrac Custom Newspapers	4,144	1,296	$4,500.00	$1.09
1	Sociological Collection (EBSCO)	6,007	1,557	$6,500.00	$1.08
2	Health Source: Nursing/Academic Edition (EBSCO)	2,881	1,611	$3,000.00	$1.04
3	PapersFirst (OCLC)	964	0	$1,000.00	$1.04
4	GPO Monthly Catalog (OCLC)	978	0	$1,000.00	$1.02
5	Newspaper Source (EBSCO)	3,213	3,263	$3,000.00	$0.93
6	Professional Development Collection (EBSCO)	8,608	5,964	$6,500.00	$0.76
7	Student Resource Center GOLD (InfoTrac)	4,042	1,055	$3,000.00	$0.74
8	Health Reference Center Academic (Gale)	4,146	4,962	$3,000.00	$0.72
9	Applied Science & Technology Abstracts (EBSCO)	3,376	8	$2,000.00	$0.59
0	World Cat (OCLC)	122,797	0	$ 70,000.00	$0.57
1	Business Source Premier (EBSCO)	71,865	91,136	$ 35,000.00	$0.49
2	Psychology & Behavioral Sciences Collection (EBSCO)	21,401	19,146	$6,500.00	$0.30
3	Academic Search Premier (EBSCO)	153,925	198,200	$40,000.00	$0.26
4	MEDLINE (OCLC)	6,919	0	$1,500.00	$0.22
5	MEDLINE (EBSCO)	12,471	2	$1,500.00	$0.12
6	ArticleFirst (OCLC)	12,417	0	$1,000.00	$0.08
7	ERIC (OCLC)	25,249	0	$1,500.00	$0.06
8	ERIC (EBSCO)	26,028	7,724	$1,500.00	$0.06
9	Encyclopedia Americana (Grolier)	204,993	77,210	$5,600.00	$0.03
	TOTALS	830,920	494,820	$892,715.00	$0.67

Figure 1-6. TexShare Database Cost Analysis (*Continued*)

Source: Vickie Drake, School of Library and Information Sciences (SLIS) 5303, University of North Texas School of Library and Information Sciences.

Program Name: Bookmobile Outreach Service	City Ranking: 15
Department: Library	Department Priority Rank: 9
Date: January 6, 2004	Cost of Package: $130,000

Statement of Purpose (What is to be accomplished): There are approximately 40,000 people in Readerville who are unable to come to the library. These include those in nursing and sheltered-care homes, day care centers, and neighborhoods that are not served by a branch or neighborhood library.

Description of Activity: The Readerville Bookmobile will make three stops per day, five days a week at the following locations to reach these unserved populations of Readerville.

- Monday: Good Shepherd Sheltered Care Center, Little Angels Day Care, and El Centro Community Center
- Tuesday: Windsor Retirement Village, Mercado Laredo, and Umojo After-School Center
- Wednesday: Vintage Retirement Community, Adult Day Care Center, and Chinese YMCA Camp
- Thursday: Carriage House Assisted Living, Rainbow Day Care Center, and Martin Luther King Recreation Center
- Friday: Goodwill Village and ABC Child Care Center; afternoon cleaning and restocking

Benefits and Desired Results: Library cards will be issued to residents and users at each facility upon request. Library staff will contact each potential user and tell them of available services, inviting them to use the bookmobile and telling them of the schedule at this stop. They will be invited to check out at least one item and return it the following week. The desired result is that 75 percent of the eligible residents and users will obtain library cards.

Related Activities: The visits to child care centers and after-school facilities will begin with a puppet show or story time to draw children to the bookmobile. They will then be invited to pick out their books.

The bookmobile is equipped with a wheelchair lift. Trained staff will go into the retirement and nursing facilities to bring residents to the bookmobile and help them get on board the wheelchair lift.

Alternatives: The library has used volunteers, including Meals on Wheels, to deliver books to shut-ins and the homebound. They are doing an excellent job of reaching individual users, but we do not have enough volunteers to reach every shut-in in Readerville.

Consequences (if the activity is not approved or is eliminated): If the bookmobile is not funded, these 40,000 residents (20 percent of Readerville's population) will be unserved by their community library.

Cost of Required Resources:

Personnel (one driver, one librarian, one clerk):	$100,000
Materials:	$ 20,000
Operations (gasoline, washing, maintenance):	$ 8,000
Programs:	$ 2,000
Total:	$130,000

Initial purchase of bookmobile: $110,000 (capital budget approved in 2003)

Figure 1-7. Decision Package Form for Zero-based Budgeting

packages. The governing authority then funds the programs in the order of the agency-wide ranking. Decisions are made on the basis of the community's goals and needs, and the decision packages are budgeted to the point that funds are anticipated for the coming year. Then a line is drawn and the governing authority ranks the decision packages in priority order below the line. If additional funding is realized, those programs will be funded.

Advantages of Zero-based Budgeting

A strong advantage of zero-based budgeting is that agencies with common goals and limited resources are more likely to pool resources and work together to accomplish the community's goals. Some examples in our experience are (1) the public library and police department's sharing costs to provide security in the area around the library, and (2) the library and recreation department's sharing costs for needed teen programming.

Disadvantages of Zero-based Budgeting

The greatest disadvantage of zero-based budgeting is that it is very time consuming. The budgeting authority (city council, school board, board of regents, corporate board) may not realize the value of the program and cut it in favor of a program from another department that is "sexier" and has more marketing appeal.

RESPONSIBILITY-CENTERED BUDGET

Responsibility-centered budgeting is frequently used in academic libraries, where each department is considered a cost center. There are three key principles that guide responsibility-center budgeting.

1. All operating expenditures and revenues for a given center should be assigned to that center.
2. Appropriate incentives should exist for each center to reduce costs and to promote a clear set of budgetary and service priorities.
3. Internal service costs should be allocated to the appropriate center as laid out in the guidelines for attributing income and assessing expenses.

If you use responsibility-centered budgeting, each department is expected to be self-supporting, with revenues covering expenditures.

Responsibility-centered budgeting encourages increased attention to generating income and containing costs. As departments raise funds through enrollment-related formula appropriations, grants, fees, or generated income, they are then responsible for the allocation and spending of those funds. Departments also charge each other for services used.

There are several key terms used in responsibility-centered budgeting; notice what they emphasize.

- Cost center (responsible for controlling costs, e.g., accounting)
- Revenue center (responsible for generating revenues, e.g., recruiting, fines, and fees)
- Profit center (responsible for generating revenues and controlling costs, e.g., library operations)
- Investment center (responsible for investments, e.g., foundation and endowments)

The University of Illinois at Urbana-Champaign uses responsibility centers in its accounting system. Figure 1-8, "Attributing Costs of Administrative and Service Units," sets forth their scheme for cost centers and assessments.

Advantage of Responsibility-centered Budgeting

The advantage of responsibility-centered budgeting is that each agency pays for all of the services it uses.

Disadvantage of Responsibility-centered Budgeting

The disadvantage of responsibility-centered budgeting is that you might get carried away with establishing cost centers and generating revenues by charging other departments within the same institution, and then all collaboration ceases. For example, the information technology department may charge the library for computer maintenance; then the library in turn charges the IT department for website development and maintenance.

A. Units Reporting to the Chancellor

Unit Code	Unit Name	Basis of Assessment to Units
0200	Office of the Chancellor	Total expenditures
0202	Equal Opportunity and Access	FTE faculty/academic/nonacademic staff
0203	Office of Development	Gift/endowment expenditures
0801	Office of Public Affairs	Total expenditures
0802	News Bureau	Total expenditures
0803	Office of Publications	Total expenditures
9101	Intercollegiate Athletics	50 percent FTE faculty/academic/nonacademic staff; 50 percent total enrollment
83xx	Leasehold, Rehab/Alterations	Net assignable square feet

B. Units Reporting to the Provost and Vice Chancellor for Academic Affairs

Unit Code	Unit Name	Basis of Assessment to Units
0204	Office of Provost and Vice Chancellor for Academic Affairs	Total expenditures
	Campuswide programs	Total expenditures
	Discovery Program	Freshmen enrollment
	General Education	Undergraduate enrollment
	Ed. Tech. Board	Instructional units
0212	Academic Human Resources	Academic FTE
0220	Chief Information Officer	Total expenditures
0221	Campus Information Technology and Educational Services	Academic FTE
0238	Comm. on Inst. Coop. (CIC)	Total expenditures
0270	Principals' Scholars Program	Undergraduate enrollment
0271	Campus Honors Program	Undergraduate enrollment
0284	Admissions and Records	Total enrollment
0285	Instructional Resources	Instructional units
0290	Management Information	Total expenditures
2601	Graduate College Administration	50 percent academic FTE; 50 percent graduate enrollment
	Facility Management and Scheduling	Net assignable square feet

Figure 1-8. Attributing Costs of Administrative and Service Units: University of Illinois Responsibility-centered Cost Centers

C. Units Reporting to the Vice Chancellor for Research

Unit Code	Unit Name	Basis of Assessment to Units
0601	Office of Vice Chancellor for Research	Total expenditures
	Critical Research Initiatives	G&C expenditures
0630	Lab Animal Resources	G&C expenditures (LAS/ACES/VetMed/Beckman only)
0633	Committee on Natural Areas	Total expenditures (academic units only)
0643	Biotechnology Center	Total expenditures (LAS/ACES/VetMed/Beckman only)
2609	Research Board	Faculty FTE
	Distributions to Units	Faculty FTE
2620	Center for Advanced Study	Faculty FTE
2652	MillerComm	Total expenditures
2660	Ancient Technologies	Total expenditures (academic units only)
2665	Fellowships	Graduate enrollment

D. Units Reporting to the Vice Chancellor for Administration and Human Resources

Unit Code	Unit Name	Basis of Assessment to Units
0301	Office of Vice Chancellor for Administration and Human Resources	Total expenditures
0340	Planning Design and Control	Net assignable square feet
0348	Environmental Health and Safety	50 percent total expenditures; 50 percent G&C expenditures
0350	Mailing Services	Total expenditures
0353	Printing Services	Total expenditures
0358	Central Stores	Total expenditures
0366	Levis Faculty Center	Total expenditures
0385	Division of Public Safety	Total expenditures
0386	Campus Parking	Total expenditures
1220	Human Resources Development	
1230	Faculty/Staff Assistance Program	FTE faculty/academic/nonacademic staff

Figure 1-8. Attributing Costs of Administrative and Service Units: University of Illinois Responsibility-centered Cost Centers (*Continued*)

Unit Code	Unit Name	Basis of Assessment to Units
1257	Benefits Center	FTE faculty/academic/nonacademic staff
8201	Operations and Maintenance Administration	Gross square feet
8205	Building Operation	Gross square feet
8220	Building Maintenance	Gross square feet
8225	General Maintenance	Gross square feet
8230	Grounds	Gross square feet
8235	Transportation	Gross square feet
8240	Heat, Light, and Power	Gross square feet
8245	Water Station	Gross square feet

E. Units Reporting to the Vice Chancellor for Student Affairs

Unit Code	Unit Name	Basis of Assessment to Units
0901	Office of Vice Chancellor for Student Affairs	Total enrollment
0921	Office of Dean of Students	Total enrollment
0925	Minority Student Affairs	Total enrollment
0935	Health Professions Information Office	
0951	Career Services Center	
0961	Office of Student Discipline	Total enrollment
0965	Counseling Center	Total enrollment
0971	Student Financial Aid	Total enrollment
0972	Student Loan Matching	Total enrollment
0981	International Student Affairs	Total enrollment
10	McKinley Health Total	Total enrollment
8555	Campus Recreation	Total enrollment
8561	Student Services Building	
8586	Housing Division	
8588	Assembly Hall	
8590	Illini Union	

Figure 1-8. Attributing Costs of Administrative and Service Units: University of Illinois Responsibility-centered Cost Centers (*Continued*)

Source: Reprinted with permission of University of Illinois Provost's Office.

BUDGETING LINGO A–Z

These are some basic budgeting terms. You will probably need to use these terms when you are creating your own budgets.

Assets: The library's *capital assets,* or *fixed assets,* are those items it owns (i.e., its property). Examples of a library's assets are the buildings, furnishings, book collection, and bookmobile. Long-term assets may be depreciated or appreciated as their value decreases or grows. For example, the value of a book collection may appreciate with age as the average cost per volume increases. The value of a bookmobile or of library furnishings will depreciate with age as the asset gets older and becomes worth less on the market.

You will also see the term *asset* on a library's financial balance sheet. In this case, an *asset* refers to revenues, or income, not to long-term *fixed assets,* such as those listed above.

Audit: An *audit* is a review of a library's financial statements. Audits may be required by legal mandates (e.g., law, regulation, or ordinance), contractual or unofficial agreement, or institutional policy. An audit can be conducted informally by in-house staff, more formally by accountants of the governing institution, or by an independent accounting agency.

The purpose of an audit is to ensure that proper financial management standards and procedures are being followed and that proper stewardship of the resources is being practiced. The audit accountant reviews financial statements and issues an opinion. When no discrepancy is found, the opinion is "unqualified." Sometimes minor improvements are noted with an unqualified rating, but if major financial reporting practices are violated a library can receive a qualified opinion and will need to address the problems and correct the reports.

The Governmental Accounting Standards Board (GASB), in its recent publication, *Audits of State and Governmental Units,* has established detailed procedures for formal audits of public libraries. The website Government Auditing Standards 2003 (the Yellow Book), at www.gao.gov/govaud/ybk01 .htm, provides details of the latest standards for auditors of grants that are partially or fully funded by government agencies. These standards pertain to auditors' professional qualifications, the quality of audit effort, and the characteristics of audit reports and ratings.

Budget: A *budget* is the best estimate of income and expenses for a set period of time, usually a fiscal year. The budget will need to be adjusted to show the actual income and expenses as they occur.

Capital: *Capital* refers to assets that accumulate over time and do not need to be spent during a single fiscal year. Examples are library buildings, book collections, and automation systems.

Cash flow: Cash flow is sometimes referred to as *liquid assets*. This is the net income that is available after expenses are paid.

Chart of accounts: The chart of accounts is a list of every item that the accounting system tracks. Accounts are divided into five basic categories:

- Assets
- Fund balances (equity/net assets)
- Liabilities
- Revenues
- Expenses

Charts of accounts specify the types of items to be included under each budget category and give each category an identifying number, which groups them with like budget categories.

A chart of accounts is needed to maintain consistency in creating and tracking the library's budget. For example, if there were no chart of accounts, an order for photocopier toner might be posted to office supplies one time and to the photocopier contract the next, or police security for a library event might get posted as an internal service charge rather than a contractual service.

A chart of accounts often uses alphanumeric descriptors to list all entries on an organization's ledger. This coded representation of elements is used to record the allocation of resources received into and going out of the library, which helps to systematize collecting and reporting financial data. The structure of the chart of accounts affects the preparation of financial statements and reports. Using a chart of accounts, classification system allows financial data stored in individual accounts to retain details of each transaction in condensed format.

Most charts of accounts implement hierarchical coding systems like the one shown in figure 1-9. In this example, a salary adjustment would be entered as 1000-1100-1199. A university accounting system, on the other hand, may look like figure 1-10.

An intercollegiate athletic department might use a hierarchical system similar to the one shown in figure 1-11.

Checks and balances: For accountability purposes, the person who orders an item should not be responsible for paying the bill. A system of *checks and balances* requires at least two people (or departments) to handle the ordering and receipt of materials and the payment using public funds. This prevents one person from having too much power and authority. This oversight system is effective in maintaining public confidence and avoiding misappropriations.

Commingled funds: If funds from multiple sources are placed into one savings or checking account, they are *commingled*. Although governments mix funds from sales taxes, property taxes, fines and fees, and other

Chart of Accounts

Description	Summary Object	Subaccount Subobject	(Line Item)
Personnel Services	1000		
Salaries and Wages		1100	
Salaries and Wages			1101
Annual Leave Taken			1102
Annual Leave at Termination			1104
Retro Pay—Straight Time			1111
Salary Adjustment			1199

Figure 1-9. Sample Chart of Accounts

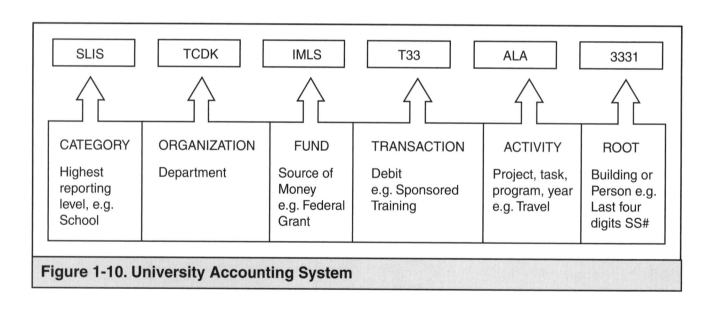

Figure 1-10. University Accounting System

sources to create a general fund account, these are all public funds. In libraries, one should not commingle or mix funds from public sources (i.e., taxes) with funds from grants, foundations, or other sources of revenue, as they each require separate accounting. Each funding source should have its own account.

Cost: The *cost* of a service includes all components of that service—the purchase price, shipping, installation cost, and maintenance. For example,

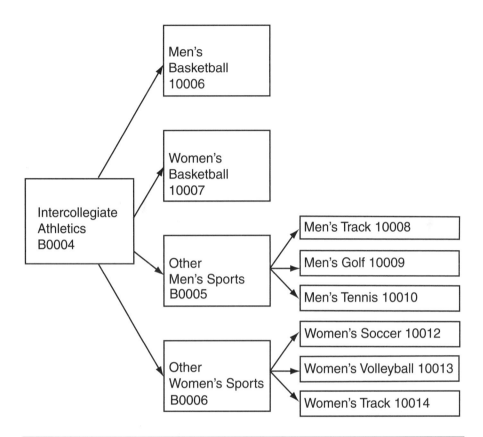

Figure 1-11. Hierarchical Chart of Accounts

the cost of an interlibrary loan includes staff time, postage, shipping bags, processing of the request, and the request forms. Thus, the entire cost of a service will probably not occur on one invoice.

Cost-benefit analysis: *Cost-benefit analysis* identifies all of the costs related to a program and the benefits derived from it. For example, the cost of providing a story time might be $10 per child, but the benefits are reading readiness, increased literacy, and socialization of children. These benefits are intangible. Cost-benefit analyses can also be tangible; for example, is it more expensive to outsource the cataloging of audiovisual materials or to have library employees catalog and process the materials in the library's technical services department? The cost of the service from each provider is divided by the number of items cataloged and processed to get the cost-benefit analysis.

Cost centers: *Cost centers* are units (usually programs) to which expenditures can be assigned in order to perform cost analysis. Examples of cost centers are a branch library, the children's department, outreach services, public programming, or a computer lab.

Deliverable: The term *deliverable* refers to the expected result or product from a consultant or vendor. For example, the building consultant is required to produce as deliverables ten bound copies of the building program and one unbound copy giving permission rights for reproduction.

Depreciation: *Depreciation* is the lowering of the value of an asset as it ages, that is, it is the amount by which the market value of purchase decreases over time. To depreciate something is also an accounting procedure (it can be entered on the books as an expense of doing business) and using the figure for tax purposes (the amount of depreciation can be a tax deduction). You can calculate this by two basic methods: *straight-line depreciation* or *accelerated depreciation*.

Note: If the value of an asset does not diminish over time, it is considered inexhaustible and is not depreciated. For example, the value of art collections, library reserve collections, and historical collections do not decrease over time; therefore, they do not depreciate.

Straight-line depreciation is the most common form of depreciation, and it assumes the asset will lose an equal amount of value each year. To calculate the annual depreciation of an asset, subtract the estimated salvage value (resale value) of the asset from the purchase price, and then divide this number by the estimated useful life of the asset.

Accelerated depreciation offers a greater tax shield by allowing faster write-offs than the straight-line method. Accelerated depreciation methods are popular for writing off equipment that may become obsolete (e.g., computers) and replaced before the end of its useful life. By averaging the cost of the asset and the cost of its repairs over its lifetime, the accelerated depreciation levels out the total cost of using the asset.

While most libraries do not need to be concerned with the taxable value of assets (and, therefore, their appreciated or depreciated value), they will need to know the current value of the assets to make decisions about insurance coverage and maintenance versus replacement of an asset.

Expenses: Expenses are monies paid. As bills come in and are paid, they are recorded as expenses. Some expenses are encumbered at the time the order is placed rather than when the materials are received. You'll learn more about encumbrances in the section on budget tracking.

Fair market value: Fair market value is the price at which the buyer and seller agree to do business.

Fee-based services: Fee-based services are those library services that (1) the library could not afford to provide without charging a fee, such as in-depth reference services provided to a business; or (2) the customer is not entitled to without payment of a fee, for example, nonresident fees for those who are not qualified through payment of taxes or tuition to make free use of a library.

Financial statements: Financial statements are disclosures and declarations of a library's financial information and status that are believed to be accurate and to impartially represent the institution's financial situation. They describe the monetary attributes of the library that are important for decision makers, trustees, library board members, partner groups, and governing bodies. In June 1999, the Governmental Accounting Standards Board (GASB) adopted Statement Number 34, Basic Financial Statements—and Management's Discussion and Analysis—for State and Local Governments. The document outlines basic financial statements and supplementary information so that financial statements are in accordance with generally accepted accounting principles (GAAP). Financial statements of public libraries should include the following:

- A management's discussion and analysis (MD&A) section providing an analysis of the library's overall financial position and results of operations,
- financial statements prepared using full accrual accounting for the library's activities, and
- fund financial statements that focus on the major funds.

For more information on this and other GASB documents, visit www.gasb.org.

Fiscal year: The fiscal year is the *budget year,* which may or may not coincide with the calendar year of January through December. Fiscal years are frequently July 1 through June 30 or October 1 through September 30.

Forecasting: Forecasting is used to make immediate projections, such as the coming budget year, as well as for predicting future trends, for example, five-year plans. It focuses on external factors that the library or governmental agency cannot control but that have a key impact on future budgets. Examples are local unemployment and tax income losses caused by anticipated plant closings, the estimated impact of the aging of baby boomers in a community, and the trends showing growth of the Hispanic population. Forecasters use statistical analysis and modeling to make their predictions.

Fund accounting: Fund accounting is the process of dividing an agency's budget into several categories. In libraries, they are usually the general fund and the capital fund, and, perhaps, the special revenue fund.

General fund: The general fund includes most income and expenses that are budgeted for a given fiscal year. Salaries, utilities, fines and fees, and sales taxes are reflected in the general budget.

General ledger: The general ledger organizes information by account. The chart of accounts (the list of items that the accounting system tracks) acts as the table of contents to the general ledger.

Income: Income is the actual money coming into the library, through fines, tax receipts, donations, nonresident cards, photocopier charges, or any other source. It is counted as income after it is received.

Lease: A lease is a contract between the owner and an agency willing to pay a specific sum of money to use the owner's property for a specific length of time. Libraries may lease property, books, equipment, or even personnel.

Liabilities: Liabilities are committed expenses, including everything from salaries to contracted lease payments for the photocopier, which appear on the library's balance sheet. They may also refer to long-term debt, for example, a mortgage on the library buildings that is being paid off by revenue bond issues.

Millage: A *mill* is one-tenth of a penny, or $1 for every $1,000 in taxable value. Property tax rates are expressed in millage. Each taxing entity (city, school district, county) levies a specific millage against property taxes. If you are voting on a 1-mill tax increase and your house is worth $100,000, you are voting on whether this issue is worth an additional $100 per year in property taxes.

NISO Z39.7 Standard: NISO, the National Information Standards Organization, last revised Z39.7, the standard for statistics, including finances, in 1995. These standards are currently under review. Library standards for financial data are important because the financial data must be recorded consistently within and among libraries so financial records can be analyzed longitudinally within an institution and comparatively among multiple libraries.

Operations budget: The operations budget is the portion of the budget that is allocated for utilities, building maintenance, travel, training, equipment, office supplies, and most other expenses that are not associated with personnel or library materials. The operations budget may be only 10 percent of the total budget, but it might provide the greatest flexibility in cutting costs.

Personnel budget: The personnel budget covers salaries, fringe benefits, and other costs related to the employment of staff.

Purchase order: A purchase order is a form provided by the library or information agency to a vendor authorizing the vendor to ship the requested item.

Recovery: Recovery refers to the efforts made to successfully retrieve missing or overdue library materials, frequently by using a collection agency or the judicial system. Recovery can also refer to cost recovery, that is, charging sufficient funds to cover the cost of providing a service.

Referendum: A referendum is an election in which the taxpayers vote on whether to increase their tax rate to a level that will permit constructing a new building or perhaps extending their service area.

Restricted funds: Funds that are restricted can only be spent according to the written intentions of the donor. For example, the principal ("corpus," or original donation) of a donation to the children's department may have to stay intact, but the interest can be spent once each year for the purchase of children's books.

Retained earnings: Retained earnings are positive cash-flow funds that are moved to a designated account for a future specified use. For example, suppose that an internal service fund charges a department $100 per month for the maintenance of the library department's vehicle, but the maintenance does not cost $1,200 every year. The internal service department does not return the balance but rather puts it into a retained earnings account that is designated for the purchase of replacement vehicles.

Return on investment (ROI): ROI measures the extent to which an organization uses its capital to generate profit. For example, if a piece of property is purchased for $100,000 and sold for $120,000, a very simple return on investment is $20,000. A detailed ROI would include expenses for the maintenance and use of the property, which are offset by the rental value of using the property.

Revenues: Revenues are the library's budgeted earnings. Anticipated property taxes, fines and fees, nonresident card receipts, and donations are counted as revenues at the beginning of the budget cycle; however, they may change as actual revenues (or income) are received. It is vital to track the difference between anticipated revenues and the actual income in order to make budget adjustments as the fiscal year progresses.

Sole source: A sole source is the only vendor who is selling a specific item or service, for example, a publisher that does not sell its books through a jobber or in bookstores.

Tax base: The tax base is the amount on which a tax rate is applied. In the public library arena, the tax base is the property in the municipality, county, district, or other taxing authority that funds the library. The school-library tax base is the school district. The public college or university will have a tax base that may encompass the entire state. Your tax base can increase because of new construction, additional industry, increased property values, annexation, or anything else that makes the value of property in your taxing area go up. Tax bases can also go down when an industry leaves or property values go down.

Taxing for Survival of Services

"As the March 2 election nears, more and more read signs proclaiming 'Yes on B for Books and Hours: Keep Our Library Strong' are popping up all over town. The campaign to pass Measure B is moving into high gear, yet the measure has opposition. . . . Measure B will appear on the ballots of voters living in Morgan Hill, Gilroy, San Martin—as part of the unincorporated area of Santa Clara County—plus Campbell, Cupertino, Los Altos, Los Altos Hills, Milpitas, Monte Sereno and Saratoga. Voters will be asked to approve a tax of $42 per year per homeowner for each of seven years. Two-thirds of voters casting ballots need to approve the measure for it to become law."

Source: Morgan Hill Times.

Tax-Rate Formula

Assessed	×	Multiplier
value	−	Exemptions
	×	Tax rate
	=	Total tax bill

Source: Copyright © 1999–2003 Normal Township, www.normaltownship.org/ Assessor/TaxRate.html.

Tax rate: The tax rate is the millage levied by each taxing body within the governmental unit. The accumulation of those tax rates becomes the home owner's tax bill. Here's how your tax bill is figured:

> Your home's assessed value times the multiplier applied by your taxing district (percentage of assessed value) minus exemptions (homestead, senior citizen) times the accumulated tax rates equals your tax bill.

Vendor: A vendor is a company or individual that provides a service for a cost. The vendor may be a book publisher, a window-washing service, or any other firm with which the library does business.

SUMMARY

This chapter described some basic concepts in library budgeting and introduced you to common terms, types of budgets, and some basic budgeting practices. Reviewing this chapter will help you become familiar with the various types of budgets. This chapter also touched on the importance of reliability in accounting information, the need to follow standards, and the importance of well-documented practices to establish financial management integrity. The budget can be viewed as a tool for accountability of financial management practices, a means to communicate financial management goals, as well as an established method to control monies and resources used to operate a library. Learning to wield the budget wisely is part of monitoring financial resources effectively and reporting judiciously. You will learn more about this in the next chapters.

2 HOW DO LIBRARIES BUDGET?

OVERVIEW

Think of the budget as a road map for navigating the library's and institution's financial environment. Along with the library mission statement, the budget is one of the library's most important planning tools because it enables the library administration and the governing bodies to keep track of financial resources, forecast the financial future, and guide the service direction of the library.

The budget states your institution's service goals in monetary terms. That is, the budget communicates the costs associated with pursuing the library's mission and achieving its goals and objectives, along with monitoring upsets as well as progress toward service goals. For example, if the library experiences unexpected increases in utility expenses over the summer, the administration will know to cut back other expenses in order to balance the total budget by the end of the fiscal year. At the same time, the budget informs the governing bodies that the library needs to address rising utility costs in future budgetary cycles. How you meet, prioritize, and communicate the library's budget demands and fluctuations over time determines how you will meet your service mission in the future.

Tracking library budget components is central to the responsible financial management of libraries. In this chapter, you will learn how to create a budget. First comes an explanation of the components of the budget. Next, you will learn about the steps in creating and adopting a library budget, as well as the tasks associated with the process. The final sections of the chapter outline some considerations and practices to consider in the budget preparation process, such as requirements for a records retention policy, recommendations on how to present the budget effectively to governing authorities, and guidelines for going through the public ratification process.

LIBRARY BUDGET COMPONENTS

The budget for a library or information agency normally has four or five significant components, depending on the organization:

- Personnel
- Materials
- Operations
- Internal services
- Capital budget

PERSONNEL

Personnel is the largest single component of the budget, with 60 to 70 percent of the library's operating expenses generally allocated to personnel. (See figure 2-1.)

The personnel budget includes all salaries, overtime, worker's compensation, benefits, and other employee-related expenses, whether the employees are part- or full-time. If you have to make major budget cuts, it is almost impossible to make them without cutting personnel (instituting a hiring freeze, cutting overtime, laying off staff, or cutting part-time hours).

> School library salaries are usually shown in the budget for the school or the district, not in the school library budget.

MATERIALS

The materials budget includes all of the costs involved in building the library collection: books, serials (newspapers, journals, other periodicals), videos, DVDs, CDs, databases, electronic resources, leased services, and so on. A sample high school materials budget is shown in figure 2-2.

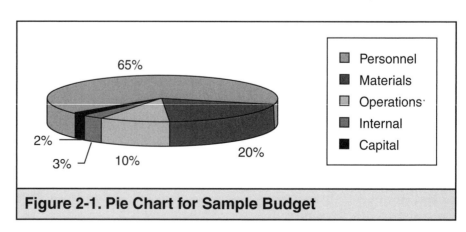

Figure 2-1. Pie Chart for Sample Budget

Table III.24—High School Libraries 1999–2000 Budget	School Budget		All Other Sources		Total	
	$ Means	%	$ Means	%	$ Means	%
Total operating expenditures	$22,625.68	100.0%	$4,557.78	100.0%	$27,174.66	100.0%
Books as reported in budget category 12-6669	$13,375.73	59.1%	$3,618.72	79.4%	$16,994.45	62.5%
Newspapers and magazines as reported in budget category 12-6399	$2,290.12	10.1%	$36.78	0.8%	$2,326.60	8.6%
Electronic format materials (software, CD-ROM, laser discs)	$1,299.16	5.7%	$95.92	2.1%	$1,395.08	5.1%
Nonprint materials (audio, video, microform)	$1,546.03	6.8%	$345.27	7.6%	$1,882.81	6.9%
Electronic access to information (online databases, searching, Internet access)	$1,362.12	6.0%	$276.48	6.1%	$1,638.59	6.0%
Other operating expenditures	$2,752.52	12.2%	$184.61	4.1%	$2,937.13	10.8%
Total capital outlay	$5,371.54	100.0%	$4,802.06	100.0%	$10,134.24	100.0%
Equipment (computers, CD-ROM drives, VCRs)	$3,595.36	66.9%	$3,699.13	77.0%	$7,264.17	71.7%
Other capital purchases (furniture, shelving)	$1,776.18	33.1%	$1,102.93	23.0%	$2,870.07	28.3%
Total budget	$27,997.22		$9,359.84		$37,308.90	

Figure 2-2. Sample High School Library Materials Budget

Source: Ester G. Smith, "Texas School Libraries: Standards, Resources, Services, and Students' Performance," Texas State Library and Archives Commission Website, 2001, www.tsl.state.tx.us.ld/pubs/schlibsurvey/appendix. html.

Librarians have primary control over the materials budget and should negotiate with vendors to get the best prices. Although books have their list prices, you can join with other libraries in a consortium, federation, district, or state to negotiate a standard low discount and free shipping from a jobber who is eager to get that contract. We have negotiated up to a 46 percent discount with free shipping from major jobbers. Keep in mind that the lowest price is not necessarily the best choice.

When purchasing materials, one of the libraries I worked in sent identical orders for a mix of children's books, videos, textbooks, bestsellers, and other materials to three or four of the top jobbers every other year (there were several branches, so these were items that we could use in quantity). We then tracked the arrival time of each item, the shipping cost, the discount, and the fill rate for each order. We then used those data in selecting our vendor for the coming two years. When we joined a consortium, we continued this practice and passed the information on to the consortium's vendor-selection committee so everyone could realize the same (or better) discount.

One of our decisions was not buy DVDs or videos until they had been in the video rental stores for six weeks. We then purchased the used videos (which the rental stores had returned) from a local distributor at a very low cost. These decisions helped relationships with the rental stores and still let us have new videos in the collection.

The materials budget is generally 15 to 20 percent of the total library budget, and it is an easy target for budget cuts. When you defend the materials budget, please remember that if you don't buy something at this point, you may never buy it. It is highly unlikely that there will be a sudden windfall in future budgets that would permit you to pick up items you were unable to purchase in low-budget years. Even if that were to happen, many of the items would probably be out of print. There are also some materials, such as periodicals, that cannot be purchased at a later date.

There are various ways to stretch the materials budget. When you are trying to stretch it, evaluate the use of periodicals and newspapers that are purchased in hard copy, the quantities of individual titles of books or audio-visual materials purchased, the potential savings in leasing high-demand items until the demand is filled (then returning them . . . if you then keep them, you will pay more than if you had bought them in the first place), and other options that might be available to your library. Ask yourself the following questions:

- Do you have standing orders for items that are published every year (travel guides, encyclopedias, directories) but that you could maybe purchase every other year to save money?

- Could you change some of your subscriptions from one year to three years and, by renewing one-third of the subscriptions each year, stretch your periodical subscriptions budget?

- Are you still buying a journal that was the favorite of a faculty member or law partner who retired five years ago and no one else cares whether you have it?

- Can you share any of your database costs?

- Are you being good stewards of your materials budget?

OPERATIONS

The operations budget includes those items that are not related to salary, materials, internal service charges, or capital expenditures. That leaves utilities, office supplies, printing, janitorial supplies, technical services supplies for processing of library materials, bindery expenses, furniture, travel, staff development and training, equipment, maintenance contracts, postage, telecommunication charges . . . and the list goes on. Your operations budget will be 10 to 25 percent of your total general budget. See figure 2-3 for a sample operations budget.

Because the operations budget is frequently the smallest part of the library's budget, you cannot really cut it sufficiently to realize a 10 or 15 percent reduction in the overall budget. Communities sometimes think that if they close a branch or if they close the library a few hours a week, they will save enough on utilities and other related costs to realize the mandated reduction. However, reductions of the magnitude of 10 to 15 percent require cutting staff; that's where the bulk of the budget is located.

Still, the library staff can control most of the operations items. There are many ways you can realize savings in the operations budget:

- Purchase commonly used items (toilet paper, copy paper, light bulbs) jointly or in bulk.
- Invest in a motion-detection system that turns off lights in rooms not in use (do not install in restrooms—lack of motion does not mean lack of occupancy!).
- Lease or outsource copiers rather than buy them.
- Analyze the cost breaks between photocopying and outsourced printing.
- Use one-color printing on colored paper rather than multicolored ink on white paper.
- Install double entry doors to keep out cold and heat.
- Analyze all costs (e.g., is it really necessary to rebind periodicals now that they are available electronically?).
- Train the trainer (send one staff member who returns to train others).
- Charge for some services that were previously provided for free (e.g., copies from public printers, replacement library cards, meeting room rental, and reserves).

INTERNAL SERVICES

The internal services portion of the budget covers those costs that other departments within your governing agency charge to the library's budget. It is

OPERATING BUDGET			
Operating Income	2000 Actual	2001 Budget	2002 Budget
Municipality	$ 33,700	$ 35,500	$ 37,300
County	$ 9,500	$ 10,000	$ 10,500
State/library system	$ 950	$ 1,000	$ 1,050
Federal (LSTA)	$ 950	$ 1,000	$ 1,050
Funds carried forward	$ 475	$ 500	$ 525
Fines	$ 850	$ 900	$ 945
Donations	$ 500	$ 500	$ 500
Fees/other*	$ 100	$ 100	$ 105
Transfer from gift fund	$ 475	$ 500	$ 525
Operating income total	$ 47,500	$ 50,000	$ 52,500
Operating expenditures	2000 Actual	2001 Budget	2002 Budget
Salaries and wages	$ 21,850	$ 23,000	$ 24,150
Employee benefits	$ 6,650	$ 7,000	$ 7,350
Books	$ 6,365	$ 6,700	$ 7,035
Periodicals (including electronic)	$ 1,330	$ 1,400	$ 1,470
Video materials	$ 950	$ 1,000	$ 1,050
Audio materials	$ 380	$ 400	$ 420
Software and other electronic materials	$ 475	$ 500	$ 525
Contracted services	$ 950	$ 1,000	$ 1,050
Staff and board continuing education	$ 950	$ 1,000	$ 1,050
Public programming	$ 475	$ 500	$ 525
Telecommunications	$ 1,425	$ 1,500	$ 1,575
Utilities	$ 3,800	$ 4,000	$ 4,200
Equipment repair	$ 475	$ 500	$ 525
Supplies	$ 1,425	$ 1,500	$ 1,575
Operating expenditures total	$ 47,500	$ 50,000	$ 52,500
Capital income	2000 Actual	2001 Budget	2002 Budget
Municipality	$ 2,000	$ 3,000	$ 3,000
Capital expenditures	2000 Actual	2001 Budget	2002 Budget
Computer equipment replacement	$ 2,000	$ 2,000	$ 2,000
New shelving		$ 1,000	$ 1,000
Capital expenditures total	$ 2,000	$ 3,000	$ 3,000
Total of all expenditures	$ 49,500	$ 53,000	$ 55,500

Figure 2-3. Sample Operating Budget

a transfer fund between departments within the governing entity. Examples might include janitorial services (if you share with other departments), library vehicle maintenance, computer maintenance, building maintenance, and security. Generally, including these costs in the internal services portion means that they are not in the operating or personnel portions of the budget. Even though it may seem that internal service charges keep increasing and are out of your control, consider it your job to scrutinize these costs.

Internal service departments estimate their budgets for the coming year, and then they prorate and levy portions of their budgets to other departmental budgets. Because everything is apportioned to other departmental budgets, the governing body does not scrutinize the internal services departments' budgets. This could mean that some staff are getting raises while your department has to deal with cutting staff to provide the funds for their raises. Internal service funds also frequently have contingency accounts (i.e., savings or "retained earnings") while your department is looking for places to cut expenses.

Question your internal service charges whenever they do not make sense. For example, suppose you find that the library is being charged 10 percent of the cost of maintaining the city's fleet of vehicles when all you have is access to a pool car. You might save money by pulling out of fleet access and renting a car when you need one (or reimbursing staff for use of their personal vehicles). If the library operates a service that benefits the entire organization, that service could be prorated as an internal service charge and the cost spread among other departments. Examples are libraries that run the website for the entire organization. In university library budgets, materials purchased for various departments are charged back to that department through an assessment to that department's budget.

CAPITAL BUDGET

The capital budget, frequently referred to as the capital improvement program (CIP), is not part of the general operating budget, and the funds from the two budgets cannot be commingled. It is frequently difficult for library staff and the community to understand why there are funds available for building a new library but not for staffing and operating it. The capital budget is funded through referenda, designated funds and donations, or budget transfers based on long-range planning. These funds carry over from fiscal year to fiscal year, whereas the operating budget is expended each year and does not carry forward. Capital funds are normally invested until used.

Capital budgets are used for constructing or renovating buildings, purchasing a new automated system, or other major expenditures that have a multiyear lifetime. They can be used to acquire and develop land or to pay for consultants, architectural services, construction, furnishings, or an opening day collection for the new building. However, although the book collection may be capitalized for insurance purposes, the individual books do not have a lifetime that can be justified as a capital expense.

STEPS IN BUDGETING

The steps to preparing a library budget are fairly standard, although not every institution will need every step. For example, if you work in an academic library you may not have public hearings. However, in general, the following steps are followed:

1. Forecast anticipated revenues and expenditures.
2. Analyze data.
3. Prepare the budget.
4. Present the budget.
5. Hold public hearings.
6. Adopt the budget.

Then the cycle repeats itself.

FORECASTING

To forecast is to estimate the revenues and expenditures that will be available during the budget year. So, for example, if property values go up 2 percent and salaries are increased 4 percent, will you have adequate funds to cover the anticipated budget? Governments use forecasting software for this step. If you use forecasting software you can plug in numbers, and then whenever you type in different numbers, the program recalculates and changes the results. You then continue adjusting until you reach a level that the governing agency finds acceptable.

Within the library system, you can use forecasting to make logical predictions about the future cost of materials, services, and labor. Book and serials vendors often forecast price increases by subject area and publisher, which can assist the library administration when they do their own forecasting. The most common method used to forecast expenditures such as serials, monograph purchases, and even labor costs is to create a price index based on the past year's costs and current fiscal trends as well as expected discount rates and currency exchange rates where appropriate. The following is a checklist of items that will be helpful when forecasting expenditures:

- Assessment of needed materials, services, facilities, and human resources
- Past budgets, financial reports, expense records, and contracts

- Inventory findings and collection development policy
- Inflation rates and exchange rates for materials and services purchased
- Recent publication data on areas of concentration within the collection

It is important to remember that forecasting is an *informed* prediction of future costs. Sometimes it is tempting to just make an educated guess, but real forecasting takes the guesswork out of the prediction of the fiscal future and relies on more quantitative measures. The greatest advantage of taking proper forecasting steps is that there is a level of accountability and justification if predictions go awry. The weight given to the various indicators listed above (needs assessment, historic budget documents, published inflation rates, etc.) must rely to some degree on the judgment of the administration and the community-specific characteristics. In the end, forecasting is still largely a judgment call, but it is grounded in proper documentation and, thus, less of a target for derision or questioning of motives.

ANALYSIS

Budgeting begins with sound financial planning. Be sure that you address the considerations in the following checklist of considerations when you are developing your budget:

- What are the governing authority's mission and goals?
- How do the library's mission and goals reflect the needs and priorities of its community?
- What programs and services do you need to add or expand to achieve those goals?
- What programs or services no longer reflect the needs and priorities of the community? How can you eliminate or curtail these programs? How can you reallocate the resources that were supporting these unnecessary programs or services so that they support needed programs?
- What changes do you anticipate in the coming budget year? Who will retire? Is postage increasing? What do you anticipate will be the increase in health insurance or worker's comp? Are you opening a new building? For which items in last year's budget was your estimate off?

Involve the staff in budget planning. They know where there is waste; they know where there are shortages. If you ask them, they will tell you.

Sources of Data for Estimating Expenditures

- Announcements of increases in postage rates or utilities (or other disposable resource)
- Letters from vendors announcing an increase in journal costs or the addition of shipping charges
- Notifications of increases in employee benefits or union contract agreements
- Copies of warranties giving dates when the library takes over maintenance of a product (maintenance contracts)
- Employee feedback about department/branch costs, items needed, and anticipated financial changes
- Past year's budget and expenditures
- Staff contracts (recruitment expenditures as required)
- External labor and equipment costs and vendor contracts
- New legislative mandates
- Anticipated training and travel expenditures
- New projects and marketing
- Budgets of other libraries of same size and equal level of services

BUDGET CALENDAR

The budget calendar is used to schedule and communicate the activities involved in preparing the library's budget. It may be no more than a list of key actions and decision points (dates). The budget-activity calendar reminds the administration of tasks and deadlines and can also be used to make assignments and note the progression of budget development and approval.

Each library has unique needs and deadlines, but the stages are similar for most libraries. Most libraries will complete four phases in the budgeting process: planning, preparation, review, and adoption. Libraries must also implement a means of continuous evaluation and monitoring, which you will learn about in Chapter 3. Fine tuning of start and ending dates and allocation of time to various tasks are at the discretion of each library and its governing body.

PREPARATION

Keep a budget folder or electronic file throughout the year. This file is where you should put articles about increases in postage rates or utilities, letters from vendors announcing the increase in journal costs or the addition of shipping charges, notifications of increases in employee benefits or union contract agreements, and copies of warranties giving dates when the library takes over maintenance of a product. Refer to this information for estimating expenditures.

Although the director is ultimately responsible for the budget, each department head and supervisor should have a budget folder of items needed, costs, and anticipated financial changes. Begin the budget with the known costs and those that you probably cannot change. These include rent, lease payments, repayment of bonds, salaries and benefits for full-time personnel, maintenance contracts, and utilities. Then plug in the variables (materials budget, travel, equipment replacement, supplies, new purchases). Usually salaries and benefits will represent 60 to 70 percent of the library's budget, followed by 15 to 20 percent for library materials. That leaves 10 to 25 percent of the budget for office supplies, equipment, maintenance contracts, memberships, fees, bindery charges, travel, electronic service charges, utilities, internal service charges from other departments, postage,

Worth checking out . . .

Black, W. K. "The Budget as a Planning Tool." *Journal of Library Administration* 18, no. 3/4 (1993): 171–88.
Seer, Gitelle. "Special Library Financial Management: The Essentials of Library Budgeting." *The Bottom Line: Managing Library Finances* 13, no. 4 (2000): 186–92.

janitorial services, furnishings, printing, repayment of bonds, and any other costs.

Keep *all* budget preparation documents readily available until the year for which you are budgeting has ended. Then follow the retention schedule for records mandated by your institution. It is not unusual to be told to change salary increases to 2.5 percent when they had been figured at 4 percent, or to receive an additional amount of money midyear that can be used for an item that was deleted from the original budget presentation. If you have the original preparation sheets (even if they are on self-sticking notes and scratch pads), you can make these changes with minimal effort. Figure 2-4 shows the Record Retention Schedule that the Delaware Association of Nonprofit Agencies recommends.

PRESENTATION

For the budget presentation, you will use the format that your governing agency stipulates. This is your opportunity to explain how the proposed budget is based upon a community-needs assessment, follows the library's strategic-planning process, carries out the library's vision and mission statements, and helps meet the community's goals.

Follow all of the guidelines that your governing authority provides, and do not deviate from the required format. They base their decisions on comparable material from several competing agencies and have chosen a format that will work best for them. There are several things you can do to increase the likelihood of their approving your budget.

- Keep the presentation simple, and stick to the information that is essential to getting your message across.
- Show that you understand your governing agency's priorities. Explain your budget in terms of the city's, county's, school district's, or university's priorities. Show how the library is helping to meet those goals and objectives.
- Be honest. Do not exaggerate. Do not mislead.
- Be able to justify each item in your budget.
- If asked, be prepared to tell which items could be cut and what the ramifications of those cuts would be.
- Be prepared with anecdotal evidence of what each service has provided to the community. If an opportunity arises, use that story or testimony effectively.
- Know the facts about your library and each branch or unit. What is the average cost of a book? How many items per capita circulated last year? How many people visited the library? How many people used the library's

Steps in Detailed Budget Preparation

1. Gather all of your sources of data for preparing the budget.
2. Analyze and validate the accuracy of previous budgets against actual expenditures.
3. List, and be prepared to justify, anticipated expenditures.
4. Determine cash flow (know when money will be received and spent during the fiscal year). Financial management software can aid in generating a cash-flow projection.
5. Compile your data and select the appropriate budget type(s) as well as the level of detail and definition of categories required.
6. Prepare the detailed budget (use spreadsheet or financial management software).
7. Distribute budget to key staff members for review.

Records Retention Schedule			
Federal, state, and local governments often mandate the retention of records. The following table provides you with the minimum requirements.			
Accident reports/claims (settled cases)	7 years	Correspondence (routine) with customers and/or vendors	2 years
Accounts payable ledgers and schedules	7 years	Deeds, mortgages, and bills of sale	Permanently
Accounts receivable ledgers and schedules	7 years	Depreciation schedules	Permanently
		Duplicate deposit slips	2 years
Audit reports	Permanently	Employment applications	3 years
Bank reconciliations	2 years	Expense analyses/expense distribution schedules	7 years
Bank statements	2 years		
Capital stock and bond records; ledgers, transfer registers, stubs showing issues, records of interest coupons, options, etc.	Permanently	Financial statements (year-end, others optional)	Permanently
		Garnishments	7 years
Cash books	Permanently	General/private ledgers, year-end trial balance	Permanently
Charts of accounts	Permanently	Insurance policies (expired)	3 years
Checks (canceled— see exception below)	7 years	Insurance records, current accident	Permanently
Checks (canceled for important payments, for example, taxes, purchases of property, or special contracts. Checks should be filed with the papers pertaining to the underlying transaction).	Permanently	Minute book or directors, stockholders, bylaws, and charter	Permanently
		Notes receivable ledgers and schedules	7 years
		Option records (expired)	7 years
Contracts, mortgages, notes, and leases (expired)	7 years	Patents and related papers	Permanently
		Payroll records and summaries	7 years
Contracts, mortgages, notes, and leases (still in effect)	Permanently	Personnel files (terminated)	7 years
		Petty cash vouchers	3 years
Correspondence (general)	2 years	Physical inventory tags	3 years
Correspondence (legal and important matters only)	Permanently	Plant cost ledgers	7 years

Figure 2-4. Record Retention Schedule Recommended by the Delaware Association of Nonprofit Agencies, http://www.delawarenonprofit.org/FinMgmntFaq2.html

Records Retention Schedule

Federal, state, and local governments often mandate the retention of records. The following table provides you with the minimum requirements.

Property appraisals by outside appraisers	Permanently	Scrap and salvage records (inventories sale, etc.)	7 years
Property records, including costs, depreciation reserves, year-end trial balances, depreciation schedules, blueprints, and plans	Permanently	Stenographers' notebooks	1 year
		Stock and bond certificates (cancelled)	7 years
Purchase orders (except purchasing department copy)	1 year	Stockroom withdrawl forms	1 year
		Subsidiary ledgers	7 years
Purchase orders (purchasing department copy)	7 years	Tax returns and worksheets, revenue agents' reports, and other documents relating to determination of income tax liability	Permanently
Receiving sheets	1 year		
Retirement and pension records	Permanently		
Requisitions	1 year	Time books/cards	7 years
Sales commission reports	3 years	Trademark registrations and copyrights	Permanently
Sales records	7 years		

Figure 2-4. Record Retention Schedule Recommended by the Delaware Association of Nonprofit Agencies, http://www.delawarenonprofit.org/FinMgmntFaq2.html (*Continued*)

online resources? What is the average cost for each interlibrary loan? How do your salaries and other costs compare with those of surrounding libraries?

• Be prepared for unexpected surprises and "opportunities." If you had an extra $100,000 in your budget, how would you spend it? How could your current staff handle running the school's technology center next year? What would your department need to take charge of the city's website? Stay cool, breathe deeply, and answer with honesty. This is your opportunity to shine!

Figure 2-5 is an example of a PowerPoint presentation or outline for a budget presentation.

PowerPoint Example/Outline

FY2005 BUDGET RECOMMENDATIONS
CITYVIEW PUBLIC LIBRARY SYSTEM

Vision statement: "Providing lifelong learning and informed citizenship"

FY BUDGET GOALS AND OBJECTIVES
- Provide basic library services that meet the expectations of Cityview citizens with a structurally balanced budget
- Address environmental and economic constraints and opportunities
- State resource needs of the library system

TODAY'S SITUATION
- Overview of library system (use brief bullets, discuss details verbally)
- Strengths (e.g., location, facilities)
- Weaknesses (e.g., limited staff, limited hours)
- Opportunities (e.g., increased demand for library services, technology)
- Threats/concerns (e.g., tax base, security, assessed valuation down)

HOW DID WE GET HERE?
- Any relevant historical information (wage freezes, library branch openings)
- Highlight previous budgets (relate how you used the money you asked for last time)
- Assumptions that are no longer valid (legislative mandate, tax base increase)
- Resulting challenges

BUDGET HIGHLIGHTS
- High-level financial plan
- Overview of proposed budget (use several slides to cover this material if necessary)

KEY ISSUES
- State specifics of funding challenges and facts on costs
- Facilities and technology
- Personnel
- Programs
- Outsourced/contract services
- State risks and negative consequences of not funding library budget programs

RECOMMENDATION
- Recommend adoption of proposed budget
- Summarize the results if ratified
- Wish list for windfall or next year's budget

Figure 2-5. Sample Outline for Budget Presentation

PUBLIC HEARINGS

Public budgets must, by law, give the public an opportunity to give their opinions before the budget is adopted. Notice of these hearings should be publicly posted (for example, as in figure 2-6) with an overview of the budget so the public can decide whether they want to attend. The public hearings are normally held near the end of the budget process, perhaps within the month before the fiscal year begins.

Public hearings are informational, political, and accountable reports to the city's, school's, or university's constituency. Even though they are mostly routine, sometimes members of the public do come to protest or support an action being taken (especially if taxes are being raised or a library branch is being closed).

PUBLIC HEARING NOTICE

Anytown City Council and Anytown Public Library

Public Hearings on the 2006 Public Library Budget and Services

[Weekday], November 4th, 2005, at 5:30 p.m.

Council Chambers

Room #, City Hall Court House

PUBLIC HEARING PURPOSE:

To Hear Concerns and Comments from the General Public and Interested Organizations and Groups Regarding the Public Library 2006 Budget, Service Levels, and Financing Plans for Library Services.

All concerned citizens and patrons may attend this meeting and comment on spending and service delivery plans for the Public Library.

The Public Hearing has been set for [Weekday], November 4th, 2005, at 5:30 p.m. in the Council Chambers.

Please review the following overview of the Proposed 2006 Library Budget. Comments and questions are welcomed regarding Library finances and services. With valuable input from interested citizens, organizations, and groups, the City Council and Library Board hope to be able to consider additional options for being responsive to the service and information needs of Anytown residents and taxpayers.

Figure 2-6. Public Hearing Notice

Positive Consequences . . . Letting Patrons Know the Value of Their Tax Dollars

Stanislaus County "Library Tax" Up for Renewal

It is reasonable to ask "How much of a difference has the 'library tax' made for the county library?"

The answer: A lot! The revenue generated annually is close to $8 million, providing 75 percent of library funding. In 2002–03 this has enabled the libraries countywide to stay open 569 hours per week. In 1994–95, opening hours had been cut back to 240. In addition, children's story times, which had been eliminated, were restored, and so were reference services, which had also been severely curtailed. . . .

While all this was accomplished, the burden on the individual taxpayer has been hardly noticeable.

Source: H. Dieter Renning, "We'll All Benefit from Measure P," *Turlock Journal*, Wednesday, February 4, 2004, www.turlockjournal.com/printer/article.asp?c+93721.

MINUTES

Board of Trustees
Regular Meeting
Tuesday,
September 14, 2004
Readerville
District Public Library

A Public Hearing on the proposed 2005 Library Budget was called to order at 7:30 p.m. by the Board President. Present were Smith, Brown, Burton, Stewart, Dawson, and Anderson. Also present were City Attorney Davis and Library Director Blue.

Davis pointed out that the public hearing was on setting the millage rate for 2005 as well as the annual budget. Blue briefly reviewed the proposed budget. Following comments and questions from trustees, the hearing was opened for public comment. There was none, and the hearing was closed at 8:40 p.m.

The Public Hearing adjourned.

ADOPTION

At the end of the budget process, the budget for the next fiscal year is adopted. Usually adopting the budget is simply an agenda item at the end of the public hearing or a scheduled and publicized public meeting. Sometimes governing authorities get bogged down in the budget process and run out of time before the budget must be adopted. If the government does not adopt the budget before the fiscal year, the government will not have operating funds for salaries and other expenses when the year begins.

BUDGET CYCLE

The budget cycle will last ten months or so in most governmental entities. If you are a library director, much of your life will be spent in preparing and defending budgets. Some governments have adopted a biennial (two-year) budget cycle. You can see Minnesota's two-year budget at www.budget.state.mn.us/budget/index.shtml. Figure 2-7 shows the budget calendar for county governments in the State of Texas with assigned responsibilities.

SUMMARY

Conscientious budget preparation and development are critical to the library's achieving its service goals and determining its response to a needs assessment; it is also critical to the future direction of the library's mission. This chapter outlined a framework for examining the budget process. You have learned how budgeting provides information for internal management and how it communicates library fiscal practices and institutional goals in monetary terms to the governing bodies and the library staff. You have reviewed basic budget components and walked through the library budget creation and ratification process. Following the requirements and recommendations for effective budget preparation and documentation enables the library administration to have the greatest success in using the budget as a management tool to communicate financial management goals to library staff and governing bodies.

County of Good Public Servants Budget Calendar		
Date	**Action**	**Official**
January 1	Assessment date	Chief appraiser
January	Prepare preliminary revenue estimates (revenue estimating is really a year-round process.	Budget officer department heads
February	Establish budget policy.	Budget officer governing body
	Establish budget calendar with governing body.	Budget officer
	Develop budget format and outline of contents.	Budget officer
	Begin preparing statistical and other supplementary information.	Budget officer
March 1	Communicate budget policy and calendar to department heads and all employees.	Budget officer
	Distribute departmental request forms.	Budget officer
March/April	Help departments complete request forms.	Budget officer
May 15	Chief appraiser submits estimate of total appraised value to appraisal review board for review and determination of protests.	Chief appraiser
May	Revise revenue estimates.	Budget officer department heads
May	Prepare preliminary budget.	Budget officer with department heads
	Revise departmental estimates and/or develop spending alternatives for governing body's consideration.	Budget officer
June	Governing body reviews budget.	Governing body
July	Departmental hearings	Budget officer department heads
July 25	Deliver certified appraisal roll to tax assessor.	Chief appraiser

August 1	1. Deliver the appraisal roll to the court showing:
	  • Total appraised, assessed, and taxable values
	  • Total appraised, assessed, and taxable values for new property
	2. Certify a collection rate for the current year.
		Tax assessor

Figure 2-7. Texas Budget Calendar for County Governments

	County of Good Public Servants Budget Calendar	
Date	**Action**	**Official**
August 7	Calculate, publish, and present to the court: 1. Effective tax rate, rollback rate, and calculation methods 2. Estimated amount of unencumbered interest and sinking, and maintenance and operations balances 3. Schedule of debt obligations 4. Projected sales and use tax to reduce property tax 5. Amount of increase (decrease) based on effective tax rate 6. Information on transferred departments or functions 7. Information on tax effect of transferred departments of functions	Person designated by the court
August	Complete proposed budget.	Governing body
August	File proposed budget with county clerk and make it available for public inspection at least fifteen days prior to public budget hearing.	Budget officer
August	Decide whether it is necessary to increase taxes by more than 3 percent over the effective tax rate.	Governing body
August/ September	Hold public hearings for tax increase; if necessary, vote on tax increase.	Governing body
	Hold public hearing on budget.	Governing body
	Adopt budget.	Governing body
August/ September	Levy taxes before September 30, or the sixtieth day after the date the certified appraisal roll is received. (If not, the tax rate for the county for that tax year is the lower of the effective tax rate calculated for that tax year or the tax rate adopted by the county for the preceding tax year.)	Governing body
	File copy of adopted budget with county clerk and county auditor (if required).	County clerk
Figure 2-7. Texas Budget Calendar for County Governments (*Continued*)		

Source: Carole Keeton Strayhorn, Texas Comptroller of Public Accounts, www.window.state.tx.us/lga/budgetco/ ch5.html.

3 HOW CAN A LIBRARY MONITOR ITS BUDGET?

OVERVIEW

If you are a library manager, by the time the library's budget is final you are tempted to celebrate and then put the budget on a shelf because you know that the process will begin again in another couple of months. However, now you have to monitor the budget.

There will be many variations to the budget throughout the year as staff changes, temperatures cause variations in utility bills, and the bills actually come in to be paid. You might experience an across-the-board budget cut midway into the year, or there is always the possibility that you will get lucky: additional revenues might come in, and the governing authorities will permit you to increase the budget. In this chapter you will learn how to monitor the budget as you order materials, react to internal and external developments, and observe the actual changes in accounts.

REQUISITIONS AND PURCHASE ORDERS

After the budget has been approved and the fiscal year has begun, it is finally time to spend the appropriated funds! Your governing authority will have specific rules for purchasing items for the library. Some governments permit the library director or financial officer to use a government purchasing card (credit card) to make repetitive local purchases (e.g., office or janitorial supplies) or to pay for travel (e.g., plane tickets or hotel reservations). Other purchases will be handled using purchase orders (see figure 3-1) and requisition forms (figure 3-2), which are frequently created and approved online rather than with paper forms.

Generally, the department sends the requisition to the purchasing authority (e.g., the finance department or purchasing department), directing them to purchase a specific item. A purchase order is then issued to the vendor who can provide the requested product. Although an account clerk

Purchase Order Request Form

Req. No. _____   Purchase Order No. _____

Account No. _____   Account Name _____

Professor's Name _____   Signature _____

Your Name _____   Your Email _____   Your Phone Number _____

Date _____

Special Instructions:

Item No.	Description	Quantity	Unit (each, pkg, case)	Per-Unit Price	Line Item Total Price

☐ In Stock   ☐ Lead Time _____   Total Price _____

Shipping Preference   ☐ Ground   ☐ Express

Complete Name of Vendor: _____   Name of Contact: _____

Address of Vendor: _____   Contact's phone number: _____

_____   Contact's fax number: _____

Please attach any web printout or email or faxed quotation received from vendor.

Figure 3-1. Purchase Order Request Form

may create the requisition or purchase order entries, the director will ultimately be responsible for these expenditures and should approve them.

A library should always have a system of checks and balances for purchases using public funds. Governments and other agencies have detailed purchasing manuals giving the thresholds and procedures for purchasing items (with and without bids), awarding contracts, and selecting vendors. As a manager, you will be responsible for following proper procedures when handling public funds. If you are considering something that you would not want to see in tomorrow's headlines, don't do it!

*Michigan***Tech.**
Michigan Technological University

Requisition #:	R _____
Purchase Order #:	P _____
Blanket Order #:	BL _____

PURCHASE REQUISITION

This is NOT a purchase order

Suggested Vendor:

Vendor Code: _____
(if known)

Vendor Name &
Address:

Phone: _____
Fax: _____
Ship-To Code: _____

Transaction Date: _____
Deliver By: _____
Requestor: _____
Phone: _____
Organization Name: _____

Line Item	Comm Code	Item Description	Unit	Qty	Unit Price	Total
1						

Total from Page 1:   Total from Page 2:   Grand Total:

Accounting Data to Be completed by Requisitioner

	Index	Organization	Account	Accounting Split Detail	
				Amount	Item Numbers
Seq 1:					
Seq 2:					
Seq 3:					

Purchasing Office Use Only:

FOB: _____   Disc: _____
Carrier: _____   Ship to: _____
Buyer: _____   Date: _____

Accounting Office Use Only:

Budget checked by: _____
Date: _____

Approval Signatures

1. *Are there any live mammals?   _____
2. *Computer Acquisition Committee approval number for computer-related
   purchases over $49,999.99:   _____

< $5,000
-or-
$5,000+ &
Bank Orders

_____   _____
Financial Manager (Account Custodian)   Date

_____   _____
Dept. Head, Chair, Director, Dean   Date

*Other   _____   _____
Date

Figure 3-2. Purchase Requisition

Source: http://www.admin.mtu.edu/pur/pdf/purchase_requisition.pdf.   (Rev. JUL-2003)

Michigan Technological University

Use this page for additional purchase requisitions. The total from this page will be added to your total from the first page. Please make sure you turn in both pages.

PURCHASE REQUISITION

Page 2

Line Item	Comm Code	Item Description	Unit	Qty	Unit Price	Total
					Total—This Page:	

Figure 3-2. Purchase Requisition (*Continued*)

APPROVAL AND PAYMENT OF BILLS

After you have received all of the items you ordered and have verified that they are what you ordered and in proper condition, you should authorize payment of the bill. As the person financially responsible for the budget, you should not authorize payment for any item that has not been received. If there are discrepancies, contact the vendor and make arrangements for the return of defective merchandise, replacement goods, or cancellations and deductions from the bill. Only then should you approve payment for the goods received.

Most governments have laws requiring that vendors be paid within thirty to forty-five days after the receipt of goods. My personal experience is that it is easiest to set aside a specific time every week to approve requisitions and process payments.

> Fugitive librarian Dorothy "Dot" Corbett turned herself in to Bethel Park police late yesterday afternoon. . . .
>
> On Thursday, police issued a warrant for her arrest on six counts each of theft, theft by deception and receiving stolen property in connection with $27,500 missing from a library account.
>
> *Source*: Mary Niederberger, "Bethel Park Librarian Returns, Surrenders to Police," *Post-Gazette,* Tuesday, March 2, 1999, www.post-gazette.com/regionstate/19990302librarian5.asp.

ENCUMBRANCES

Encumbrances are funds that are committed but not yet spent. For example, you always encumber twelve months of salary expenses and set the funds aside to pay future salaries for library staff. As you monitor financial records, you track the actual expenses against the encumbrance to realize the amount that is saved or that exceeds the budget as a result of fluctuations in actual time worked, hiring, resignations, and other activities covered by that budget category.

The library materials budget is the most challenging encumbrance. The encumbrance is placed against the budget when the materials are ordered and includes all anticipated expenses (including shipping and handling), assuming that all materials on the order are received.

Then, as the materials arrive (sometimes over six to eight weeks), you track the actual cost against the encumbrance and the balance in the account remains encumbered. When you receive the last shipment against that order, you will subtract all of the actual costs from the total encumbered funds, and then put the balance back into the materials budget to be spent. If actual costs were higher or shipping charges were not anticipated correctly, you will have to deduct the actual costs from the remaining budget.

Many libraries try to encumber their materials budget within the first nine months of the fiscal year so there is not a large balance during the budget-planning process, and the bills are paid by the end of the fiscal year. Funds do not normally carry over from one fiscal year to the next. Periodical and standing orders are the easiest to encumber at the beginning

> "Cities and villages and other units of government must now comply with the Illinois Prompt Payment Act which became effective July 1, 1987. (See Ch. 85, par. 5601 et. seq. of the Illinois Revised Statutes.)" The law resulted from the complaints of some vendors who experienced delays in receiving payment for goods or services purchased by local governments.
>
> The Local Government Prompt Payment Act requires specific action to be taken by local governments when purchasing goods or services.
>
> *Source*: "Prompt Payment of Bills and Compensation," www.lib.niu.edu/ipo/im870925.html.

of the fiscal year, and they may have the greatest fluctuation in cost from year to year.

ACCOUNTING SYSTEMS

Accounting systems are generally of two types: accrual and cash. If you use accrual-basis accounting, you record income when it is earned (rather than when it is received) and expense the item when it is ordered (rather than when the payment is made). Cash-basis accounting is like checkbook accounting. You record the income when it is received, and deduct the expenses when they are actually paid.

If you are using accrual accounting and you order a computer in November, the funds you use to pay for it will be counted as expended in November, not when the computer and invoice actually arrive. If you use cash-basis accounting and order that same computer in November, if it arrives and is paid for in February, the funds will not be counted as expended until February.

Or, to take another example, perhaps the library's allocation from the state library arrives on June 10, but, using the accrual method, it is not accrued and cannot be spent until the end of the month, when the revenues for the month of June are all posted. Using cash-basis accounting, that allocation would be available on the day that it is deposited in the bank.

Accrual accounting makes it possible to track encumbrances and track expenses against those encumbered amounts. If an unexpected donation is received, cash accounting will permit expenses against that donation when it is deposited in the bank. Accrual accounting will need to accrue the income and then "realize" it, perhaps causing a month's delay before the funds are available for expending.

City and state governments currently use the modified accrual method of the Governmental Accounting Standards Board (GASB), found at www.gasb.org. The modified accrual basis records supplies and other consumables, for example, toilet paper, computer supplies, and processing supplies, when they are purchased, as you would do if you used cash-basis accounting. Blanket orders and periodical subscriptions are other examples of items for which the funds are accrued when they are ordered.

Using pure accrual-basis accounting, you would track those supplies (which with the modified accrual accounting would be charged at the point of purchase) by estimating how much would be used each month and charging the expense to that month. Under the pure accrual method, quantity purchases might not all be charged to the same budget year.

FUND ACCOUNTING

Most libraries will have several funds that cannot be commingled; each requires separate accounting and reporting. For example:

- Photocopy revenues (which may require collection and payment of a sales tax)
- Fine money (which is deposited with the governing agency as revenue)
- Friends of the Library used-book sale money (which is given to the Friends treasurer)
- State or federal funds (which require tracking for those governments)
- Endowments or grants (which have specified uses and reporting forms)
- Capital funds (used for building or large projects)
- General fund (the monies in the general operating fund, which is the annual or biennial budgeted amount)

The governing authority may track some of these funds (fine money, photocopy revenues, general fund, and capital funds), but the library may need to do its own tracking of ear-marked state and federal funds, endowments, and grants.

STATEMENTS AND RECONCILIATION

When the monthly or quarterly financial statements arrive, take the time to review them. Look for anything that seems unusual, especially trends that are going in an unexpected direction. Mistakes are easily made and just as easily corrected, but they have to be caught in a reasonable time. Finding a mistake in your library's favor in last year's statements will not make those funds available this year. It is good to have at least two people (you and your account clerk or financial manager) review the statements to look for errors or trends. Having more than one person examine the statements also provides a system of checks and balances to prevent misappropriations or embezzlement. Embezzlement is a serious federal crime, and it carries heavy penalties: stiff fines, imprisonment, or both. Many library governing authorities have adopted the American Library Association's Code of Ethics (see figure 3-3) as an ethical framework.

American Library Association

Code of Ethics

As members of the American Library Association, we recognize the importance of codifying and making known to the profession and to the general public the ethical principles that guide the work of librarians, other professionals providing information services, library trustees, and library staffs. Ethical dilemmas occur when values are in conflict. The American Library Association Code of Ethics states the values to which we are committed, and embodies the ethical responsibilities of the profession in this changing information environment. We significantly influence or control the selection, organization, preservation, and dissemination of information. In a political system grounded in an informed citizenry we are members of a profession explicitly committed to intellectual freedom and the freedom of access to information. We have a special obligation to ensure the free flow of information and ideas to present and future generations. The principles of this Code are expressed in broad statements to guide ethical decision making. These statements provide a framework; they cannot and do not dictate conduct to cover particular situations.

I.

We provide the highest level of service to all library users through appropriate and usefully organized resources; equitable service policies; equitable access; and accurate, unbiased, and courteous responses to all requests.

II.

We uphold the principles of intellectual freedom and resist all efforts to censor library resources.

III.

We protect each library user's right to privacy and confidentiality with respect to information sought or received and resources consulted, borrowed, acquired, or transmitted.

IV.

We recognize and respect intellectual property rights.

V.

We treat co-workers and other colleagues with respect, fairness, and good faith, and advocate conditions of employment that safeguard the rights and welfare of all employees of our institutions.

VI.

We do not advance private interests at the expense of library users, colleagues, or our employing institutions.

VII.

We distinguish between our personal convictions and professional duties and do not allow our personal beliefs to interfere with fair representation of the aims of our institutions or the provision of access to their information resources.

VIII.

We strive for excellence in the profession by maintaining and enhancing our own knowledge and skills, by encouraging the professional development of co-workers, and by fostering the aspirations of potential members of the profession.

Adopted by the ALA Council, June 28, 1995.

Figure 3-3. The American Library Association Code of Ethics

Source: American Library Association. *Intellectual Freedom Manual*, 6th ed., pp. 407–8.

AUDIT PROCESS AND PREPARATION

An audit is a comprehensive analysis, by a professional or a governing body, of your financial management procedures and activities. The auditor produces a report, with a variety of supplements and recommendations, that indicates how well your library is managing its resources. In most libraries, the audit is included with the parenting government's audit. If the library is private or self-governing (e.g., a district library), the library director will need to arrange for an annual financial audit. See figure 3-4 for text from the Government Auditing Standards and figure 3-5 for a sample report from an independent auditor.

ANNUAL REPORTS

Library directors are required to complete an annual report for the governing agency and to their constituency. In the annual report you will include financial income and expenses for the year, circulation and other library-use statistics, and names of those responsible for library operations (director, board chair, etc.).

To save time and maintain consistency, it is important that the statistics in the local library's annual report be compiled using the same method that is required by the local governing authority, the regional system, the state, the accrediting agency, and the national government. Before you start to collect statistics or compile financial data, review the various annual reports to see which data will be needed. When comparable data are collected, you will find that annual reports are very useful for comparing data with other libraries of the same type and size. A sample Texas Academic Library Statistical Report form to be completed by the local academic library is shown in Appendix B. Examples in the sidebar "Compiling Statistical Reports" show how the local academic library annual report is then used to populate the state and federal reports.

BUDGET MONITORING

Once the budget year begins, you will continually be monitoring the budget. As you compare actual expenses against the amount budgeted, you may find it necessary to transfer funds from one area of the budget to another. Some agencies permit moving funds on a quarterly basis, some semiannually. If you

---

U.S. Code Section 641. Public money, property or records

Whoever embezzles, steals, purloins, or knowingly converts to his use or the use of another, or without authority, sells, conveys or disposes of any record, voucher, money, or thing of value of the United States or of any department or agency thereof, or any property made or being made under contract for the United States or any department or agency thereof; or Whoever receives, conceals, or retains the same with intent to convert it to his use or gain, knowing it to have been embezzled, stolen, purloined or converted—Shall be fined under this title or imprisoned not more than ten years, or both; but if the value of such property does not exceed the sum of $1,000, he shall be fined under this title or imprisoned not more than one year, or both. The word "value" means face, par, or market value, or cost price, either wholesale or retail, whichever is greater.

Worth Checking Out . . .

Library of Congress Financial Statements: www.loc.gov/fsd/fin/.

Government Auditing Standards

Generally Accepted Government Auditing Standards (GAGAS)

Financial Audits

2.4 Financial audits include financial statement and financial related audits.

a. Financial statement audits provide reasonable assurance about whether the financial statements of an audited entity present fairly the financial position, results of operations, and cash flows in conformity with generally accepted accounting principles.[1] Financial statement audits also include audits of financial statements prepared in conformity with any of several other bases of accounting discussed in auditing standards issued by the American Institute of Certified Public Accountants (AICPA).

b. Financial related audits include determining whether (1) financial information is presented in accordance with established or stated criteria, (2) the entity has adhered to specific financial compliance requirements, or (3) the entity's internal control structure over financial reporting and/or safeguarding assets is suitably designed and implemented to achieve the control objectives.

2.5 Financial related audits may, for example, include audits of the following items:

a. Segments of financial statements; financial information (for example, statement of revenue and expenses, statement of cash receipts and disbursements, statement of fixed assets); budget requests; and variances between estimated and actual financial performance.

b. Internal controls over compliance with laws and regulations, such as those governing the (1) bidding for, (2) accounting for, and (3) reporting on grants and contracts (including proposals, amounts billed, amounts due on termination claims, and so forth).

c. Internal controls over financial reporting and/or safeguarding assets, including controls using computer-based systems.

d. Compliance with laws and regulations and allegations of fraud.

Figure 3-4. Government Auditing Standards

1. Three authoritative bodies for generally accepted accounting principles are the Governmental Accounting Standards Board (GASB), the Financial Accounting Standards Board (FASB), and the sponsors of the Federal Accounting Standards Advisory Board (FASAB). GASB establishes accounting principles and financial reporting standards for state and local government entities. FASB establishes accounting principles and financial reporting standards for nongovernment entities. The sponsors of FASAB—the Secretary of the Treasury, the Director of the Office of Management and Budget, and the Comptroller General—jointly establish accounting principles and financial reporting standards for the federal government, based on recommendations from FASAB.

Source: http://www.gao.gov/govaud/ybk01.htm.

are overspending in one area, you must underspend in another because the bottom line of the budget does not normally change after it has been adopted.

Above all, the budget must balance! If revenues increase, you may have an opportunity to increase spending in that budget year, but you will need approval from the governing authority. If you receive gifts or donations,

To the Librarian of Congress and the National Digital Library Trust Fund

We have audited the accompanying statement of financial position of the National Digital Library Trust Fund (the Fund) as of September 30, 2003, and the related statements of activities and cash flows for the year then ended. These financial statements are the responsibility of the Fund's management. Our responsibility is to express an opinion on these financial statements based on our audit.

SUMMARY

As stated in our opinion, the financial statements are presented fairly, in all material respects, in conformity with accounting principles generally accepted in the United States of America.

Our consideration of internal control over financial reporting resulted in no material weaknesses.

The results of our tests of compliance with certain provisions of laws and regulations disclosed an instance of noncompliance, described below, that is required to be reported herein under *Government Auditing Standards* issued by the Comptroller General of the United States:

   Noncompliance with Congressional Accountability Act of 1995.

The results of our tests disclosed no other instances of noncompliance that are required to be reported under *Government Auditing Standards.*

The following sections discuss our opinion on the Fund's financial statements, our consideration of the Fund's internal control over financial reporting, our tests of the Fund's compliance with certain provisions of applicable laws and regulations, and management's and our responsibilities.

OPINION ON FINANCIAL STATEMENTS

We have audited the accompanying statement of financial position of the Fund as of September 30, 2003, and the related statements of activities and cash flows for the year then ended. These financial statements are the responsibility of the Fund's management. Our responsibility is to express an opinion on these financial statements based on our audit.

We conducted our audit in accordance with auditing standards generally accepted in the United States of America and the standards applicable to financial audits contained in *Government Auditing Standards* issued by the Comptroller General of the United States. Those standards require that we plan and perform the audit to obtain reasonable assurance about whether the financial statements are free of material misstatement. An audit includes examining, on a test basis, evidence supporting the amounts and disclosures in the financial statements. An audit also includes assessing the accounting principles used and significant estimates made by management, as well as evaluating the overall financial statement presentation. We believe that our audit provides a reasonable basis for our opinion.

In our opinion, the financial statements referred to above present fairly, in all material respects, the financial position of the Fund as of September 30, 2003, and the changes in its net assets and its cash flows for the year then ended in conformity with accounting principles generally accepted in the United States of America.

Figure 3-5. Independent Auditor's Report

Our audit was performed for the purpose of forming an opinion on the basic financial statements taken as a whole. The accompanying supplemental information contained in the consolidating schedules of financial position and activities is presented for purposes of additional analysis and is not a required part of the basic financial statements. Such information has been subjected to the auditing procedures applied in the audit of the basic financial statements and, in our opinion, is fairly stated, in all material respects, in relation to the basic financial statements taken as a whole.

INTERNAL CONTROL OVER FINANCIAL REPORTING

In planning and performing our audit, we considered the Fund's internal control over financial reporting in order to determine our auditing procedures for the purpose of expressing our opinion on the financial statements and not to provide assurance on the internal control over financial reporting. Our consideration of the internal control over financial reporting would not necessarily disclose all matters in the internal control over financial reporting that might be material weaknesses. A material weakness is a condition in which the design or operation of one or more of the internal control components does not reduce to a relatively low level the risk that misstatements in amounts that would be material in relation to the financial statements being audited may occur and not be detected within a timely period by employees in the normal course of performing their assigned functions. We noted no matters involving the internal control over financial reporting and its operation that we consider to be material weakness. We noted other matters involving the internal control over financial reporting that we have reported to management of the Fund in a separate letter dated February 27, 2004.

COMPLIANCE WITH LAWS AND REGULATIONS

The management of the Fund is responsible for complying with laws and regulations applicable to the Fund. As part of obtaining reasonable assurance about whether the Fund's financial statements are free of material misstatement, we performed tests of its compliance with certain provisions of laws, regulations, contracts, and grants, noncompliance with which could have a direct and material effect on the determination of financial statement amounts. However, providing an opinion on compliance with those provisions was not an objective of our audit and, accordingly, we do not express such an opinion.

The results of our tests of compliance with the laws and regulations described in the preceding paragraph disclosed an instance of noncompliance, described below, with the following laws and regulations that are required to be reported under *Government Auditing Standards.*

* During fiscal year 2003, the Fund was not in compliance with the "Congressional Accountability Act (CAA) of 1995." In the CAA, Congress made its facilities and employees subject to the same safety laws that applied outside the Legislative Branch. In 1997, other provisions of the CAA applied fire safety standards to Congressional buildings. The Office of Compliance conducted a year-long fire safety investigation that culminated in a report issued in January 2001 that identified numerous safety hazards in the three Capitol Hill Buildings utilized by the Fund.

The results of our tests disclosed no other instances of noncompliance that are required to be reported under *Government Auditing Standards.*

This report is intended solely for the information and use of the Librarian of Congress, management of National Digital Library Fund, and Congress, and is not intended to be and should not be used by anyone other than these specified parties.

Figure 3-5. Independent Auditor's Report (*Continued*)

it may be best to deposit those funds in a separate account (accounts for the Friends, a foundation, etc.). Governing authorities find it very tempting to cut the budget proportionate to the amount of the gift!

BUDGET CUTS AND INCREASES

If revenues fall below those anticipated or an emergency expense occurs (e.g., a lawsuit, hurricane, riot, or air conditioner replacement), the total budget may need to be altered midyear. This is a good reason to encumber major expenses—the funds are earmarked before possible cuts occur. When the anticipated budget falls short, the governing authorities will be looking for unencumbered funds remaining in budgets. If you have been meaning to buy new shelving or hire an authorized staff member, you may find that line item frozen. We have all read newspaper stories of hiring freezes, moratoria on travel, cutbacks in library hours, and so forth, when anticipated revenues suddenly fall short of budgeted amounts.

Sometimes, however, there *is* a budget increase—from savings, special appropriations, or "found" money. One city received a huge settlement from a utility company that had been underestimating its franchise payments. Midyear, that money was suddenly available for reallocation. You should always have a wish list ready in case a sudden windfall comes your way!

REVISION PROCESSES

The process for budget revisions is similar to the process for the original budget approval. The library submits the revised budgets to the governing agency, the revisions are incorporated into the total budget, and there are negotiations to get to the required bottom line. Then there will be a public hearing on the revised budget with approval by the governing authorities. The revised budget is then used to adjust departmental budgets so they reflect the new figures, which become effective immediately. Resulting hiring freezes, closures, or cutbacks will also need to take place immediately to realize the projected savings.

Compiling Statistical Reports

Forms That Collect Texas Library Statistics: www.tsl.state.tx.us/ld/pubs/als/about.html.
National Center for Educational Statistics: www.nces.ed.gov/surveys/libraries/academicpeer/.
Texas Academic Library Statistics: www.tsl.state.tx.us/ld/pubs/als/index.html.
Examples of Texas Public Library Statistical Reports and the local library report form are found at
www.tsl.state.tx.us/ld/pubs/pls/2002/2001tplstats.pdf.
Comparative data can be found at http://nces.ed.gov/surveys/libraries/publicpeer/.

FINANCIAL MANAGEMENT SOFTWARE

Financial management accounting systems automate the accounting cycle for library directors and library systems and assist in budget monitoring. There are built-in functions in the software that enable automatic posting to accounts, generation of financial statements, password-protected data-entry screens, and so forth. In most circumstances, the parent organization dictates which financial-management system the library is to use. Staff will be required to acclimate to these systems and report as mandated by governing body policy.

Budget Cuts across the Nation

Beginning March 3, 2003, the District of Columbia Public Library will institute newly reduced public service hours in most of its locations. The reduction was voted on by the Board of Library Trustees in an effort to absorb the city's cut of $587,159 from the library's Fiscal Year 2003 budget in response to falling District revenues, following two additional budget reductions carried over from FY 2002.

Source: DC Public Library Services, *Library News,* February 21, 2003, www.dclibrary.org/news/cut-hours.html.

"ALA has found that libraries in at least 41 states (82 percent) report funding cuts of as much as 50 percent. Most of the data accumulated from published reports reflects deep cuts to library budgets on the federal, state, and local levels."

Source: "ALA's Report on Library Funding in the United States: 41 States Report Cuts," www.ala.org/ala/news/libraryfunding/libraryfunding.htm.

The ALA report lists the following general trends:

"—Libraries report reductions of library personnel; salary freezes; reductions in operating hours

(including some library closings); elimination of some programs and services such as bookmobiles and interlibrary loans; decreased books and materials budgets; minimal hiring of library professionals and staff; and an increased dependence on volunteers and part-time employees.

"—There is an increased trend in fundraising by Friends organizations, volunteers, and community supporters. More importantly, revenues from these campaigns are supplementing operating expenses instead of supporting programs, services, or long-term projects.

"—A small number of libraries are reporting positive impacts such as new construction of libraries, expansion of hours, small pay increases, and reinstatement of previously cut hours or services."

Source: "Colorado Budget Cuts," www.lrs.org/documents/closer_look/budgetcuts.pdf.

14

This section is for those of you with the good fortune to be able to work with your parent organizations to select or customize an integrated financial management system, those of you in stand-alone libraries (e.g., district libraries or some special libraries), or those of you required to manage special funds (e.g., grants or foundations) in separate accounting systems. If you are looking to purchase financial management software in the near future, this section will help you determine your organization's financial management software needs. It also includes a list of questions and features to consider, and resources for current literature on financial management packages.

CONDUCTING A FINANCIAL MANAGEMENT SOFTWARE NEEDS ASSESSMENT

You know the current financial management system is not working. Before you purchase a new software system, it is important to do a "needs assessment," a detailed analysis of the problems, so that you can determine the best resolution. When you conduct your needs assessment, do not assume that a new software package will automatically solve all your problems. The goal of a needs assessment is to provide an analysis of your current financial management system and its components. You should gather information that will help you select the best software from different sources:

- Interview all personnel who interact with the accounting system, from a data-entry clerk to the library director, to identify what is working and which needs are not being met.

- Identify all accounts, subaccounts, programs, and documentation that will be monitored and flowchart all financial processes.

- Delineate any problems with the way tasks are currently accomplished, the way the system functions, and any recurrent bottlenecks.

- Evaluate possible improvements to procedures, technologies, skills/training, task assignments, and any other aspects to the current system.

The best solution to the problem does not necessarily involve purchasing a new software package. But a needs assessment of your financial management system can serve as a good starting point for a request for proposal (RFP) for a new system. There are literally thousands of features available in the current systems; figure 3-6 lists some general questions to consider.

Why not just use a simple spreadsheet or a general ledger, calculator, and a pencil?

- Often these can't meet the regulatory needs of the funding bodies without significant effort by clerical/accounting staff.
- Human error is less likely in a computerized system.
- Audit and reporting are far more time consuming in a paper-based or spreadsheet system.
- There is no built-in flexibility to do analysis over multiple budget cycles.

Compatibility with staff	Are accounting personnel familiar with the software and comfortable with implementing the accounting package? Does staff have the computer skills to operate the software? Is the staff trained in the discipline of managing financial accounts, for example, accurate monthly financial statements and timely reconciliation of monthly bank statements?
System requirements	What equipment and computer operating system(s) do you have? Is the software compatible? Will the library need to invest in new equipment to install the software? Evaluate your computers (operating systems, RAM-processing speed, servers, etc.) and network to ensure they are adequate and compatible. The installation specifications for most packages are listed on their marketing brochures and within the technical specifications.
Security	Access and password issues: Do you want access to the financial management system over the network? Some software will allow you to customize the screens and account access by the user. Think about stability and back-up issues.
Cost	For most packages, the costs are comparable to the organization's size and needs; the larger the organization, the greater the needs, the higher the costs. What is your budget for the software and will there be additional funds each year if you purchase a modular financial management system that can be upgraded?
Reporting	What are your reporting requirements? Define your institution's reporting needs, for example, need for customizable or flexible reporting, list-specific reporting requirements, need for retrospective reporting of prior budget cycles, etc. Are there templates or can the reports be customized? Which report templates will you use? Will these reports address special regulatory mandates such as nonprofit IRS forms, and will the data export to these forms? Have you reviewed a print-out of all sample report templates for suitability and completeness? Are you able to integrate with report writers such as Excel with ODBC, Crystal Reports, or Microsoft Business Solutions for Analytics—FRx Pro to generate financial statements?
Support	Will your library support the software internally, or are you going to need long-term help from the vendor who installs it? Well-established packages with a large support network offer more support to larger organizations. Does it have an adequate "help" feature? Line-by-line help access?
Integration of multiple accounts/ Fund accounting	How many funds do you have? How independent are they? Do you need fundraising software, fund-accounting software, or both? If both, do they need to be connected? Do you need to maintain separate balance sheet data (assets, liabilities, fund balance) for multiple accounts? Although some organizations, such as Friends of the Library or other special groups, can use software designed for households or small businesses, (e.g., Quicken or Microsoft Money) larger organizations and those with more complicated accounting situations need fund-accounting software that will manage multiple levels of accounts, subaccounts, departments, and programs. Many packages are eliminated because of the restrictions to the number of levels and relational tables that can be created in the account number structure.
Data entry	Is it real time or batch processed? Is the screen customizable? Are there task-oriented data-entry screens? Can different screens be assigned by group?

Figure 3-6. Questions for Selecting Financial Management Packages

HOW TO EVALUATE THE SOFTWARE

After you've narrowed the features and functionality you require, you should base your evaluation on the following sources of information:

- The library accounting staff's interaction with the products (demos and trial versions are often available, or individual staff members may have prior experience),
- information from the literature and marketing materials of the companies,
- information from each vendor's website, and
- comparative evaluations from the literature (some useful websites are listed in a sidebar).

When reviewing the literature, be wary of all marketed features until you have actually seen them demonstrated or done a hands-on evaluation yourself. Once you have narrowed your selections, you may ask vendors to provide a "scripted demo" of their product. For the scripted demonstration, the library provides a detailed outline for various vendors to follow when they demonstrate their products. The demonstration should simulate the library's actual operational needs, and you should provide a sample of your actual institutional data to use with software files and report templates. For example, the library might require that the vendor show how the equipment tracks purchase orders, deducts balances from encumbrances, notifies vendors that

---

Some Sources of Library Management Software

Library management software packages: www.allwonderssoftware.com/library.html.
Sources of library management software: www.capterra.com/library-automation-software.
Additional sources: http://acqweb.library.vanderbilt.edu/pubr/opac.html.

Worth checking out . . .

"Closing the Accounting GAAP and Donor Divide: A Guide to Selecting Software for Your Nonprofit's Fiscal and Development Departments." www.npowerny.org/tools/af_report.pdf.
Comparative features chart highlighting nonprofit financial management software is available annually (October) at the CPA Technology website at www.cpata.com/tables/. The PDF file for 2003 is available at www.cpata.com/tables/images/2003/notforprofit.pdf.
"How to Select Financial Management Software." www.allianceonline.org/FAQ/financial_management/what_accounting_software.faq.
"Financial Management." *Financial Executive* 18, no. 4 (June 2002): 18.
Myaing, Robin T. "How to Select Financial Management Systems Software." *The Government Accountants Journal* 45, no. 2 (Summer 1996): 24.

backorders of longer than sixty days have been cancelled, reports average discounts received on orders from a vendor, and so forth. You should ask all vendors to demonstrate the same processes so you can compare them.

Automated systems negate the need to manually track expenses, costs, revenues, inventories, and payroll in ledgers, but you still have to understand the processes. The computer is only a tool to streamline and systematize these financial management processes. The strength and integrity of the library's financial management rest in the hands of those who understand the processes and interact with the automated system on a daily basis.

SUMMARY

Responsible monitoring of the budget is important in showing governing officials and constituents that their tax dollars and other funding are providing an efficient and cost-effective library service. Responsible budget monitoring includes putting into place a system of checks and balances, standardized forms, processes that can be tracked and audited, and developing financial management systems that work best to meet the library's needs.

SPECIAL TOPICS IN FINANCIAL MANAGEMENT FOR LIBRARIES

4 OUTSOURCING

OVERVIEW

There are many controversies over outsourcing, and the term has often been given a bad name. But many libraries have found that outsourcing some library tasks and services is the most cost-effective use of library resources. In this chapter you will read about the pros and cons of outsourcing, the impact outsourcing has had, and an overview of areas that libraries have decided to outsource, including selection of materials, technical services, and even the management of library services. At the end of the chapter you will find a checklist of issues, questions to consider before outsourcing, and a list of additional services you may want to consider outsourcing.

THE OUTSOURCING CONTROVERSY

Outsourcing library services is not a new concept. Libraries have contracted bindery services and the production of catalog cards for decades. Outsourcing first became controversial in the 1980s, when libraries began contracting core services. The outsourcing controversy became really heated in the late 1990s, when the first libraries became totally privatized, beginning with the public library in Riverside County, California, and their outsourcing of the management of the public library to Library Systems and Service, Inc. (LSSI). The privatizing of materials selection in Hawaii resulted in a controversy that cost State Librarian Bart Kane his job.

However, there are definite financial advantages to outsourcing library functions. You can select vendors that specialize in particular services and do them more efficiently than library staff, who have additional responsibilities. Also, you pay only for the services rendered rather than a yearly salary and benefits.

On the other hand, you are sacrificing some control. You will also be working with a for-profit organization. You risk the vendors' cutting corners, going out of business, or being purchased by another company that may not have the same interest in or understanding of your needs. Finally, your governing authority's guidelines for selecting a vendor may not necessarily work to your advantage. The pros and cons of outsourcing are summarized in a sidebar.

OUTSOURCING TERMINOLOGY

There are some specific contractual terms used in outsourcing that you will want to know.

Outsourcing: The contracting, to external companies or organizations, of functions that would otherwise be performed by library employees. A library might outsource its audiovisual processing, cataloging, janitorial services, or photocopier services.

Privatization: The shifting of policy making and management of library services, or the responsibility for the performance of core library services in their entirety, from the public to the private sector. A library that is privatized is managed by a private business but still functions as a public, academic, or special library. The library employees are hired and policies are made by the private company.

Core services: Those professional activities that define the profession of librarianship. These include collection development and organization, gathering and providing information, making the collection accessible to all library users, providing assistance in the use of the collection, and providing oversight and management of these activities.

Pros and Cons of Outsourcing

"Pros" of Outsourcing

- Outsourcing can save time and money.
- Private vendors specialize in particular services and can do them faster, better, and less expensively than library staff, who can then be freed to perform other duties.
- Vendors can be hired to do specific jobs, whereas staff must be paid salaries and provided with benefits all year long.

"Cons" of Outsourcing

- Quality control is harder to maintain.
- The vendor may not understand your needs.
- Vendors may cut corners to save money and increase profits.
- The library may lose some positions, which could lower staff morale.
- Vendors can go out of business or be sold during the contract.
- Vendor services must usually be put out for bid, and you may be required to accept the lowest responsible bidder—this may not be the best service.

In the following pages, you will read about some of the most frequently used types of library outsourcing. Figure 4-1 shows the results of a survey on outsourcing that the Urban Libraries Council conducted in 1998.

MATERIALS SELECTION

Libraries have long used vendor approval plans to assist with materials selection. In the 1950s, Emerson Greenaway, librarian of the Philadelphia Free Library, founded the Greenaway Plan, blanket ordering from publishers to help libraries acquire new books rapidly. Some Greenaway plans are outright purchases; the libraries trust the publisher to send any new books in specific subject areas. Others are approval plans in which publishers send the books and libraries keep those they want for the collection and return the remainder.

Opening Day Collections are frequently purchased to stock a new library (perhaps a new branch or school) with a basic collection. The materials, selected by the jobber according to the library's preapproved profile, arrive cataloged, processed, and ready for shelving.

TECHNICAL SERVICES

In the 1990s, libraries began to eliminate their entire technical services departments and outsourced those services to the private sector. Three prominent outsourcing cases are outlined in the article "Outsourcing Library Technical Services: What We Think We Know and Don't Know" by James H. Sweetland (see Worth Checking Out . . .).

Approval Q & A

Nardini, Robert F. "Approval Plans." *Encyclopedia of Library and Information Online*, 2003. www.ybp.com/ybp/pdf/approval_dekker.pdf, 133–39.

Examples of Standing Order Plans and Approval Plans

Blackwell's approval plan: www.blackwell.com/level4/ApprovalPlans.asp.
Brodart's service for new school openings: www.books.brodart.com/schools/newschools.htm.
Brodart's McNaughton plan: www.books.brodart.com/products/mcnaughton.htm.
Ebsco sample issue and book program: www.ebsco.com/sip/about.asp.
Books on Tape: http://library.booksontape.com/ldiscount.cfm.

Outsourcing Survey: Results at a Glance

One hundred twenty-seven members of the Urban Libraries Council were sent questionnaires in the spring of 1998. Of the 127 addressees, 72 returned them, for a response rate of 56.7 percent.

A. Future of Outsourcing

Half of the respondent libraries anticipate outsourcing more functions in the future; 47 percent anticipate outsourcing about the same amount as they currently outsource. No library anticipated outsourcing fewer functions.

B. Outsourcing

Frequency of Outsourcing

At respondent libraries, an average of 7.5 functions are outsourced to some extent. Only one library reported outsourcing no functions.

Functions Most Frequently Outsourced

The following functions were outsourced by 50 percent or more of respondent libraries:

Binding	82%
Materials processing	68
Grounds maintenance	63
Custodial	63
Internet service provision	61
Computer training	58
Security	56
Cataloging	51

Percentage of Function Outsourced

Often outsourcing of a function is selectively done. Only for the following functions is over half the work outsourced by libraries that outsource them:

Binding	97%
Internet service provision	92
Security	85
Grounds maintenance	83
Integrated systems	81
Custodial	72
Payroll	71
Fundraising	70
Subscription check-in/maintenance	68
Web page design and maintenance	60

Outsourcing Service Providers

Overwhelmingly, commercial vendors are chosen as the providers of outsourced services (71 percent). Other providers include government agencies (15 percent), library consortia (5 percent), other nonprofit agencies (5 percent), and other libraries (3 percent).

Only in the cases of payroll and other personnel services were government agencies more often the service provider (63 and 50 percent, respectively). This may relate more to governance structure than to choice.

Figure 4-1. Urban Libraries Outsourcing Survey

Annual Cost

The average annual cost of outsourced functions ranges from $6,278 to $173,884. The costliest outsourced functions are shown here.

Function Outsourced	Average Cost
Integrated systems	$173,884
Custodial	$168,214
Security	$130,371
Materials selection/collection development	$128,226
Subscription check-in	$106,158
Materials processing	$86,920

Length of Outsourcing

Outsourcing is an established practice in respondent libraries. All but two of the functions queried about have been outsourced by libraries that outsource them for an average of five or more years. Those two functions are more recent technological innovations—Internet service provision and web page design and maintenance. Over half of outsourced functions have been outsourced for an average of ten or more years.

C. Reasons and Results

Mandated by Governing Body

Outsourcing is not significantly driven by government mandates. In more than a quarter of the libraries, government mandates accounted for outsourcing only three functions: cataloging, for 35 percent of those who outsource it; payroll, for 31 percent of those who outsource it; and other personnel functions, for 28 percent of those who outsource it.

Reasons

The most important reason cited for outsourcing twelve of the seventeen functions outsourced was better use of staff. Increased efficiency and better customer service were the next most often cited reasons and were considered at least moderately important. Cost savings was generally cited as a slightly to moderately important reason.

Results

Generally, libraries rated the result of outsourcing in close correlation to their reason for outsourcing. For example, libraries that outsource binding indicated better use of staff as a very important reason for outsourcing the function (3.8 on a 4.0 scale, with 4 ranked as very important). These same libraries said that outsourcing of binding performed very well vis-à-vis this reason (3.7 on a 4.0 scale, with 4 ranked as very well).

A slight divergence can be seen only when a better relationship with the governing body is cited as a reason for outsourcing. Libraries indicated this was generally a not very important to a slightly important reason (average of 1.1 to 2.4 on a 4.0 scale, with 1 not at all important). Consistently, however, libraries indicated a better relationship with a governing body as a more important result of outsourcing (a range of 2.2 to 3.1, with 3 being a good performance).

Figure 4-1. Urban Libraries Outsourcing Survey
(*Continued*)

Source: "Outsourcing in Metropolitan Libraries," outsourcing survey result, Urban Libraries Council, www.urbanlibraries.org/standards/outsourc.html.

1. Wright State University, the first university to eliminate the cataloging department and outsource cataloging (1993).

2. Baker and MacKenzie Law Firm, whose Chicago office fired its entire library staff of ten and replaced them with a library management company (March 31,1995), and then reversed the decision four years later by hiring in-house library staff.

3. The State of Hawaii, which in 1995 outsourced not only cataloging but also selection. This resulted in a great controversy over the materials that vendor Baker & Taylor selected, led to State Librarian Bart Kane losing his job, and caused the state to pass legislation requiring that local librarians have input into materials selection.

Although the savings in outsourcing seem to be significant (cheaper labor, no benefits), there are also concerns about the decline of quality. Some libraries only outsource some parts of technical services, such as the processing of audiovisual materials or items that require special types of library supplies. Think about the following questions before outsourcing any of your library functions.

Questions to Ask before Outsourcing Technical Services Processes

Why outsource?

What is the objective for outsourcing any or all of a particular library's technical services activities? Broward [Community College] identified two measurable objectives: (1) realigning technical services staff to public services; and (2) making books available sooner to end users. Clear goals of what is to be achieved by outsourcing are necessary before starting an outsourcing program.

What are the costs?

What are the current costs to acquire and process materials? Knowing your current staff and processing costs will help you identify potential areas for savings. In some areas, your library may be processing items faster and cheaper than a vendor would be able to.

What is my current workflow?

Are there areas in the current technical services workflow that could be streamlined? By knowing your current workflow, you may isolate processes that could be streamlined or eliminated. What tasks in your current workflow can only your staff perform? What can be eliminated without a loss of necessary information? Are there pieces of your workflow that are more suitable for outsourcing than others?

Who will manage the process?

Who on staff will manage the process from start through execution and ensure compliance? Local staff will still be necessary to manage the contract, receive items, and so on. You may unpack a shipment of books and have them go directly to the shelf, but is that really advisable without quality-control procedures?

What will be the impact on staff?

How will staff adjust to the changes that outsourcing will bring? Do they see themselves as part of the process?

What is essential to my library?

The more customization your library has performed in classification—such as call number formatting—the more difficult and costly it is to duplicate when titles are outsourced. Do the call numbers on labels need to be formatted a certain way? Must all titles on a particular subject be classed together, regardless of changes to the Library of Congress or Dewey classification?

Which vendor or vendors should I use?

The choice of vendor or vendors will most likely result from your experiences or the experiences of others with a particular vendor. Because Broward had no experience with outsourcing, they chose to limit their initial foray to one vendor. This allowed them to concentrate on finding solutions to problems that arose and to have a clearer understanding of all the ramifications of outsourcing.

Which formats of materials should I outsource?

The choice of formats to outsource depends on a variety of factors. Broward chose to outsource only the book format, as that format represented a majority of their orders, and timely processing was critical for them. Local staff was adequately handling other formats; therefore, Broward chose not to outsource those formats. Do you have backlogs in a particular format? Could trade materials be outsourced to free up staff to concentrate on other projects? Do you order formats that need a particular expertise to catalog or process that is not found on your staff?

What are your obligations as an LINCC library or an OCLC member?

As an LINCC library, you are governed by the Guidelines for the Responsible Use of LINCC. As an OCLC member, you are also governed by your membership obligations for use of OCLC MARC records. [LINCC connects community colleges in Florida.]

What are your institutional obligations?

You may be governed by agreements with other libraries, or your business office may have procedures and practices that preclude taking full advantage of some automated ordering or invoicing processes.

Source: Quoted from "Outsourcing Technical Services: Broward Community College/Davie Campus Library—Considerations for LINCC Libraries," www.ccla.lib.fl.us/docs/reports/Outsourcing.pdf.

The checklist in figure 4-2 is designed for public libraries, but it can be used for other libraries as well. You will find it helpful whenever you are thinking about outsourcing any library function to be sure that you consider every aspect of the decision before signing a contract.

LIBRARY MANAGEMENT

We've discussed the outsourcing of various aspects of library services, but some communities, colleges, and schools have outsourced (privatized) the entire management of their libraries. They pay a flat fee to a vendor to run the library, hire the staff, and maintain the facilities. Outsourcing of library management has been very controversial in library circles since the Riverside County (CA) Public Library was privatized in 1997. The library outsourced management to Library Systems and Service, Inc., a group of

---

Worth Checking Out . . .

Outsourcing Library Technical Services (PowerPoint): www.nelinet.net/ahirshon/outsourc/.

"Planning and Implementing an Outsourcing Program." www.ala.org/ala/oif/iftoolkits/outsourcing/
    planningimplementing.htm.

"Public Libraries: Outsourcing Technical Services." www.unt.edu/slis/students/projects/5320/appleby.htm.

Sweetland, James H. "Outsourcing Library Technical Services: What We Think We Know and Don't Know."
    The Bottom Line: Managing Library Finances 14, no. 3 (2001): 164–77.

	Outsourcing: A Public Library Checklist 10/12/00	Yes	No
Issues and Questions	Is the activity core to the library's mission?		
Fundamental Issues	Is the activity considered for outsourcing "inherently governmental" and therefore not appropriate for outsourcing?		
Legal Issues	Have all applicable local and state general laws and regulations been adequately addressed?		
	Have all applicable contracting and procurement regulations been adequately addressed?		
	Have all current collective bargaining contracts and related issues been adequately addressed?		
	Does the administrative entity considering the proposed outsourcing have the authority to make the decision and enter into a contract?		
Economic and Quality of Service Issues	Will greater efficiencies result?		
	Will cost savings result?		
	Are provisions in place to monitor and verify that the anticipated cost savings actually occur?		
	Will the result be more timely completion of activities?		
	Will specialized skills or technical expertise be obtained that are not currently available?		
	Will the activities and processes that the library continues to conduct be improved through more efficient and effective completion of the contracted activities?		
	Will service to the public improve?		
Policy Issues	Will library governing board responsibilities be affected?		
	Will library advisory board responsibilities be affected?		
	Will the outsourcing contract allow the agency to respond to changing situations?		
	Will the library's free library service policy or statutory requirements be affected?		
Political Issues	Have the library governing and advisory boards been involved in the planning and decision making?		
	Do the library governing and advisory boards support the outsourcing decision?		
	Are outsourcing decisions being driven by external political influences?		
	Has the local community been involved in the outsourcing decision-making process?		
	Is the community comfortable with the proposed outsourcing?		
Organizational and Staff Considerations	Have organizational issues resulting from the proposed outsourcing been adequately considered?		
	Will organizational restructuring be required?		
	Will staff be replaced or transferred to the employment of the contractor?		
	Have library staff been informed of the proposed outsourcing of activities?		
	Have library staff had the opportunity to participate in the planning and decision-making process?		
	Do library staff support the proposed outsourcing of activities?		

Figure 4-2. Public Library Outsourcing Checklist

		Yes	No
Administrative Issues	Will library administration be responsible for monitoring contractor performance?		
	Have adequate provisions been made to administer the outsourcing contract?		
Contract Considerations	Are the contract specifications for the activity proposed for outsourcing sufficiently clear and appropriate?		
	Are the scope and scale of the contract specifications for the activity proposed for outsourcing clear and appropriate?		
	Does the proposed contract include specific provisions to adequately insure sufficient quality of service and performance?		
	Does the proposed contract provide adequate provisions for monitoring contractor's performance and correcting contractor's failure to meet performance requirements?		
	Does the proposed contract provide a reasonable process for terminating the contract for cause?		
	Do contract renewal provisions provide the agency with realistic options to seek a new vendor or bring the activity back in house?		
	Is the agency prepared to reassume responsibility for the contracted functions or activities should the contractor fail to meet the performance terms of the contract?		
	Does the contract provide sufficient protection from contractor low-balling, that is, offering a low initial-year price to get the contract, then increasing the price when the agency no longer has the capacity to bring the activity back in-house?		

Figure 4-2. Public Library Outsourcing Checklist (*Continued*)

Source: Public Library Association, *Outsourcing: A Public Library Checklist* (Chicago: American Library Association, 2000), www.ala.org/ala/pla/plaorg/reportstopla/outsourc.pdf.

former library directors. Riverside County was the first, largest, most visible, and, ultimately, most controversial example of outsourcing an entire library system.

OUTSOURCING OTHER SERVICES

There are certain services that libraries traditionally outsource; this is usually because the vendor can provide the needed services at a lower price. You may also need these outsourced services only infrequently; therefore, it is not effective to keep staff employed to do the specialized duties. Among the frequently privatized library services are the following:

- Custodial services
- Security services
- Digitization of photos or records

- Photocopier service
- Vending and coffee machine services
- Laundry services (providing clean rugs, towels, and rags)
- Window washing (especially high windows)
- Carpet cleaning and floor refinishing
- Plant and landscaping care
- Pest control
- Repair of audiovisual equipment or materials
- Disaster recovery
- Elevator maintenance
- HVAC maintenance and changing of filters
- PC repair
- Inspections: boiler, fire extinguishers, roof, and termites
- Training

There are key considerations other than cost when you are deciding to outsource:

- Cost effectiveness
- Staffing issues
- Expertise of vendor

Worth Checking Out . . .

Ball, D. "A Weighted Decision Matrix for Outsourcing Library Services." *The Bottom Line: Managing Library Finances* 16, no. 1 (2003): 25–30.

DiMattia, S. (2001). "Lancaster Public Library, TX, Outsourced to LSSI." *Library Journal Online,* retrieved March 14, 2005. www.libraryjournal.com/article/CA149798?display=searchResults&stt=001&text=ca1149798.

"Library Outsourcing: A New Look." www.infotoday.com/searcher/apr02/ebbinghouse.htm.

LSSI (Library Systems and Service, Inc.): www.lssi.com/6.html.

Outsourcing in law firm libraries: www.llrx.com/features/outsourcing.htm.

Outsourcing of library management: www.ala.org/ala/ors/reports/outsourcing.htm.

Worth Checking Out . . .

Dobb, Linda S. "Bringing It All Back Home: Insourcing What You Do Well." *The Bottom Line: Managing Library Finances* 11, no. 3 (1998):105–10.

Tennant, R. (1999). "Outsourcing digitization." *Library Journal Online,* retrieved March 14, 2005. www.libraryjournal.com/index.asp?layout=articlePrint&articleID=CA156509

- Effect on community
- Local control
- Legal issues
- Accountability
- Performance
- Evaluation
- Standards
- Stability

SUMMARY

Outsourcing is a controversial topic. In some cases, you may find that outsourcing is the best decision for the library because it saves money, provides improved service, and frees staff to offer more services to the library public. Outsourcing can also impede services, especially if the outsourcing agency goes out of business, provides inferior products, or does not meet deadlines. Deciding upon a vendor for outsourcing requires the same due diligence as choosing any other provider of library services.

5 PROTECTING LIBRARY PROPERTY

OVERVIEW

In this chapter, you will learn about the librarian's responsibility of stewardship in protecting the collection and conserving library resources. As a librarian, you need to balance your responsibility to give patrons as much access to the collection as possible with your resolve to safeguard your collection and limited resources for the greater good of all and for future generations. This requires you to maintain a delicate balance between the two often-conflicting agendas. This chapter discusses areas in which proper stewardship and planning can ensure the greatest protection for your library's limited resources while promoting accessible collections. This stewardship includes several key activities:

- recovering overdue materials and stolen or mutilated items, and the various ways you can accomplish this;
- adopting security measures to protect the collections;
- insuring collections and what you should consider before doing so;
- developing a checklist for conservation and emergency preparedness; and
- conducting a collection inventory, how to do it, and its benefits.

If you plan and maintain prudent stewardship of your library materials, you will be able to identify potential threats to your collection and find cost-effective solutions for security and conservation needs.

In East Peoria, Illinois, in the 1970s, we had a bookmobile driver named Erv. Erv had delivered milk in his earlier career, and part of his job was collections. He had a great rapport with the children of the community because he drove the bookmobile, which visited schools. After completing his bookmobile route, Erv would spend a couple of hours knocking on doors and collecting overdue materials. Frequently the children were home alone, so they would warmly greet Erv, then run to the shelf, top of the refrigerator, or wherever the overdue items were kept, and return them. The return rate was excellent. However, that was a safer time in a smaller community. I would not recommend door-to-door collectors today. —Dr. Arlita Hallam

RECOVERING OVERDUE LIBRARY MATERIALS

There are several options for the recovery of overdue library materials.

1. Appoint library-collection staff.

    The library hires a staff member whose job is to collect overdue library materials. The staff member calls the customer at home and makes arrangements to have the item returned. It is a good idea to have this step in place before making a referral to a collection agency or court system.

    After confirming that the customer has the material, the staff member's message is, "We're scheduled to turn your overdue materials over to the collection agency or court system tomorrow, and I wanted to give you one more opportunity to return them before you incur the additional fines and fees. Is there any way you can bring it in tonight?" Frequently the response is deep gratitude and the return is very rapid.

2. Refer overdue materials to a collection agency.

    Collection agencies are more prevalent today, including some that specialize in collecting overdue library materials for a set fee. The collection agency charges approximately $10 per account, which the delinquent customer must pay. The agency sends overdue notices, makes phone calls, conducts skip traces (for those who have left the area) and, after 120 days, files a credit report against the customer. Their estimated recovery rate is 50 to 75 percent.

3. Refer overdue materials to a court system.

    Many communities have a municipal court or county court system that will handle failure to return public property as part of their caseload at no additional charge. The library staff prepares the forms, which are provided by the court system, and gives them to the court system to be delivered to the delinquent customer. This should be the third or fourth step in the recovery system, after making efforts to notify the customer by mail and telephone and after sending a bill and waiting a reasonable time for a response. Failure to respond to the court summons will result in a warrant for the person's arrest—for failure to appear in court.

    Frequently, the warrant is not served upon the customer immediately, but will show up if the customer is stopped for any other reason or is involved in an accident. Then there are court costs in addition to the recovery costs of the overdue materials that must all be paid before the person is released. This is a very effective collection system (probably 90 to 95 percent effective), but obviously arresting people for overdue library materials can also result in negative publicity.

4. Withhold grades and transcripts.

Schools and universities have the ability to hold grades and transcripts until students return their overdue library materials and pay their fines. This is highly effective because students are unable to register or get their transcripts until their accounts are paid.

5. Offset debts against payments.

Some governmental agencies are able to offset debts (including those for overdue library materials) against payments such as tax refunds, final government checks, or other agency payments to the individual.

6. Refer to fines as "extended-use fees."

An innovative and positive spin to handling overdue fines is to call them *extended-use fees*. When the library material becomes overdue, it begins accumulating extended-use fees until it is returned. This terminology sounds like a benefit to the library customer rather than a penalty.

7. Institute amnesty days.

Libraries have used amnesty days with varying levels of effectiveness. The library announces an "amnesty day, week, or month" to the public and publicizes it widely. Delinquent customers are encouraged to bring back their overdue library items, and all fines will be purged. There may even be a newspaper story on the longest-overdue item returned.

The "down" side of amnesty days is that they cannot be scheduled regularly, or customers will just hold on to their overdue materials so they can return them on an amnesty day without paying a fine. The result is that materials are kept overdue even longer.

8. Conduct skip chases.

Skip chase is a location service that collection agencies offer. However, by using the some of the resources listed in figure 5-1, librarians can conduct their own skip chases to locate missing customers who have overdue materials.

You can use these resources to find the address of a patron who has moved.

✓ Post office (request forwarding address on items mailed)
✓ Department of Motor Vehicle License and Registration Records
✓ Emergency contact on library card application or transcripts
✓ Directory assistance and new city telephone directories
✓ Internet search:

AnyWho

White Pages: www.anywho.com/wp.html
Yellow Pages: www.anywho.com/yp.html
Toll free: www.anywho.com/tf.html
Reverse lookup: www.anywho.com/rl.html
International: www.anywho.com/international.html
AT&T: www.att.com/directory/
Teldir: www.infobel.com/teldir/teldir.asp?page=/eng/

InfoSpace

White pages: www.infospace.com/redirs_all.htm?pgtarg=ppli
Yellow pages: www.infospace.com/redirs_all.htm?pgtarg=ylwi
Reverse directory: www.infospace.com/redirs_all.htm?pgtar+reve
International: www.infospace.com/intl/int2.html?XNavigation=int

Yahoo! People Finder

White pages: http://people.yahoo.com
Yellow pages: http://yp.yahoo.com/Yahoo

Figure 5-1. Finding Library Patrons Who Have Moved

THEFT AND MUTILATION OF PUBLIC PROPERTY

So far, in the situations we have been discussing, you know who checked out the missing or overdue library materials. However, you will no doubt experience actual theft of library materials as well. You will not know who has the item, but it is missing and presumed stolen. There is also something called *theft by conversion* of public property; this covers long-overdue items that are presumed stolen because they have not been returned after a series of contacts and bills.

Theft and *mutilation* are legal terms that convey the intent of the abuser. The fact that library materials are missing does not necessarily mean that they were stolen. They may be misplaced, or a customer may have reported an item lost and then paid for it, but it was not properly withdrawn from the library's database.

Frequently, theft is discovered when a collection of library materials is found at a pawn shop, at a flea market, or in a police raid. Our library first discovered that many of our videos had been stolen when the thief tried to sell them to a pawn shop. The pawn shop owner noticed that the library ownership identification had been cut off the video cases, and notified police.

Attempted theft is frequently discovered when customers exit the library and pass through security systems. You should have a written policy outlining what the staff member on duty should do when the security alarm rings (see figure 5-2 for the basic components of a policy). Should the procedure be to call the police, detain the customer and check that all materials were checked out properly, or wave the person on through, assuming that the equipment is malfunctioning? Figure 5-3 is the Alliance Library System's (East Peoria, IL) policy defining theft of library property and detailing how security officers or staff members should handle any instances of suspected theft.

SECURITY SYSTEMS

Manufacturers of library security systems claim to offer an 80 to 85 percent reduction in thefts. The security system is installed at the exit doorway of the library to pick up electromagnetic or radio-frequent signals from tags or strips placed in the library materials. If the materials are checked out properly, the signals are desensitized so that they will not set off the security system. Some types of security systems include:

- **Access management systems:** Patrons leave a credit card or identification card (driver's license) at the library entrance when signing in to use the library. This method is frequently used in rare book libraries or library computer labs.

- **Closed-circuit television:** Video surveillance cameras are installed throughout the library, around the exterior of the building, and in parking lots to deter theft and

---

Theft at Widener

French historical materials dating from the late eighteenth century have been reported stolen from Harvard's Widener Library. Harvard College Library officials suspected theft when a number of empty book covers were discovered in the Widener stacks on Thursday, April 19. A subsequent inventory conducted by library staff confirmed that a total of forty-six items including pamphlets, journals, and books from the French Revolution and Napoleonic periods, valued at approximately $10,000, were missing. The Harvard University Police Department is investigating the case and is working with library officials to gather information for the involvement of other law enforcement agencies. Book dealers, research libraries, and dealers specializing in French antiquities have been notified.

Source: "Theft at Widener," *Harvard University Gazette*, May 3, 2001, www.news.harvard.edu/gazette/2001/05.03/02=theft.html.

Worth checking out . . .

Peoria (IL) Public Library. "Theft of Library Materials or Property."
www.alliancelibrarysystem.com/safeharbor/index.cfm?sectionID=163.

In Northeast Document Conservation Center Emergency Management Technical Leaflet 12, Section 3, titled "Collections Security: Planning and Prevention for Libraries and Archives," Karen E. Brown details the elements of good security planning. Below is a list of the six basic components she identifies for effective security planning. For more detailed description of each of these components, visit www.nedcc.org/plam3/tleaf312.htm.

Effective Security Planning

1. Prepare a written security policy. If appropriate, form a security planning group to help develop policies and procedures. Always insure that the policy is endorsed at the highest managerial level.
2. Appoint a security manager to develop and implement your security plan.
3. Perform a security survey to assess your needs.
4. Initiate preventive measures:

   a. Eliminate weaknesses to insure the security of the building.
   b. Install appropriate security systems.
   c. Insure that collection storage is secure and that good records are kept.
   d. Establish patron regulations.
   e. Establish staff regulations.

5. Identify likely emergencies and plan your response to any breach of security. Tell staff what to do, practice response plans, and coordinate plans with outside officials.
6. Maintain and update your security plan.

Figure 5-2. Basic Components of Security Planning

crime. A security guard then watches the monitors and sends someone to investigate suspicious activities.

- **Radio-frequency identification (RF-ID):** Library cards contain RF-ID chips that record patron activities in the library and also serve as library cards when patrons check out materials. All library materials also have RF-ID chips as well. If the patron leaves the library without checking out the items, the system has a record of the patron's name and the materials involved.

- **Robotics:** Robots in stacks can detect mutilation or other inappropriate activities and report the activity.

- **Network security:** You might want a system that thwarts digital vandals as well. There are systems that do this.

THEFT OF LIBRARY PROPERTY

POLICY

Taking any material or property owned by the library without properly checking it out is theft, and is against the law. See 720 ILCS 5/16B-1.

Examples of theft include, but are not limited to, the following:

1. Knowingly and intentionally removing any library material from a library facility without authority to do so.
2. Knowingly and intentionally concealing any library material upon his or her person or among his or her belongings with intent to circumvent checking out that material.
3. Using a stolen or fraudulent library card.
4. Failing to return checked-out library material as described in the above citation.
5. Leaving the library facility with any material not intended for circulation, example, rare documents, local history/genealogy, special collections or equipment.

PROCEDURE

WHO	WHAT
Security officer/staff member	If a person caught violating this policy seems harmless, the staff member should explain that the action/theft is against the law and must stop. The incident should be reported to the staff person in charge who will determine if the police will be notified. If the person is acting in violation of this policy and obviously not approachable, the staff member should call the police immediately. The staff member involved will send a written incident report form detailing the incident to the director. The Library will post a copy of the Protection of Library Materials Act 720 ILCS 5/16 B-1 at each entrance and at each circ desk, as required by that act.

WHAT TO SAY

"My name is _____, and I work here at the library. Theft of library property is against the law, and I need you to stop. My supervisor will be here shortly."

Reprinted with permission of Alliance Library System, 600 High Point Lane, East Peoria, IL 67611.

Figure 5-3. Policy on Theft of Library Materials

Dynamic route filters can automatically detect suspicious activity and deny a patron access to a machine to prevent an automated attack on a site. Firewalls monitor all activity with an application gateway and act as gatekeepers for information that gets in and out of a network.

For descriptions of some specific systems, see figure 5-4.

Checkpoint Systems, Inc.
101 Wolf Drive
Thorofare, NJ 08086
Phone: 800-257-5540
Fax: 856-848-0937
Contact: Nicole DeFeo
Contact phone: 856-251-2178
E-mail: library.info@checkpt.com
Web address: www.checkpointlibrary.com

Choose from a number of theft detection systems to protect your collection from "unauthorized" removal. Checkpoint's systems offer unique designs and reliable protection—safe for books, audiocassettes, videos, CDs, computer software, and patrons.

Gressco, Ltd.
328 Moravian Valley Road
Waunakee, WI 53597
Phone: 800-345-3480
Fax: 608-849-6304
Contact: Sales
Contact phone: 608-849-6300
E-mail: info@gresscoltd.com
Web address: www.gresscoltd.com

Kwik Case®—a magnetic, keyless theft protection system for audiovisuals that works with electromagnetic or radio frequency tags. Polycarbonate cases allow media to be displayed, thus increasing circulation, eliminating double storage, and reducing checkout time.

ID Recall Systems
1540 Pine Crest Drive
Grants Pass, OR 97526
Phone: 800-779-5669
Fax: 541-471-4113
Contact: Sales
E-mail: info@idrecall.com
Web address: www.idrecall.com

ID Recall Systems provides security gates; desensitizer/resensitizer work stations; and tattle tail, spine, CD, and video security strips.

Sentry Technology Corporation
350 Wireless Blvd.
Hauppauge, NY 11788
Phone: 631-232-2100, 631-739-2000, and 800-645-4224
Fax: 631-232-2124
Web address: www.sentrytechnology.com/cprofile.htm

Sentry Technology Corporation offers electronic article surveillance and closed-circuit television equipment.

3M Library Systems
3M Center Building 225-4N-14
St. Paul, MN 55144-1000
Phone: 800-328-0067
Fax: 800-223-5563
Web address: www.3m.com/us/library

3M Detection Systems are the worldwide industry standard for protecting all of your library materials. Completely safe for all media (print and nonprint), they help ensure that no materials leave the library that are not properly checked out. Video security system and voice alarm are optional.

Figure 5-4. Security Equipment and Systems

INSURANCE

Insurance costs need to be considered as part of the library's financial planning. The entity to which the library belongs (city, county, university, school district) may be self-insured, but you still need to know what is covered by that insurance. If the library pays for insurance policies, it is important to know what is covered and what is not. Make sure that you can answer the following questions:

- Does the insurance have a deductible? Does the library have an amount of money set aside to cover that deductible?

- Is the reported value of the collection, furnishings, and so on up to date?

- Could you document your holdings if necessary? It is a good idea to keep an off-site video of the library in case the building is destroyed. This simple project can be done by having a student or employee walk through the library with a video camera and describe each room while panning it with the camera.

- Do you have a disaster recovery plan? Are the contact numbers for disaster recovery experts (for freeze-drying wet materials, water-extraction equipment, etc.) kept off-site so you could find them in a hurry? Is a computer tape of library holdings kept off-site and periodically updated? See figure 5-5 for a checklist of how to respond to an emergency.

- Does the library's insurance cover all liabilities, including leased space, vehicles, employees' or customers' personal property, items on loan from others, vandalism, theft, earthquake, flood, fire, explosions, and water damage?

- Should library employees or officers be bonded?

Worth checking out . . .

Boss, Richard. "RFID Technology for Libraries." www.ala.org/ala/pla/plapubs/technotes/rfidtechnology.htm.

Brown, Karen E. "Collections Security: Planning and Prevention for Libraries and Archives." www.nedcc.org/plam3/tleaf312.htm.

"InfoSyssec: The Security Portal for Information System Security Professionals." www.infosyssec.net/infosyssec/secpol1.htm.

Recovery of Harvard University Library Collections

Checklist for First Response to an Emergency

In the event of an emergency that threatens library collections, take the following steps:

Step 1—Make sure staff members are safe.
Take appropriate measures to protect the lives and health of all staff members, including your own.

Step 2—Make a rapid assessment of the emergency situation.
If possible and safe to do so, quickly assess the source of the danger to the collections and the extent of the damage.

Step 3—Protect the collections from further damage.
If possible and safe to do so, take appropriate steps to protect the collections, for example, cover them with plastic sheeting.

Step 4—Notify, or verify notification of, people and programs that are designated to respond in an emergency.

- Library administration
- Facilities
- Library's local Emergency Response Team

Step 5—Notify LCET (HUL-wide Library Collections Emergency Response Team).

LCET Cell Phone
If the is no response in ten minutes, call the
University Operations Center.
Alternatively, during business hours, call
Preservation Center or Conservation Services.

Step 6—Work with facilities staff members to stabilize the environment.
If possible:

- Lower temperature below 65 degrees F.
- Lower relative humidity below 35 percent.
- Move air gently through affected area(s).

Step 7—Do a comprehensive assessment of damage to the collection(s).

- Identify the types of materials and estimate quantities:

  - Bound volumes
  - Unbound paper
  - Microforms
  - Photographic prints and negatives
  - Videotape, audiotape
  - Motion picture film
  - Other

Figure 5-5. Steps for Responding to an Emergency

- Identify the nature of the damage, for example, materials might be:

  ○ Damp
  ○ Wet
  ○ Smoke damaged
  ○ Fire damaged
  ○ Dirty
  ○ Contaminated by bacteria or other dangerous substance(s)

- Photograph affected areas.

Step 8—Determine if an outside commercial response service is required.
Library's administration, in consultation with LCET (HUL-wide Library Collections Emergency Team), determines if the type or amount of collection damage exceeds the library's capability to respond.

Step 9—If an outside service is required, arrange for purchase of services.
Library's administration contacts the appropriate offices:

- Financial services
- Insurance office

Step 10—If an outside service is not required, implement salvage activities.
Library's local Emergency Response Team should, in consultation with LCET (HUL-wide Library Collections Emergency Team):

- Gather supplies.
- Remove damaged collections.
- Salvage damaged items.

Step 11—Keep detailed records.
Record:

- Areas/ranges affected
- Items affected
- Locations of items being salvaged
- Salvage methods

Figure 5-5. Steps for Responding to an Emergency (*Continued*)

Source: Reprinted with permission © 2004 by the President and Fellows of Harvard College.

INVENTORY

There was a time when conducting library inventories was entirely manual and took years. Staff walked through the library with boxes of shelf-list cards, trying to find every volume that was supposed to be there. The word *inventory* was enough to cause staff to think of early retirement.

The Northeast Document Conservation Center provides assistance to libraries with collection-threatening emergencies. Call 978-470-1010, day or night, seven days a week. After center hours, you will be referred to a second telephone number to reach a staff member. Please do *not* request disaster assistance via e-mail, since it is not monitored twenty-four hours a day.

Sources of Additional Information

NEDCC's Emergency Management Technical Leaflets
Collections Security: Planning and Prevention for Libraries and Archives. www.nedcc.org/plam3/Index3.htm.
Preservation of Library and Archival Materials: Emergency Management. www.nedcc.org/plam3/tleaf312.htm.

Other Sources

Conservation OnLine has a section on disaster planning and recovery with additional links at
　　http://palimpsest.stanford.edu/bytopic/disasters/.
Federal Emergency Management Agency (FEMA): www.fema.gov.
Illinois Cooperative Extension Service Disaster Resources Home Page: www.ag.uiuc.edu/~disaster/prep.html.
The Inland Empire Libraries Disaster Response Network (IELDRN): www.ieldrn.org/.
Library Administration and Management Association/Library Organization and Management Section
　　(LAMA/LOMS) Risk Management and Insurance Committee: www.ala.org/ala/lama/lamacommunity/
　　lamacommittees/liborg/libraryorganization.htm.
National Fire Protection Agency (NFPA): www.nfpa.org/catalog/home/index.asp?cookie%5Ftest=1.
National Task Force on Emergency Response. "Heritage Preservation." www.heritagepreservation.org/
　　PROGRAMS/taskfer.htm.
Walsh, Betty. "Salvage Operations for Water-Damaged Collections." http://palimpsest.stanford.edu/
　　waac/wn/wn10/wn10-2/wn10-202.html.

Now, with handheld scanners and computers as well as barcodes and radio-frequency identification, which can track materials and furnishings from acquisition through disposition and check-in through check-out, inventories are much easier to maintain. Most automation systems have an inventory module.

The greatest value of a periodic (annual, biennial) inventory today is that you can identify items or equipment that have disappeared from the library. Finding the source of theft will help you to guard against future losses.

Before you even begin the inventory, there are certain steps in the process that you need to think about:

- Make a plan and time schedule. Decide whether to perform a partial or full inventory, and whether to close the library or keep circulation open. If you leave the library open and circulate items during inventory, there will be some discrepancies in your missing items and inventory that will need to be rectified.

- Know the functionality and features of the inventory control software that is installed in your system, become familiar with the barcoding hardware/scanner, and do a basic workflow analysis to determine the best method to inventory the materials in each department.

- Back up the collection and circulation files, and have several copies of current backups on hand. Also back up the system collection data, the circulation data, and the full system. Make several copies of each and store them in a safe location, with at least one set of backups stored off-site.

- Revise the status of any item you already know needs updating, and add any new materials to the collection. You may choose to weed damaged items or items with low circulation rates before inventory.

- Log items in each section of the library into an inventory log by scanning the barcodes or radio-frequency identification (RF-ID) codes.

- Manage the circulation materials. Check in all materials that have been returned to the library during inventory, and clear up any conflicts not resolved during inventory.

- Create and print all remainder reports.

After you have completed the inventory, you will still have lists to clean up, and you will realize that some materials are simply "missing." It is generally prudent to wait a period of time, perhaps a year, to see if the missing items are found; if not, then withdraw them from the library database. Data relating to the missing items should be carefully analyzed.

- Is there a preponderance of missing items in one subject area or in a less-monitored area of the stacks?
- What percentage of the collection is missing?
- What is the dollar value of the missing items?
- Should the missing items be replaced?
- What percentage of the collection do you have to replace each year because of theft?
- Does the amount of theft warrant installing a security system or hiring a security guard?
- What do you consider an acceptable loss rate? five percent of the collection? one percent?
- What are the adverse effects of installing multiple theft-reduction methods (security system, guards at the doorways, alarm systems, etc.)?

As a former library director, I have been very successful in disposing of donated property and keeping the funds for the library. In one city, a large doll collection had been donated to the library fifty years earlier and had been stored in the library's attic. After unsuccessfully searching for heirs of the donor, we obtained permission to sell the collection and to use the $12,000 in proceeds to purchase children's library materials. —Dr. Arlita Hallam

In another city, a storage company donated a large collection of linguistics books to the library. The company had established that the former owner was dead with no known heirs, had cleared all of the legal hurdles, and so could make the donation. The library sold the collection to a university library for $13,000 and bought new library materials with the proceeds.

SALE AND DISPOSAL OF PUBLIC PROPERTY

A process that is somewhat related to the inventory and an aspect of collection management is weeding the collection and removing materials that are no longer appropriate. You will have to dispose of such items and materials properly.

Every entity has rules governing the sale and disposal of public property, including library books no longer needed in the collection. It is the responsibility of the library administration to know those rules and follow them. You may give permission to Friends of the Library, or another library-related entity, to sell surplus library materials, but there must be legal backing to such an arrangement, approved by the library's parent governing body.

The decisions guiding the disposal of public property will be guided by the following criteria:

- Is the property actually surplus (no longer needed)?
- If it is no longer needed by one location/branch, can another use it?
- Can another agency within the same government use the item?
- Does another governmental entity need the property that your library is disposing of?
- Does a nonprofit entity need the property?
- Can you sell the item and keep the proceeds in the library budget?
- What approvals are needed to gift the item to an outside agency?
- What steps do you need to follow to remove the item from inventory and asset records?

It is never appropriate to give public property to a library staff or family member. In some jurisdictions, employees and their family members are not even allowed to bid on public property being auctioned. Improper disposal of public property is not a new problem for managers, as demonstrated in the impeachment of President Andrew Johnson, a section of which is quoted here (see sidebar). On the other hand, you can't really justify storing an unused item forever just because it is too much trouble to dispose of it properly!

FINES AND FEES

Although everyone likes to think of library services as "free" because they are usually tax-supported, libraries also charge for services. Fee-based services, processing fees, and late fines have been charged to patrons in public libraries as ways to restrict use—or misuse—of materials and to supplement costs associated with particular services. If you offer fee-based services or materials you are faced with policy decisions, pricing issues, fee collection, as well as financial record keeping of the special-services funds. In the following sections, you will learn about some of the issues that fee-based services entail. You will also find some suggestions for cost recovery for special library services as well as ways to collect library fees and fines.

FINES

To encourage borrowers to return materials promptly, most libraries charge a nominal fee for each day that a circulating item is kept past its due date. The amount may vary depending on the format of the material checked out. Overdue fines for items on reserve are often charged by the hour. Patrons can avoid fines by renewing items on or before the due date. Most automated circulation systems are programmed to block a borrower's account if unpaid fines accumulate beyond a certain amount. To make a fine sound less punitive, some libraries call it an "extended-use fee." (See figure 5-6 for an example of late charges and fees.)

I do impeach Andrew Johnson, Vice President and acting President of the United States, of high crimes and misdemeanors:

I charge him with a usurpation of power and violation of law:

In that he has corruptly used the appointing power;

In that he has corruptly used the pardoning power;

In that he has corruptly used the veto power;

In that he has corruptly disposed of public property of the United States.

In that he has corruptly interfered in elections, and committed acts which, in contemplation of the Constitution, are high crimes and misdemeanors.

Source: www.worldwideschool .org/library/books/hst/ northamerican/HistoryoftheImpeachmentofAndrewJohnson Presidentofthe UnitedStates/ chap4.html. (Emphasis added.)

FEES

Fees are a sum of money paid for a service. The amount may be fixed, depending on the type of service, or variable, depending on the amount of time required to perform the service. In some libraries, document delivery service is fee based. Some libraries charge fees to borrow items from a rental collection composed of duplicates of items in the regular collection. However, for the most part, libraries in the United States are committed to offering basic services at no charge to their clientele. Persons who live outside a public library's service area, or those who are not faculty or students entitled to use the resources and services of an academic library, may have to pay a fee for limited borrowing privileges.

Information Service Rates	
Cornell University—School of Industrial and Labor Relations 10 percent discount for ILR alumni	
Professional time	**$135/hr**
Special rate *For labor unions and small businesses* *with fewer than fifty employees*	**$75.00/hr**
Online searches	**per vendor charge**
Same-day service *When request received before 1 p.m.* *Eastern Time*	**$35.00 surcharge**
Document Delivery Service	
Per document	**$25.00**
Fax/scan *Up to thirty pages*	**$10.00**
Postage/delivery	**per carrier** (no charge for regular mail)
All document delivery in accordance with copyright laws.	
Figure 5-6. Sample Fees for Special Information Services	

Source: Reprinted with permission of Martin P. Catherwood Library, Cornell University.

MANAGEMENT OF FINES AND FEES

Fines and fees are considered part of the library's revenues, but libraries usually do not keep them. They are normally turned in to the university's, city's, or school's general operating fund to be reallocated with other fines and fees (parking tickets, usage fees, permits, etc.).

Unless the fees are designated for library services, such as in academic libraries, it is generally in the best interest of the library to have all fines and fees commingled with those coming from other governmental departments. The fines and fees that a library collects are not adequate to operate the library. However, if the library does keep its fines and fees, those departments that generate major fines and fees (tax, police, building officials) are likely to want to keep theirs as well. This would cut the amount of general revenues available for all operations and, thus, hurt the library.

Library patrons sometimes think they are "helping the library" by keeping items overdue, assuming that the fine money can then be used to buy new books. If your library does not keep fines, it is important to dispel that erroneous notion.

Some libraries have chosen to not charge overdue fines; they feel it is not worth the added work. This does not mean there is no penalty for overdue items; these libraries do deny borrowing privileges to those who have not returned items by the due date. Still other libraries provide incentives for returning library materials on time.

Publicity about the Patriot Act has also made customers aware that many libraries only retain patron information for overdue library materials. These libraries delete the links between customer and material when the customer returns the item on time or pays any overdue fines.

FEE-BASED LIBRARY SERVICES

Fee-based services operate like small businesses within the library. In public libraries, one fee-based service might be a business reference service that does in-depth research and reports for local businesses that cannot afford their own corporate libraries. In academic libraries, fee-based services might provide extensive reference services to the community or to alumni of the institution.

Worth checking out . . .

American Library Association, Office for Intellectual Freedom. *Guidelines for Developing a Library Privacy Policy*, August 2003. www.ala.org/ala/oif/iftoolkits/toolkitsprivacy/guidelineslibraryprivacy.doc.

In establishing how much to charge, you should plan to recover the total cost of the service provided, including benefits, space, overhead, and database charges. The companies or individuals who use the service are normally billed on an hourly basis for the services they receive. Libraries charge for a full range of additional services, for example:

- Photocopying
- Renting meeting rooms
- Printing
- Interlibrary loan
- Reserving books
- Recovering overdue materials
- Replacing lost library cards
- Repairing or replacing lost or damaged materials
- Renting art prints, best sellers, or other special collections (It is important to have at least the same number of "free" best sellers in the circulating collection. The Friends or foundation might operate the rental collections.)
- Selling office supplies

Library Uses Positive Reinforcement to Reduce Overdues

In December 2003, five Georgia Southern students won $30 gift certificates to the University Store in a drawing conducted by Henderson Library. The students were selected at random from among the 3,577 students who had borrowed at least one library item during the 2003 fall semester, and had no overdue library loans during the same time period. The rewards are part of an experiment to determine whether positive reinforcement might be as or more effective in minimizing overdue library materials than are more traditional punitive methods, such as charging fines.

Henderson Library has not charged fines in more than ten years, although they have been a familiar tradition in most American libraries for more than a century. Despite the prevalence of fines policies, there is a controversy regarding whether they are effective. The empirical evidence is weak at best. Further, many librarians, particularly those who work in public libraries, contend that library fines present obstacles to information access for those who can least afford to pay them. Henderson Library's experiment is intended to determine whether positive reinforcement offers a feasible and effective alternative.

The early results are encouraging. The fall of 2003 was the first semester the reward system was in place for student borrowers, and Henderson Library recorded a 5.5 percent decline in undergraduate overdue loans, and a 14 percent reduction in graduate student overdues, compared with FY 2003. The Library will continue the experiment in the spring of 2004. Costs of the system are minimal, consisting primarily of the gift certificates and a few minutes of staff time to run the computer reports needed to identify reward eligibility and to conduct the drawing.

Source: Quoted with permission from http//library.georgiasouthern.edu/cio/cio107.html# reinforcement.

Portland State University: Late Charges and Fees	
Material	**Late Charges**
General collections	$.25/day per item
Summit loans	$.50/day for first ten days $1/day for next fifteen days $20 maximum
Interlibrary loans	$.50/day per item $10 maximum
Recalled items	$.25/day per item
Course reserves	two-hour item: $1/hour for first hour $.25/hour per hour after first hour late
	2-day item: $2/day for two-day item NO LIMIT ON MAXIMUM FINE
Study room keys	First day: $1/hour Second day: $5/hour Third day: $10/hour

Appealing Charges

You may appeal if you believe library charges have been mistakenly assessed or extenuating circumstances warrant charge cancellation or reduction. Appeals should be made within thirty days of the original billing by the Business Office. Notices of overdue materials are sent as a courtesy reminder to your e-mail account. Nonreceipt of an overdue notice does not exempt you from late fees or charges. It is your responsibility to ensure your current e-mail address is in your PSU record.

You can appeal library charges by submitting a Petition for Waiver of Library Charges. You can pick up a copy of this form at the Circulation Desk. Reasons generally not acknowledged as valid for canceling or reducing library charges include the following:

- Lack of knowledge of library policy
- Disagreement with library fine/fee structure
- Inability to pay library fees or charges
- Material loaned to a third party
- Nonreceipt or late receipt of library reminder notice
- Returning items to library other than PSU library
- Being out of town
- Forgetting the due date
- Term breaks, leaves, vacations, exams
- Transportation problems

Returning a book with one of these reasons will not reduce your library fines.

Figure 5-7. Sample Policy for Overdue Materials

MRSC Fee Schedule For Nonmunicipal Government Users	
Service	Charges/Restrictions
Library Loans	$7 per item
BBS Access to Library Bibliographic Information	$150 per year
On-site Library Use (covers staff time to select and res helve materials)	$20 per visit
Document Delivery	As specified
Photocopies	25 cents a page, $2 minimum One-day rush—$15 surcharge Two-day rush—$7.50 surcharge
Normal deadlines within three to five working days	
Fax	$1.00/page (inside Washington)
Delivery	Actual cost of whatever service is used
Invoice fee	$2 (not applied to prepaid orders)
Research by Library Staff	$65 per hour
Note: Online Searching MRSC now has the capability to perform searches on DIALOG, LOCAL EXCHANGE, and LOGIN. Charges for conducting online searches would cover the actual cost of the online search plus staff time; $65 per hour for staff time plus search charges.	
Fee Collection: MRSC will accept prepayment (cash or check) or invoice the user. If invoiced, MRSC will charge an additional $2 processing fee.	
Municipal Research and Services Center, 2601 Fourth Avenue, Suite 800 • Seattle, WA 98121-1280	

Figure 5-8. Sample Fees for Nonmunicipal Government Users

Worth checking out . . .

Martin, Murray S., and Betsy Park. *Charging and Collecting Fees and Fines: A Handbook for Libraries.* New York: Neal-Schuman, 1998.

- Providing pay telephones or coin-operated typewriters or computers
- Library services for nonresidents

The Municipal Research and Services Center in Seattle, Washington, allows nonmunicipal residents to use their services for a fee. They have adopted the fee schedule depicted in figure 5-8. Figure 5-7 is a schedule for information services for an academic library.

SUMMARY

One of the big challenges that a library manager faces is balancing responsible stewardship of the library facilities and collection with positive customer service and good public relations with the community. This means having policies and procedures for all aspects of caring for the collection, from recovering overdue materials and preventing theft and mutilation of library property to being prepared for disasters, taking inventory, and knowing how to dispose of public property. Fortunately, there are many resources for dealing with these issues.

The purpose of library fines and fees is not punitive. The only purpose for these charges is to recover library materials and the costs of services so that the user of a service or the patron who does not return materials—not the public at large—pays the costs of providing the specialty fee-based service or of recovering an overdue library item.

CAPITAL PROJECTS

OVERVIEW

Capital projects are major expenditures that are usually spread over several years: the time it takes you to accumulate the funds, plan the project, actually begin to implement the plan, and finally complete it. The capital project may be a new library building or renovation, or it may be the installation of a new automation system. Because the capital project is a major and very visible expenditure, your decisions will be open to scrutiny by the media and the general public.

In this chapter, you will learn what a capital project actually entails: a needs assessment, a building program, estimating costs, renovations and remodeling, and other considerations. Sample budgets and checklists will help you grasp the scope of a capital undertaking.

COMMUNITY NEEDS ASSESSMENT

Construction of a new library building (or any capital project) really begins with a community needs assessment and the acknowledgment that a new library (or other project) is needed. Sometimes the needs assessment is conducted in conjunction with a larger master plan for a new campus or an enlarged service area. It is important that you be included in the master plan so that the library becomes a priority and part of the governing agency's long-range plan.

In the needs assessment, you will evaluate the community's changing demographics, shifting populations, current building inadequacies, staffing shortages, available resources, and comparative standards and data. When the library's community needs assessment has been completed, a consultant is usually brought in to work with library staff and community leaders to prepare the building program. Figure 6-1 details the components of a community needs assessment. Your needs assessment is, of course, part of your

---

What Is Included in a Community Needs Assessment?

Definition and Purpose

A needs assessment process reveals the influences acting on the library. Information collected shapes the services and programs that best fit the library's strengths and budget. Ultimately, it informs a vision for future development.

Results of a needs assessment can be used in a variety of situations:

- Commencing a strategic planning process
- Determining change in a user community
- Making changes in a library's collection, services, and so on
- Determining adequacy of facilities, technology, and so on
- Establishing satisfactory staffing patterns and library hours

Essential Data

- Local information and demographics cited from census/vital statistic records, library statistics, community development plans, and/or other existing data sources
- Internal (library) and external (community) scanning results
- Community input
- Analysis of data (e.g., identification of common threads or issues)
- Library vision statement linking data to the library's direction

Data Collection Options

Careful consideration should be given to which data collection techniques are employed. Using only one technique may provide limited information while using too many can be expensive and time consuming. The online resources below provide several articles with pros and cons of the various techniques, which include the following:

- Surveys: mail, telephone, e-mail
- SWOT (strengths, weaknesses, opportunities, threats) exercise
- Key informants
- Community forum/focus groups
- Census and/or public records
- Citizen advisory groups
- Town meeting

Online Resources and Examples

Arizona State Library, Archives and Public Records

Needs Assessment Information
Part of Collection Development Training
www.dlapr.lib.az.us/text/cdt/commneeds.htm

Community Analysis Methods and Evaluative Options: The CAMEO Handbook

Prepared by The Consulting Librarians Group, Sandra M. Cooper, Nancy Bolt, Keith Curry Lance, Lawrence Webster, in cooperation with MGT of America, Inc., for the Library of Virginia
http://skyways.lib.ks.us/pathway/cameo/index.htm

Figure 6-1. Components of a Community Needs Assessment

Florida Cooperative Extension's Electronic Data Information Source

Conducting a Community Needs Assessment: Primary Data Collection Techniques
Keith A. Carter and Lionel J. Beaulieu
http://edis.ifas.ufl.edu/pdffiles/HE/HE06000.pdf

Iowa Community Education Association

Community Needs Assessment article
www.iowacommunityeducation.org/ceneeds.html

Library Research Service

Resources for Community Analysis—Colorado and National
www.lrs.org/asp_public/community.asp
Community Survey Form
www.lrs.org/asp_public/ca_form.asp

Montana Department of Commerce

Community Needs Assessment Techniques
www.commerce.state.mt.us/CDD/Includes/CDBG/Needs Assessment/03ExA.pdf

Upper Hudson Library System

Community Analysis Community Survey Form
www.uhls.org/uhls/communityanalysis/

Western Rural Development Center

Coping with Growth Series—Community Needs Assessment Techniques
http://extension.usu.edu/files/SGuide.pdf

Figure 6-1. Components of a Community Needs Assessment (*Continued*)

Source: Reprinted with permission of the Idaho State Library, 325 W. State St., Boise, ID, www.Lili.org.

overall planning. Figure 6-2 shows where the needs assessment fits in the strategic planning process. As you can see, these are ongoing processes, and you will have to monitor your progress and reevaluate as needed.

Worth checking out . . .

Two Good Examples of Needs Assessments
Moline Public Library: http://www.rbls.lib.il.us/mpl/needs.html.
School District 128 Needs Assessment: www.district128.org/board/fiveyearplan.asp.

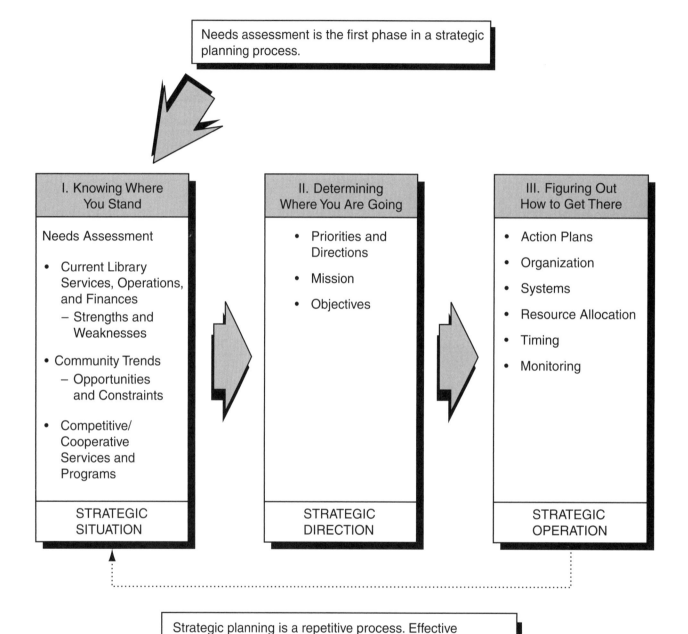

Figure 6-2. Needs Assessment as Part of Strategic Planning

Why Do a Needs Assessment?

Direct Benefits
- Provides a strong basis for planning and budgeting
  - Developing short- and long-term plans
  - Dealing with competing needs
  - Setting priorities
  - Allocating scarce resources
- Tough decisions where a needs assessment can help:
  - Reducing service levels
  - Adding services
  - Closing branches
  - Opening branches

Indirect Benefits
- Raising your profile/marketing your library
- Building partnerships
- Educating many groups
  - Public
  - Staff
  - Board
  - County council
- Improving communications
- Developing staff skills and knowledge

Source: Oxford County Library System, Southwestern Ontario, Canada, www.ocl.net/needs/one.html#exhibitthree.

BUILDING PROGRAM

The purpose of a building program is to analyze the space needs for each current and future function of the library, whether you are planning a new library, an addition, or a renovation. Your result is a list of areas, uses, and furnishings for those functions; how the areas are to be used; and the square footage needed to provide the library service. Those square footages are then added together, with an additional factor for unassigned space (ductwork for heating and air conditioning, stairwells, restrooms, elevators, interior walls, etc.), to come up with the total size (square footage) needed for the new library or addition.

Your building program will also include estimated construction costs, giving you an idea of the amount of money needed to construct the library building that will best serve the community's needs. In addition to the construction, there will be estimates for other components of the project, for example, the land, parking, furnishings, and equipment.

Most libraries do not have a capital fund to which they can charge consultant fees while they are still working on the building program; if yours is one of those that does not yet have a capital fund, you will need to charge the cost of the consultant to contractual or professional fees. You will need to develop a request for proposal (RFP) to solicit proposals from consultants. ALA's Library Administration and Management Association (LAMA) has compiled a "Library Building Consultants List," which is available at https://cs.ala.org/lbcl/lbcl2.htm. For a sample consultant RFP, see Appendix C.

ESTIMATING COSTS

Once you have completed the building program, you will be able to calculate cost estimates for land acquisition, site preparation, construction, furnishing, equipment, and staffing of the new facility. The new library may be more efficient than the former, but it will also be used twice as heavily just because it is new. Therefore, budget for an increase in staff for the new facility.

One way to estimate building costs is to review the annual December issue of *Library Journal* (www.libraryjournal.com/article/CA339603). You will find building costs for new construction and renovations for all types of libraries. A division of square footage into total costs will give a good per-square-foot estimate for construction in your geographic area. See the tables at the end of the *Library Journal* article for cost data.

To calculate the estimated costs for a new library, multiply the square footage for the library by the cost estimates for library construction in your area. (You will already have put these figures into your building plan.) For example: $100,000$ square feet $\times$ $\$200$ per square foot $=\$20$ million.

The public will remember two figures: the size of the library and the estimated cost. Whenever one of these figures changes, you can expect a newspaper story. To avoid negative publicity, when you are speaking publicly about the size and cost of the library, try to speak in terms of ranges or estimates.

The actual cost of the library needs to include more than bricks and mortar. Here are some approximate percentages for the costs you need to consider:

- Seventy-five percent of the cost will be construction,
- Eleven percent will cover equipment and furnishings,

Here are some good examples of building programs and space-needs guidelines:

College of Charleston Libraries: www.cofc.edu/~library/addlestone/program/index.html.

Dahlgren, Anders C. "Public Library Space Needs: A Planning Outline/1988" (formulas). www.dpi.state.wi.us/dlcl/pld/plspace.html.

"Determining Space Needs" (formulas). www.lva.lib.va.us/whatwedo/ldnd/govadmin/pfle/Appendix_C.pdf.

Glenview (IL) Public Library: www.glenview.lib.il.us/gplpgrm.pdf.

"Library Building Checklist." www.ki-inc.com/files/librarybuildingchecklist.pdf.

"Library Building Program Components." http://cml.ci.cerritos.ca.us/media/pdfs/301_7.pdf.

"Library Space Planning Guide." http://webjunction.org:21080/orig/ct/6181.pdf.

Library Space Planning Guide Worksheet: http://webjunction.org:21080/orig/ct/6182.xls.

- Seven percent will cover the site, and
- Seven percent covers other costs (architect's fees, engineers, etc.).

"Cost Estimating Simplified" is an excellent website funded by the Institute of Museum and Library Services (IMLS). You can find it at www.librisdesign.org/docs/cost_estimating.doc?bbatt=Y. In this publication, Nick Butcher explains how cost estimates are established for each of the twenty items listed below.

1. Foundations
2. Vertical structure
3. Floor and roof structure
4. Exterior cladding
5. Roofing and waterproofing
6. Interior partitions, doors, and glazing
7. Floor, wall, and ceiling finishes
8. Function equipment and specialties
9. Stairs and vertical transportation
10. Plumbing systems
11. Heating, ventilation, and air conditioning (HVAC)
12. Electric lighting, power, and communication
13. Fire-protection systems
14. Site preparation and demolition
15. Site paving, structures, and landscaping
16. Utilities on-site
17. Off-site development
18. Off-site utilities
19. General conditions
20. Contractor's overhead and profit or fee

Source: This material was created by Nick Butcher and Linda Demmers and provided through the Libris Design Project (http://www.libris design.org/), supported by the U.S. Institute of Museum and Library Services under the provisions of the Library Services and Technology Act, administered in California by the state librarian. Any use of this material should credit the authors and funding source.

For an example of a school library renovation/addition, see the cost estimate for the Natick (MA) High School Library: http://natickhighschool.net/report/6.1.cost_est_schemeA.pdf.

Linda Demmers provides an example of cost estimating through Library Construction 101, also funded by IMLS. The cost estimates for a $22,000,000 library ($185 per square foot) are delineated in figure 6-3, and figure 6-4 presents a sample budget for a new building.

Budget Cost Plan COMPONENT SUMMARY		
Area: 87,500 square feet (SF)		
	$/SF	$×1000
1. Basement excavation and foundations	7.69	673
2. Vertical structure	10.95	958
3. Floor and roof structures	18.89	1,653
4. Exterior cladding	26.3	2,301
5. Roofing and waterproofing	12	452
Shell (1–5)	68.99	6,037
6. Interior partitions	7.3	639
7. Interior finishes: floors, walls, ceilings	11.46	1,003
Interiors (6–7)	18.77	1,642
8. Function equipment and specialties	6.93	606
9. Vertical transportation	5.28	462
Equipment and Vertical Transportation (8–9)	12.21	1,068
10. Plumbing	4.53	396
11. Heating, ventilation, and air conditioning (HVAC)	26.75	2,341
12. Electrical and communications	26.5	2,105
13. Fire protection	2.8	245
Mechanical and Electrical (10–13)	58.14	5,087
Total Building Construction (1–13)	158.1	13,834
14. Site preparation and demolition	1.11	97
15. Site development	7.81	683
16. Site utilities	2.75	241
Total Site Construction (14–16)	11.67	1,021
TOTAL BUILDING AND SITE (1–16)	169.77	14,855
General conditions	7.00%	11.88	1,040
Overhead and profit	5.00%	9.08	795
PLANNED CONSTRUCTION COST		190.74	16,690
Design contingency	10.00%	19.07	1,669
Allowance for rising costs	3.00%	6.29	551
Budget FOR CONSTRUCTION		216.11	18,909

Figure 6-3. Sample Cost Estimate for a New Library Building

Source: Library Construction 101. Fall 2002. This material has been created by Nick Butcher & Linda Demmers and provided through the Infopeople Project (http://www.infopeople.org), supported by the U.S. Institute of Museum and Library Services under the provisions of the Library Services and Technology Act, administered in California by the state librarian. Any use of this material should credit the author and funding source.

Library Construction 101: Project Budget with Cost Estimate Details

Cost/Square Feet		Budget Activity Details		Cost	Percentage of Total
$185.00	**New Construction**			$11,251,700	51.04%
	$9.00	Contractor's Overhead and Profit @ 5 percent	$547,380.00		
	$27.00	Electrical, Lighting, Power, and Communications	$1,642,140.00		
	$15.00	Exterior Cladding	$912,300.00		
	$5.00	Fire Protection Systems	$304,100.00		
	$21.00	Floor and Roof Structure	$1,277,220.00		
	$14.00	Floor, Wall, and Ceiling Finishes	$851,480.00		
	$3.00	Foundation	$182,460.00		
	$12.00	Function Equipment and Specialties	$729,840.00		
	$18.00	General Conditions @ 11 percent	$1,094,760.00		
	$28.00	HVAC	$1,702,960.00		
	$6.00	Interior Partitions, Doors, and Glazing	$364,920.00		
	$6.00	Plumbing Systems	$364,920.00		
	$6.00	Roofing, Waterproofing, and Skylights	$364,920.00		
	$6.00	Stairs and Vertical Transportation	$364,920.00		
	$9.00	Vertical Structure	$547,380.00		
$30.00	**Site Development**			$1,824,600	8.28
$23.02	**Site Acquisition**			$1,400,000	6.35
	$23.02	Site Acquisition (General)	$1,400,000		
$39.89	**Furniture and Equipment**			$2,425,969	11.01
$0.30	**Technology Installation**			$18,200	0.08
	$0.08	Building Access Systems (Key Card)	$5,000		
	$0.04	Building Security System Equipment Installation	$2,200		
	$0.12	Computer Equipment Installation	$7,500		
	$0.06	Telephone Equipment Installation	$3,500		
$5.00	**Technology Cabling**			$304,100	1.38
$2.00	**Signage**			$121,640	0.55
$2.15	**Works of Art**			$130,763	0.59
$17.20	**Architectural and Engineering Fees**			$1,046,104	4.75
	8.00 Percent of Construction Contract				
$1.08	**Professional Construction Cost Estimator**			$65,382	0.30
$6.45	**Construction Management**			$392,289	1.78
$3.19	**Interior Design Fees**			$194,078	0.88
	8.00 Percent of Furniture and Equipment Cost				
$7.60	**Planning and Administration**			$462,000	2.10
	$0.20	Acoustical Consultant	$12,000		
	$0.08	ADA Consultant	$5,000		
	$0.16	Appraisal	$10,000		
	$0.04	Art Consultant	$2,500		

Figure 6-4. Sample Project Budget with Cost Estimate Details

Cost/Square Feet		Budget Activity Details		Cost	Percentage of Total
	$0.21	Asbestos Study	$13,000		
	$0.13	Audio-Visual Consultant	$8,000		
	$0.08	Building Security Systems Consultant	$5,000		
	$0.74	Ceremonial Expenses	$45,000		
	$0.07	Energy Audit	$4,500		
	$0.36	Environmental Assessment	$22,000		
	$0.13	Feasibility Analysis	$8,000		
	$0.13	Financial Consultant	$8,000		
	$0.33	Fundraising Consultant	$20,000		
	$0.07	Geotechnical (Soil Engineering) Report	$4,500		
	$0.06	Historical Consultant	$3,500		
	$0.30	Land Surveys	$18,000		
	$0.44	Landscape Architect	$27,000		
	$0.66	Legal	$40,000		
	$0.20	Library Building Program Consultant	$12,000		
	$0.26	Library Technology Consultant	$16,000		
	$0.28	Lighting Consultant	$17,000		
	$0.66	Permit and Utility Connections Fees	$40,000		
	$0.74	Signage Consultant	$45,000		
	$0.43	Special Testing and Inspection	$26,000		
	$0.08	Structural Engineering Study	$5,000		
	$0.49	Testing and Inspections	$30,000		
	$0.12	Title Report and Insurance	$7,000		
	$0.13	Traffic Engineering Consultant	$8,000		
$0.16	**Relocation**			$10,000	0.05
	$0.05	Computer Equipment Moving	$3,000		
	$0.03	Equipment Moving	$2,000		
	$0.08	Furniture Moving	$5,000		
$0.94	**Collection Moving Costs**			$57,000	0.26
	190,000	Items Moved			
	1	Number of Times Items Moved			
	$0.30	Cost per Item Moved			
$21.50	**Contingency**			$1,307,630	5.93
	10.00 Percent of Construction Contract				
$345.47	**Project Cost Subtotal**			$21,011,455	95.32
$16.97	**Inflation**			$1,032,090	4.68
	2.40 Percent Inflation Rate for Twenty-four Months				
$362.44	**Project Cost Estimate**			**$22,043,545**	**100%**

Figure 6-4. Sample Project Budget with Cost Estimate Details (*Continued*)

Source: Library Construction 101 Summer 2002–Spring 2003. This material has been created by Linda Demmers using the Libris Design software and provided through the Infopeople Project (http://infopeople.org/), supported by the U.S. Institute of Museum and Library Services under the provisions of the Library Services and Technology Act, administered in California by the state librarian. Any use of this material should credit the author and funding source.

SITE ACQUISITION AND DEVELOPMENT COSTS

Keep in mind that the cheapest site may not necessarily be your best choice. Because the choice of the library site will probably be the most controversial aspect of library construction, it is important that you examine all cost factors closely. Ask yourself these questions:

- What do you need to do to the site so that you can build on it (drainage, landfill, leveling, clearing of debris, tree removal and relocation, access roads, etc.)? What are those costs?
- Are there adequate utilities to the site, or do they need to be extended or enlarged? Include those costs.
- How was the site used in the past? If there was a gas station, junk yard, garbage dump, or any use that could have contaminated the land, you will need to have it cleaned before you can start to build.
- Is there a building that needs to be demolished? Does it have asbestos or any toxic materials that need to be removed?
- Does the property need to be condemned? Is so, there will be additional legal costs.
- Will the site permit surface parking, or will a parking garage be needed?
- Do soil borings and engineering studies show that the soil will support the structure, or are there added costs for diverting ground water or pilings?

Even though an average library site cost is 7 to 10 percent of the cost of the project, the perfect building site could cost as much as 50 percent of the project. If a more expensive site requires less development, attracts more people, and provides a better location for the next twenty years, it may be the best bargain. Because the library needs parking and room for expansion, setbacks, and other auxiliary space, it is a good rule of thumb to purchase three to four times the amount of land needed for the library's footprint (first floor). If you are purchasing the land from an individual or corporation that can benefit from tax write-offs, consider offering a price lower than market value and a receipt for the remaining amount as a donation to the library. Libris Design's Web page lists criteria to be used when selecting a library site (see figure 6-5 or go to www.librisdesign.org/docs/site_selection.doc?bbatt=Y).

Site Selection Criteria
1. Geography Evaluate proximity to other civic services, schools and transit.
2. Land Acquisition Costs Compare initial cost, long-term lease cost, or other arrangement.
3. Soil/Structural Implications Assess soils report and anticipated structural footings.
4. Infrastructure Estimate extent of new or modified infrastructure needs (water, powertel/data, gas, vaults, utility reroutes).
5. Topography Gauge extent of site grading needed to prepare site.
6. Project Approvals Compare environmental, design, and city approvals process.
7. Site Fit Check library building program on the site's buildable area.
8. Parking Check parking requirements based on local codes and recommendations. Factor in costs for structure if needed.
9. Site Amenities Assess opportunities for accommodating gardens and gathering places.

Figure 6-5. Criteria for Site Selection

Source: "Site Selection for Libraries," material created by Lisa Padilla, AIA, and provided through the Libris Design Project (http://www.librisdesign.org/), supported by the U.S. Institute of Museum and Library Services under the provisions of the Library Services and Technology Act, administered in California by the state librarian. Reprinted with permission.

FURNITURE, FIXTURES, AND EQUIPMENT

Furniture, fixtures, and equipment (frequently referred to as FF&E) will come to approximately 11 percent of the project's total budget. The percentage will vary because some of the costs will be considered construction costs rather than FF&E costs. For example, furniture that is built into the building (counters, circulation desks, cabinetry) is part of the construction costs. Carpeting, wall coverings, light fixtures, and window treatments may also be included in construction, or they may be considered FF&E.

Even though you might be tempted to put all the money into the construction and "make do" with existing furniture until future budget funds are available, you are better off including all furnishings (including computers and wiring) when the new building is constructed. Purchasing all of the furnishings at one time takes advantage of discounts of up to 30 to 40 percent and helps guarantee that the furniture you need will be available and will match the colors used in the interior.

It is also advisable to purchase additional fabric, carpet tiles, shelves, and furniture to store and use for replacements. Dye lots and finishings change over time, so you probably won't be able to match the original colors exactly.

When you select furniture and furnishings, the first thing you should check for is durability. Library furniture gets hard use from both customers and custodians. Again, the low bid may not be the best economy if you have to replace the furniture in two or three years.

PROFESSIONAL FEES

You can figure on professional fees costing another 7 percent of the library building project. These fees include engineers, architects, interior designers, automation consultants, audiovisual consultants, acoustic consultants, lighting consultants, construction managers, legal counsel, financial counsel, landscape engineers, and others who have the expertise to assist with the library's project.

When selecting your architects and other consultants, interview those who have recent experience in designing libraries. They bring valuable knowledge to the project that other architects (yes, even the local favorite) will not have. Your architect needs to understand the function, flow, staffing, usage, and operating costs of running a library, which is not like a typical office building.

Good consultants can actually save you money because they have access to wholesale prices on quality materials that will be efficient and effective for library use. You should certainly resist the temptation to turn the interior decoration of the library over to a board member who has a lovely home or asking the local garden club to do the landscaping.

Here are some excellent guidelines for choosing furniture:

Infopeople library furniture guidelines: www.infopeople.org/training/past/2002/lib_furniture101/.

Libris Design furniture program: www.librisdesign.org/docs/furniture.html.

North Carolina State contract for library furniture (note discounts): www.doa.state.nc.us/PandC/420d.pdf.

RELOCATION COSTS

The relocation costs will also be charged to the library construction budget (and if you build the new library on the same site, you will have to relocate twice). Your relocation budget may need to include funds for renovating and leasing temporary space as well as for moving materials to and from that space. There are library movers who specialize in moving collections intact and relocating materials on the shelves in the correct order. Here again, it is a false economy to deal with a household mover or volunteers who offer to box books and relocate them to the new library. The minute two books are put into a box, they are out of order. Imagine putting an entire library back into Dewey or Library of Congress order!

Library movers also know how to put library shelving back together (or move it intact) so it doesn't "domino" the first time someone leans on the end panel. For a list of reputable library moving contractors, see ALA's "Fact Sheet on Moving Libraries" at www.ala.org/ala/alalibrary/library-factsheet/alalibraryfactsheet.htm.

RENOVATION AND REMODELING

If the library's current site is ideal, you will have to decide whether to remodel or renovate the existing library or build a new one. If you are thinking of remodeling, examine all of the costs very carefully.

- Remodeling may actually cost more per square foot in construction costs than a new library because the contractor has to tear down in order to rebuild.
- There are unknowns in remodeling (asbestos and whatever else may be behind the walls and in the ceilings), so the cost estimates are frequently higher than new construction and the contingency fund must be larger.
- There are also the costs of keeping the library operational during the renovation versus relocating the library to a temporary location.
- Renovations will require upgrading of wiring, extra load handling for air conditioning and heating systems, and installation of ADA (disability) accommodations that may not have been required in the original "grandfathered" building.

Worth checking out . . .

Green Schools: www.rmi.org/sitepages/pid715.php.

Frequently, existing buildings are readapted into libraries. Grocery and furniture stores or other one-story buildings with flexible open space can be converted fairly easily into libraries. They usually have adequate parking and are located in prime locations that make them convenient, especially as neighborhood branches. Figure 6-6 is a checklist for analyzing an existing building.

BUILDING MAINTENANCE

After a building has been constructed or renovated, it must be maintained. As the librarian, you are responsible for constantly monitoring proposed installations (furnishings, light fixtures, floor and wall coverings, restroom fixtures, etc.) to make certain that they can be cleaned and replaced after the contractors are gone. The following checklist can help avoid costly maintenance mistakes:

- Make interior ledges accessible for cleaning.
- Avoid corners behind poles (they cannot be reached by vacuum cleaners).
- Keep light fixtures low enough so that they can be reached to change bulbs.
- Order light fixtures with bulbs that can be readily purchased in your community.
- Provide restrooms with soap fixtures and paper towel holders above the sink and wastebaskets in the countertop so the user does not have to move to wash and dry hands.
- Provide quiet surfaces where book trucks and other equipment are to be rolled.
- Put chair rails in meeting rooms to protect wall coverings.
- Build drains in restrooms to catch water when toilets overflow.
- Provide storage for ladders, vacuum cleaners, and buffers.

Worth checking out . . .

Dean, Edward M. "Renovation, Addition, or New Library: A Planning Process."
   www.librisdesign.org/docs/renovation.doc?bbatt=Y.

Dean's material is made available through Libris Design (www.librisdesign.org), which is supported by the U.S. Institute of Museum and Library Services under the provisions of the Library Services and Technology Act, administered in California by the state librarian.

Building Analysis Component	Issue
1. Seismic resistance capacity	Determine what measures are likely to be required to meet current codes.
2. Structural load capacity	Evaluate if the floor loading capacity is adequate for shelving throughout the existing structure to provide maximum flexibility.
3. Energy efficiency	Determine what features are particularly inefficient and need to be corrected. Retrofit features should be considered as well.
4. HVAC systems	Study the heating/cooling systems and determine if they have reached the end of their useful lives.
5. Electrical systems	Determine how extensive an upgrade will be required.
6. Lighting	Evaluate what needs to be done to provide energy-efficiency and improved quality of light. Determine if this entails replacement of entire light fixtures and their control systems. Evaluate how daylight can be introduced in an existing structure.
7. Telecommunications and information systems	Determine how easy it is to install new cabling in the existing building and how many new data closets must be added.
8. Fire alarm	Determine if this system needs to be upgraded to meet current standards.
9. Security systems	Evaluate security needs and if security cameras or other new systems will be required.
10. Plumbing systems	Determine requirements for additional toilet facilities required under current code, including the extent of the accessibility (ADA) code upgrade work.
11. Fire protection	Determine if a sprinkler system will be required if not already installed.
12. Acoustics	Determine the extent of existing noise problems that need to be ddressed.
13. Accessibility	Determine what ADA upgrades will be required to meet current codes.
14. Shelving systems	Determine if the existing shelving system meets current seismic standards and other code requirements and evaluate the feasibility of keeping the existing shelving in place.
15. Architectural systems	Conduct an overall review of the general condition of the existing building, including features such as roofing, windows, exterior sheathing, and ceilings.
16. Architectural design features	Evaluate changes that will be required to improve navigation, overall space organization, and code exiting.
17. Miscellaneous	Determine if there are any special aspects of the existing building that may have cost implications in a renovation option, such as its qualification as a registered historic structure.

Figure 6-6. Checklist of Topics and Issues for an Existing Building Analysis

- Put deep sinks in the janitor's closets.
- Install shades or protection against afternoon sun on western windows.
- Create entries with foyers and mats to catch water, leaves, and dirt.
- Locate public restrooms so they are visible from a public desk.
- Synchronize clocks so you do not need to reset them individually at the semiannual time change.
- Remember that exterior ledges, ramps, and steps beg skateboarding.
- Recognize that undivided couches and park benches may become beds for street people.
- The list goes on. During construction or renovation, keep asking yourself how each space will be used and how it will be cleaned and maintained.

THE SEVEN DEADLY SINS OF PUBLIC LIBRARY ARCHITECTURE

This is an outline of a program presented by Fred Schlipf and John Moorman at the Public Library Association national conference in Kansas City, Missouri, March 12, 1998. It is reprinted with their permission.

1. Bad Lighting
   - Glare
   - Direct glare
   - Indirect glare (veiling reflectance)
   - Glare from natural light
   - Glare from artificial light
   - Uneven lighting
   - Badly lighted perimeters and corners
   - Dark surfaces, particularly walls and ceilings
   - Inefficient lighting
   - Inflexible lighting
   - Lighting systems with slow restrike times in areas where lights need to be switched off and on frequently (like meeting rooms). Since they take a while to "restrike"—come up and go down—you have to wait before turning them on again.

- Noisy lighting
- Esoteric technology
- Skylights
- Downlighting (the truly great evil), that is, incandescent lights or other lights with a beam that goes straight down

2. Inflexibility
- Inadequate floor loading
- Bearing walls
- Incorrect column spacing in modern modular architecture
- Permanent objects in the way
- Insufficient data conduit and electrical outlets
- Access points to data conduit and electricity that place limits on space usage
- Nonexpandable buildings, because of no adjacent land or designs that defy additions
- Architectural solutions to furniture problems

3. Bad Location
- Entrances far from parking
- Locations with entrances in areas people hesitate to frequent, especially after dark
- Locations too close to schools
- Locations adjacent to other government buildings rather than retail shopping areas
- Badly lit exteriors
- Need for two entrances in order to serve both drivers and pedestrians
- Locations that would be bad for retail

4. Complex Maintenance

   Examples include the following:
- Bad floor coverings
- Bad heating, ventilation, and air conditioning (HVAC)

Worth checking out . . .

College of Charleston (SC) Library. "General Building Issues."
   www.cofc.edu/%7Elibrary/addlestone/program/general.html.

- Too many different lamps or unusual lamps
- Unnecessarily inaccessible light fixtures
- Trouble-prone restrooms

5. Insufficient Work and Storage Space
   - No provision for staff growth
   - Unrealistic predictions of storage needs
   - Use of offices for storage

6. Bad Security
   - Bad sight lines
   - Multiple entrances
   - Aisles that run the wrong direction for supervision
   - Adult pathways through children's services areas
   - Private restrooms
   - Places to spit
   - Frightening drop-offs
   - Failure to take advantage of oversight possibilities through service desk and office placement
   - No provision for theft control systems
   - Book returns that lead inside the library
   - Dead-end book aisles

7. Signature Architecture
   - Excess ceremonial space
   - Ornamental, freestanding staircases
   - Awkward or unusable interior spaces, resulting from creative but impractical footprints
   - Badly matched expansions
   - Unexpected problems with untested architectural systems

LEASING AND RENTING

Sometimes owning your building or equipment may not be the best financial decision. Sometimes you are really better off leasing or renting.

PROPERTY

If you want space in a shopping center or heavy traffic area for one of your branches or for a business-reference location, leasing may be the only way to obtain this prime space. If you do lease, you will be expected to renovate the space for library use, pay the utilities, and participate in payment of fees for common areas (such as cleaning and lighting of parking lot and sidewalk).

The lease will cover who maintains the HVAC, plumbing, roof, exterior walls, windows, and doors. When you lease or rent commercial space, you are going to be dealing with more costs than when you are renting an apartment.

Because a lease is an operating expense, not a debt, the library will not need a bond referendum or capital financing to be able to lease property. This can be a temporary way to test a location for a future branch, or it can become an ongoing solution to providing library service to prime property.

Libraries may also be lessors of property. Many libraries lease space in their buildings for coffee shops, copy services, bookshops, gift shops, and other related commercial businesses. When we visited the Vancouver Public Library, there were nineteen shops in the library's mall. Figure 6-7 shows how public-private partnerships in Maryland fund public schools.

EQUIPMENT

Libraries lease many types of equipment, from photocopiers to bookmobiles. If you lease equipment you can charge the costs to the budget's operating expenses, and you can then trade in the equipment for a new model at the end of the lease. The library does not need to be concerned with depreciation, resale, or disposal of the equipment, nor is there a need to save money for the replacement of the vehicle or equipment at the end of its life cycle. The budgeted expenses are consistent from the beginning of the lease to the end. However, when you negotiate a lease, make certain that you know what is included. Here is a checklist you can use to determine the total cost of the lease over its lifetime, and then compare those costs with the costs of owning the same item. Sometimes the lease is more economical, but sometimes it is not. A sample equipment lease is shown in Appendix D.

- Does the photocopier lease include maintenance, toner, and replacement parts?
- Does the library pay insurance or an annual maintenance fee that is not included in the lease?
- Is there a lease-purchase option?

This table provides a framework for evaluating public-private partnerships in context.	
Benefits Unique to Public-Private Partnerships	**Benefits Attributed to Public-Private Partnerships That Are Not Unique**
• Depreciation tax savings accrue to nongovernment entity that can benefit • Cost overrun risk can be shifted from counties to developer • Demographic risk can be shifted from counties to developer • Incentives to design-in savings and generate revenues can be built in • Nontraditional use of public school space during nonschool time • Nontraditional locations of school buildings • Use of performance contracting	• Interest savings from shorter maturities used for leasing contracts • Time and money savings from foregoing voter referendum for bond issue[1] • Time and money savings from circumventing existing procurement regulations • State support of public school construction via contribution of lease payments
Costs Unique to Public-Private Partnerships	**Costs Attributed to Public-Private Partnerships That Are Not Unique**
• Increased issue costs for certificates of participation and lease revenue bonds versus general obligation bonds • Increase interest costs due to nonappropriation clause in lease contracts	• Profit margins of developers are not different, in principal, from private sector returns from any public contract. Net benefit/cost to taxpayer is relevant.

Figure 6-7. Public-Private Partnerships in Maryland

1. In Maryland, bond issues for school construction do not usually require voter approval.

Source: "Innovative Partnerships—Commercial Development and Shared Use," www.puaf.umd .edu/OEP/pscfp/Funding%20Methods/Innovative%20Funding%20Options/Public%20Private% 20Partnership/Public%20Private%20Partnership%20_%20%20Analysis.pdf.

- Is there a penalty for early termination?
- What are the sales or use taxes that must be paid because of the lease?
- Can the lease be broken for nonperformance?
- Are there additional costs at the end of the lease?

OTHER LEASES

Personnel

Some libraries have transferred their employees to a human resources leasing agency that then leases the employees back to the library. If you lease personnel, you save the costs of handling payroll and other paperwork and reporting, but you have to pay an administrative fee to the leasing company. You might also lease temporary personnel to fill long-term absences or provide needed employees for a short-term project. Custodial services, landscape maintenance services, or security guards may be leased from a company that screens and trains them, then leases them to the library for a specified time.

Materials

Materials that libraries lease include multiple copies of best sellers, rotating collections of large-print books, or audiovisual materials that are needed for a short time, but can be returned when the popularity of the title has waned. If you lease materials and later decide to buy the item, you may do so, but then you lose the savings of leasing. You end up paying for the book twice (even if the lease and purchase were discounted) and processing it twice.

Examples of Library Leases

California lease-revenue bonds: http://sam.dgs.ca.gov/TOC/6000/6873.htm.
Kansas City Public Library—Central Library lease:
    www.ala.org/ala/alonline/currentnews/newsarchive/2000/september2000/kansascitybanks.htm.
Kansas City Public Library—Plaza Branch lease:
    www.ala.org/ala/alonline/currentnews/newsarchive/2002/june2002/kansascitylibrarys.htm.

Sources of Leased Library Materials and Staff

C. Berger Group. "Temporary Library Staff." www.cberger.com/jobs/.
"History of the McNaughton Plan." http://divisions.brodart.com/books/mcn/mcnhist.htm.
"McNaughton Plan" (click on the books for information). http://divisions.brodart.com/books/mcn/mcnhome.htm.

UTILITIES: CUTTING COSTS

ELECTRICITY

Design your new building to be energy efficient. Existing buildings can be retrofitted so you can save money on utilities.

1. It is easier to control north/south sun than east/west sun, so the design should place the building so it runs east/west with the bulk of the windows on the north and south sides.

2. Install window sunscreens to allow winter sun in but to block summer sun.

3. Use operable windows to let in cool breezes and periodically air out the building, especially when fumes (paint, glue) are being used.

4. Plant trees to provide shade in the parking lot and around the building.

5. Take advantage of solar energy panels to heat water as well as some areas of the library.

6. Use high-efficient T-5 or T-9 fluorescent light fixtures for the bulk of library lighting, with task lights and indirect lighting for other areas.

7. Install photoelectric sensors to automatically switch off or dim lights when the natural lighting is adequate.

8. Install motion sensors to turn off lights in meeting rooms and offices when no one has been in the room for a period of time. Do not use these in restrooms or in the public part of the library, where lights would be blinking on and off in the stacks.

9. Balance HVAC systems so that infrequently used areas are not heated and cooled at the same level as frequently used areas. Keep equipment in optimal working order.

10. Install ceiling fans in offices and meeting rooms to move stuffy air when you are not using either heating or cooling.

11. Ask your electrical company for an energy audit. If they do not do it, consider hiring a consultant to recommend energy savings measures in your existing building.

12. Make certain that the new or remodeled building is adequately insulated to save on heating and cooling costs.

13. Consider retrofitting light fixtures. Going from a 4-lamp, 40-watt T12 fluorescent fixture with magnetic ballast to a 2-lamp, 32-watt T-8 retrofit with electronic ballast and reflector system can save 68 percent on that lamp's energy. Changing exit signs from two 15 watt lamps to two .09 LED can save 94 percent.*

14. Set thermostats to adjust automatically for time of day and season of the year.

15. Keep all filters clean.

16. Minimize the use of incandescent lights that have a bulb life of 1,000 hours; fluorescent lights will last 20,000 hours. Warm white bulbs are more comfortable in a library than cool white bulbs.

17. Paint ceilings and walls white to increase light and decrease the cost of providing artificial light.

*From Carmine J. Trotta and Marcia Trotta, *The Librarian's Facility Management Handbook*. (New York: Neal-Schuman, 2001).

WATER

Even though the library may be part of a municipality, you will still receive a water bill. There are several ways that you can reduce your water bills.

1. Design landscaping so that it requires minimal watering and upkeep. Consider xeriscaping (see sidebar on page 129).

2. Where practical, install drip irrigation systems rather than sprinklers to keep plantings watered.

3. Install automatic shut-off faucets in public and staff restrooms.

Worth checking out . . .

Libris Design Group. "Daylighting Design in Libraries." www.librisdesign.org/docs/daylighting.html.
———. "Lighting for Libraries." www.librisdesign.org/docs/lighting1.html.
———. "Power and Communications Management." www.librisdesign.org/docs/power_comm.html.
———. "Sustainable Library Design." www.librisdesign.org/docs/sustainability.html?bbatt=Y.
Trotta, Carmine J., and Marcia Trotta. *The Librarian's Facility Management Handbook*. New York: Neal-Schuman, 2001.

The publications from Libris Design are provided through funding from the Institute of Museum and Library Services (IMLS) for Libris Design via a federal grant of the Library Services and Technology Act (LSTA) from the California State Library to the Cerritos Public Library.

4. Consider the use of low-flow toilets, which do not require as much water for flushing. However, keep in mind that if the toilet has to be flushed twice to be effective, no money is saved.

SECURITY AND SAFETY

The issues of library safety and security cannot be stated any better than the "Library Security Guidelines" document prepared by the Security Guidelines Subcommittee of the LAMA Buildings and Equipment Section's (BES) Safety and Security of Library Buildings Committee. They are found at www.ala.org/ala/lama/lamapublications/librarysecurity.htm. The sidebar shows a checklist of policies and procedures from this site.

Seven Guidelines for Xeriscape™ Landscaping

The seven principles of Xeriscape™ landscaping are not new; they have been practiced in the landscape industry for decades. The concept of combining all seven guidelines into one effort toward landscape water conservation is what makes Xeriscape landscaping unique. The principles are given below:

1. Planning and design are the foundation of any water-wise landscape.

2. Soil analysis will determine whether soil improvement is needed for better water absorption and improved water-holding capacity.

3. Practical turf areas suggest that turfgrasses be used as a planned element in the landscape. Avoid impractical turf use, such as long, narrow areas.

4. Appropriate plant selection keeps the landscape more in tune with the natural environment. Both native and exotic plants make up the huge variety of plants available for Xeriscape™ landscaping.

5. By simply using efficient irrigation, you can instantly save 30 to 50 percent on your water bill.

6. Use mulches in flower and shrub beds to prevent water loss from the soil through evaporation and to increase water penetration during irrigations.

7. Appropriate maintenance preserves the beauty of the Xeriscape™ landscape plus saves water. Pruning, weeding, proper fertilization, pest control, and irrigation system adjustments all conserve water.

Source: Reprinted from Texas Xeriscaping Guidelines, http://aggie-horticulture.tamu.edu/extension/xeriscape/xeriscape.html.

Examples of Xeriscaping

"Green Building" and "Xeriscaping" from the *Sustainable Building Sourcebook*.
    www.greenbuilder.com/sourcebook/xeriscape.html.
Texas Xeriscaping Guidelines: http://aggie-horticulture.tamu.edu/extension/xeriscape/xeriscape.html.
"Xeriscape Demonstration Garden." www.csu.org/csu/xeri/xeriscape.jsp.

BONDS AND REFERENDA

When libraries need to borrow money, usually for building programs, the librarian enters a new realm of the world of finance: the bond market. A bond is long-term debt security sold to an investor, who lends money, with interest, to a governmental entity to help finance the government's projects. Bonds are frequently sold to raise money for projects such as constructing buildings or roads.

Selling bonds is a complex process that requires the assistance of bond and financial counsel. Each state has different laws governing the establishment of special assessment districts (units of government that manage specific resources within a predefined geographic region), use of revenue bonds, and so on. You really do need to seek advice here; you cannot rely solely on this book because laws are different in each locale, and they do change with time. For example, because of the various propositions that have been approved in California, their libraries need to be more

---

Safety and Security Procedures and Policies Checklist

1. **Problem Situation Manual:** This is kept at each public desk and in each department with regularly scheduled review and update of materials. This would include guidelines and authority for problem scenarios.

2. **Governances Regarding Access to the Building and Library Facilities:** (Library staff are usually provided access one hour before and after closing, unless scheduled for specific work-related reasons; maintenance and security staff as scheduled. Usually library director, administrative services manager, technical services manager, and information systems manager are permitted unlimited access but should schedule themselves so security will be aware of their presence.) Have key and security code assignments and responsibilities. Schedule and sign-out book should be kept in central location near alarm-setting device. Security contact information and alarm arming should be kept with sign-out sheet for when last supervisor leaves the building.

3. **Securing Specialized Facilities or Materials:** For example, an archive room, library cell

phones or phone lines, administrative offices, and computer labs.

4. **Injury or Incident Report Procedures and Form:** All incidents should be reported immediately to the librarian in charge and administration, as well as the police emergency number, 9-911. Basic first-aid kit, emergency procedures, and emergency contact information should be made available.

5. **Natural Disaster Procedures:** For fire, flood, hurricane, tornado, and so on. Evacuation procedures/diagrams, emergency contacts, locations of fire extinguishers, and so on.

6. **Accidents with Library Bookmobile or Other Motor Vehicle Owned or Leased by the Library:** Information on what to do at the scene of the accident, insurance carrier information, policy number, and license plate numbers of vehicles in case of theft.

7. **Training Requirements and Manuals for Library Staff:** Some libraries schedule regular Red Cross and CPR training, security reviews, fire safety checks, and so on.

"creative" and use revenue bonds rather than general obligation bonds. Other communities might be allowed to simply hold a referendum and get voter approval.

Although you will be relying on professional counsel, you still need to be familiar with some of the vocabulary and learn as much as you can about bonds so that you know how to take advantage of this funding source, if necessary. You also need to know enough to be aware of when you need to seek advice and to be able to converse with a professional without being overwhelmed. Here is some information on bonds, and you will find some links to additional information in the sidebars.

GENERAL OBLIGATION BONDS

A general obligation bond is a type of government bond that is backed by the credit and "taxing power" of the issuing jurisdiction rather than by the revenue from a given project. General obligation bonds are issued by local governments after a referendum has been held and the public has approved borrowing money to make a public improvement (such as building a new library). General obligation bonds are the least expensive way for a government to borrow money because the governing jurisdiction stands behind the funds borrowed. The governmental entity tries to have the best possible bond rating when it is time to sell bonds so they can get the lowest possible interest rate. General obligation bonds are repaid from income generated by raising taxes.

BOND RATINGS

Governments are rated by Standard & Poor's or Moody's Bond Ratings from Aaa (best) to C (worst). A government will try to maintain a bond rating above A (that is, a rating of Aa or Aaa; the latter is sometimes referred to as a Triple-A rating). The lower the government's bonded indebtedness, the better their bond rating.

Information on Bonds and How They Work

The following links will answer many of your questions about the specifics of bonds:

http://personal.fidelity.com/poroducts/fixedincome/howbondswork.shtml

www.ameritrade.com/education/html/encydlopedia/tutorial3/t3_s8.html

http://ceres.ca.gov/ca.gov/planning/specific_plans/sp_part6.html

http://news:morningstar.com/classroom/print_quiz/0,3270,5384,00.html

Moody's Bond Ratings are intended to characterize the risk of holding a bond. These ratings, or risk assessments, in part determine the interest that an issuer must pay to attract purchasers to the bonds. The ratings are expressed as a series of letters and digits. Here's how to decode those sequences. (Most of this information was obtained from *Moody's Bond Record;* portions are copyright 1995 by Bill Rini. For a comparison of Moody's and Standard & Poor's ratings, see figure 6-8.)

Rating "Aaa"

Bonds that are rated Aaa are judged to be of the best quality. They carry the smallest degree of investment risk and are generally referred to as "gilt edged." Interest payments are protected by a large or an exceptionally stable margin, and principal is secure. While the various protective elements are likely to change, such changes as can be visual-

Rating	Standard & Poor's (S&P)	Moody's
Highest quality	AAA	Aaa
High quality	AA	Aa
Upper medium quality	A	A
Medium grade	BBB	Baa
Somewhat speculative	BB	Ba
Low grade, speculative	B	B
Low grade, default possible	CCC	Caa
Low grade, partial recovery possible	CC	Ca
Default, recovery unlikely	C	C

You can obtain more information on bond ratings directly from Moody's or Standard & Poor's.

Moody's Investor's Service
99 Church Street
New York, NY 10007
212-553-0376

Standard & Poor's Credit Week
25 Broadway
New York, NY 10004
212-208-1842

Figure 6-8. Bond Rating Codes

ized are most unlikely to impair the fundamentally strong position of such issues.

Rating "Aa"

Bonds that are rated Aa are judged to be of high quality by all standards. Together with the Aaa group they comprise what are generally known as high-grade bonds. They are rated lower than the best bonds because margins of protection may not be as large as in Aaa securities, fluctuation of protective elements may be of greater amplitude, or there may be other elements present that make the long-term risk appear somewhat larger than the Aaa securities.

Rating "A"

Bonds that are rated A possess many favorable investment attributes and are considered as upper-medium-grade obligations. Factors giving security to principal and interest are considered adequate, but elements may be present that suggest a susceptibility to impairment some time in the future.

Rating "Baa"

Bonds that are rated Baa are considered as medium-grade obligations (i.e., they are neither highly protected not poorly secured). Interest payments and principal security appear adequate for the present, but certain protective elements may be lacking or may be characteristically unreliable over any great length of time. Such bonds lack outstanding investment characteristics and in fact have speculative characteristics as well.

Rating "Ba"

Bonds that are rated Ba are judged to have speculative elements; their future cannot be considered as well-assured. Often the protection of interest and principal payments may be very moderate, and thereby not well safeguarded during both good and bad times over the future. Uncertainty of position characterizes bonds in this class.

Rating "B"

Bonds that are rated B generally lack characteristics of the desirable investment. Assurance of interest and principal payments of maintenance and other terms of the contract over any long period of time may be small.

Rating "Caa"

Bonds that are rated Caa are of poor standing. Such issues may be in default or there may be present elements of danger with respect to principal or interest.

Rating "Ca"

Bonds that are rated Ca represent obligations that are speculative in a high degree. Such issues are often in default or have other marked shortcomings.

Rating "C"

Bonds that are rated C are the lowest rated class of bonds, and issues so rated can be regarded as having extremely poor prospects of ever attaining any real investment standing.

A Moody rating may have digits following the letters, for example "A2" or "Aa3." According to Fidelity, the digits in the Moody ratings are in fact sublevels within each grade, with "1" being the highest and "3" the lowest. Therefore, the ratings from high to low are Aaa, Aa1, Aa2, Aa3, A1, A2, A3, Baa1, Baa2, Baa3, and so on (http://www.cftech.com/BrainBank/).

BOND RATINGS

Standard & Poor's and Moody's are the best-known and most influential credit rating agencies. Their role as raters is to assess the risk of certain bonds through the study of all information provided to the public, and to assign to the issue and issuing company grades that accurately reflect the company's ability to meet the promised principal and interest payments.

Bond prices and interest rates are broadly determined by bond categories (zero-coupon, convertible, income, for example). But an issue's exact pricing and coupon are determined by a credit rating. While Standard & Poor's warns investors that a credit rating is not a recommendation to purchase, sell, or hold a particular security, their initial ratings, and revised downgrades and upgrades, greatly affect the attractiveness of the issuance in the eyes of both issuers and holders. Bonds with higher ratings offer lower yields and easier money for the issuer. A lower rating usually results in a lower price on the bond—a less expensive purchase for the investor, but a riskier investment. In 1991, those who gambled on lower-rated bonds (junk bonds) reaped the highest total returns: an average of 34.5 percent. One year later, in a less outstanding year for bonds, junk debt took second place in the race for high returns, 18.2 percent compared to a 22.4 percent return on convertible debt.

Although somewhat different in their letter usage, Standard & Poor's and Moody's both rate bonds in descending alphabetical order from A to C. Standard & Poor's rates some two thousand domestic and foreign companies; eight thousand municipal, state, and supranational entities; and thirteen hundred commercial paper-issuing entities. Moody's rates nineteen thousand long-term debt issues; twenty-eight thousand municipals; and two thousand commercial paper issuers.

Source: http://invest-faq.com/articles/bonds-moody-ratings.html.

REVENUE BONDS

Revenue Bonds

A revenue bond is a type of government bond that is backed by the income that the projects financed by the bond are expected to generate. Some of the things that revenue bonds are used for are airports, toll roads, golf courses, or sewer and water systems. They are rarely used for libraries because libraries do not generate a revenue stream. However, revenue bonds may be used for another governmental service that does generate funds, and then these funds can be used to pay back the funds borrowed for the library. Issuing revenue bonds does not require a referendum since tax dollars are not used to repay the bonds.

Lease Revenue Bonds

You could use something called a lease revenue bond to build a library if a special assessment district constructed the building, then leased it to the library. The library would pay the lease through operating funds. This would require the existence of a special assessment district, though.

Finding an alternative way to fund a library in order to avoid a referendum usually does not look good in the public's eyes and is not advised. Even in the recent tight economy, library referenda have had a good track record of passing.

REFERENDA

Before you can sell general obligation bonds, a referendum must be held. Voters—who will be taxed to support the library (or other bond issue)—must vote on a tax increase to repay the bonds. Over the past decade, li-

> **Worth checking out . . .**
>
> "How Bond Ratings Work." http://personal.fidelity.com/products/fixedincome/bondratings.shtml.

brary referenda have had a 64 percent success rate. The referendum may be scheduled in connection with a general election (when city, county, or federal elections are being held), or there may be a special election, in which the library item is the only item on the ballot. If a special election is held, the library will also need to budget the cost of the election (polling places, judges, printing of ballots, etc.).

Friends of the Library, a foundation, or another support group usually raises the campaign funds. The library staff can educate the public about a referendum, but may not persuade them to vote one way or another. Likewise, tax funds may be used to educate the public but not to encourage them to vote for or against the proposed increase.

LEGAL ISSUES

Legal counsel will be needed throughout the bonding and building process for advice on some of the following issues:

- Wording of ballot
- Real estate transactions
- Rights of way and easements
- Title review
- Gifts (strings attached or reverter clauses)
- Compliance with environmental laws
- Compliance with public advertising for bids
- Negotiation of construction contract
- Bond counsel

Generally the attorney for the city, county, school district, or university can handle these issues, but you may need to call in special counsel for title review or issuing bonds. You may only be involved in one or two building projects or referenda in your entire career, so the advice of legal and bond counsel (usually available through your parent agency) is essential for handling the procedures correctly. Remember, always seek advice to avoid costly mistakes and embarrassments.

Worth checking out . . .

"Balloting Backs Growth."
    www.libraryjournal.com/index.asp?layout=article&articleId=CA280491&display=searchResults&stt=001&text=.
"Education Bond Issue in CA to Support Academic Libraries."
    www.libraryjournal.com/index.asp?layout=article&articleId=CA263168&display=searchResults&stt=001&text=.
"Minneapolis Revenue Bonds." www.mcda.org/Services/Business/RevBond.htm.

SUMMARY

A capital project is an enormous undertaking, and is likely to be spread over several years. Like long-term planning or developing a budget, you should start your capital project with a community needs assessment. Once you have decided what you want—for example, a new building or an addition—you will have to develop a detailed building program and a carefully considered budget. Be sure to consult experts and resist the temptation to cut corners by taking the lowest bid without scrutinizing it carefully and identifying all of the costs. Finally, if you are involved with referenda or selling bonds, be sure to seek expert investing and legal advice.

7 CONTRACTS AND RFPs

OVERVIEW

If you are the library manager in a publicly funded environment, you cannot just call your favorite architect, vendor, or engineer to do the needed work. Even if the vendor is well known in the community or is someone who has done work for the library before, there must be a well-publicized effort to solicit bids from those whom the library staff may not know. You will learn how to issue these requests for information, quotation, or proposal in this chapter.

REQUEST PROCESS

DEVELOPING THE REQUEST

There is a consultant or a provider for just about any service your library might want to offer, but it is not always easy to find out whether that service or product is (1) what you want and (2) within your financial range. There are three types of requests that are frequently used in library financial management to get that very information:

- Request for information (RFI)
- Request for quotation (RFQ)
- Request for proposal (RFP)

The requests are business documents that you send to consultants or potential vendors to solicit enough information to select the best proposal and convert the requested information into a contract. The request you send out will include background information on the potential project, a statement of the issue or problem to be addressed, the expected deliverables (written report, presentation, product), the anticipated timeline, the contact person, a response deadline, and perhaps the funds available. The request should

Sample RFPs

"9 Vendors, 3,000 Questions, and a Deadline: How to Make the Most of Your RFP Process." www.dynix.com/collateral/white papers/dynix-rfp-enu.pdf.

Sample RFI for a digital imaging system: www.rlg.org/ preserv/RLGrfi.pdf.

For a sample RFP for a building consultant, see Appendix C of this book.

Sample RFQ for outreach state planning and evaluation: http://nnlm.gov/sea/outreach/ rfqs/2004/stateplanningteams .html.

include requirements to provide shipping, insurance, installation costs, maintenance costs, and any other fees that might not be included in the base price of the item or service being acquired.

The consultants or vendors then submit a written proposal, quotation, or information in response to this request by the deadline you specify. The checklist in figure 7-1 lists the information that you would want to include in an RFP to potential building consultants. Because governments have very specific procurement rules to follow, make certain that the requirements of the RFP/RFQ/RFI match those of the library's governing entity.

PROPOSAL ANALYSIS

Do not open the proposals as they arrive. Keep all proposals unopened and in a secure place until the deadline. At that point, the library's evaluation panel opens the proposals, checks off the items included for completeness of response, then evaluates them according to a previously agreed-upon point system and chooses the top respondent. In the case of architects or automation consultants, the evaluation team may choose to bring in the top three or four respondents or visit their installations before making the final decision.

When evaluating the contracts, the extra costs—such as maintenance, shipping, and the like that were included in the request—should be included in the point system. All other potential related costs (travel, long-distance calls, training) should be specifically included before awarding the contract.

AWARDING THE CONTRACT

When you award the contract, you are creating a legally binding document in which you repeat many of the provisions outlined in the response to the requests for quotations, information, or proposal. Libraries may choose to

Further Examples of RFPs

Bloomfield Township Public Library (Bloomfield Hills, MS). Request for bids for shelving.
    www.btpl.org/answers/AV_Shelving_bid.pdf.

City of Baltimore. RFP for bindery services. www.ci.baltimore.md.us/government/finance/notices/BP-04059.pdf.

Indiana University. RFQ for Enterprise Wireless Architecture. www.educause.edu/ir/library/pdf/CSD2913.pdf.

Library of Congress. RFP for books. http://lcweb.loc.gov/flicc/rfp/lc02015.doc.

The RFP Process PowerPoint (how to develop an RFP using PowerPoint).
    www.educause.edu/ir/library/pdf/CSD2913.pdf.

University of Kansas. RFP for integrated library system. www.usg.edu/galileo/rfp/kansas/rfptoc.html.

❑ **RFP due date**

❑ **Address for submittals**

❑ **Deadline for submission of all proposal materials**

❑ **Contact information for project**

❑ **Overview of statement of work:** outlines who requests the work, name of the project, library team members for collaborative work (Friends of the Library, library board, library personnel, etc.)

❑ **Description of the library** (e.g., geographic location, demographics, population growth, economy, governing bodies, organizational chart, and/or mission statements)

❑ **Detailed project narrative that scopes the work and deliverables:** might include site selection, schematic design, project cost estimates, facility operating cost estimates, time schedule, public meetings, surveys, research, needs assessment, development of a library building program, staffing cost estimates, information for grant requests, marketing/public education, and any other collaboration that would be required by a design firm

❑ **Needs assessment expectations**

❑ **Building program statement requirements**

❑ **Governing authority and funding source** for final approval of the library building program.

❑ **Working relationship defined between consultant, library staff, and architect**

❑ **Timeline and tentative schedule**

❑ **Minimal information to request of applicants**

❑ **Firm Overview**

Name, address, phone number, website, and e-mail for firm.

Brief history of firm, including length of time firm has been in business, mission statements, and building philosophy.

❑ **Experience**

List of projects that are similar to presented building project with references.

❑ **Work Plan and Technical Approach**

Gantt chart, timeline, narrative of the proposed work plan, including methodologies and a time-phased statement of project milestones. Specify expectations for information or assistance from library staff.

❑ **Principals on Project Team**

Describe the project team and provide resumes of key members stating their role on the project, their experience, and their qualifications.

Provide a breakdown of the estimated staff time for each task outlined in the Work Plan.

❑ **Other information** that will help you to evaluate a firm.

Figure 7-1. Checklist for RFP for Library Building Consultant

---

Examples of Contract Awards

Fairfax (VA). Library and classroom furniture award contract.
www.co.fairfax.va.us/gov/psma/noa/0250758013noa.pdf.
Florida State. Contract for library technology services.
http://dlis.dos.state.fl.us/bld/Library_Tech/BLD_Tech_Procurement.html.
Louisiana State University. Contracts for computers and automation.
www.lib.lsu.edu/systems/staff/resources.html.
Vancouver Public Library. Contract award for security guards.
www.city.vancouver.bc.ca/ctyclerk/cclerk/010605/a8.htm.
Wisconsin State. Contract with Baker & Taylor for library materials.
www.dpi.state.wi.us/dltcl/rll/btcontract.html.

"piggyback" on existing county, state, or federal contracts that give larger discounts. It is good to bookmark your state contract sites and remember to check them whenever an item is needed. If the item is already on an awarded contract for your area, you should take advantage of the existing contract. This saves time and effort that you would otherwise need to spend soliciting and evaluating proposals, and you will probably get a better price.

COMPETITIVE BIDS

MATERIALS

Competitive bids are normally required for items above a certain monetary threshold, unless the library can prove that an item has a sole source (see figure 7-2). You might assume that a specific book has a sole source—its publisher. However, you might be able to obtain that book from a variety of sources: a bookstore, a jobber, or the publisher. While it is not necessary to obtain bids for every book or periodical purchased, you may be required to request bids from a variety of jobbers, with shipping costs, discounts, and supply rate being the variables that decide who gets the contract for that year.

SERVICES

You handle bids for services in much the same way as you handle bids for materials. Libraries are responsible for locating the best price and best value for public dollars. As with all other bids, the lowest price is often not the best value, so there must be other factors in bid solicitation. Which vendor is the most responsive in providing the service?

Sole Source Justification Form

This form helps both the department submitting a requisition and Purchasing comply with policies requiring justification of a sole source in order to waive the requirement for competition for purchases in excess of $50,000, or consultant agreements in excess of $15,000. Please use additional pages as necessary.

> Sole Source Justification for Requisition # _____
>
> To: _____, Buyer   Fax: _____
>
> From: _____, Department: _____
>
> Phone: _____   Email: _____
>
> We request a purchase order be issued to _____
>
>   Vendor name:
>
> in the amount of $ _____, without obtaining competition.

Please answer the following questions:

1. Under which exception to the requirement for competition are you justifying this sole source? You may select one or more. (See Blink, *Sole Source Justification,* for more information.)

   _____ personal or professional advice or expertise
   _____ product or proprietary service is unique
   _____ available from only one source
   _____ designated to be compatible with existing

2. Please explain in detail how purchase of goods or services meets the above selected criteria for a valid Sole Source Justification. (For this question, price cannot be a part of the justification.)

3. If the product or proprietary service is unique, list the most important features or performance specifications and explain why this supplier is the only possible source.

4. If designated to be compatible with existing, please describe the factors that determine the need for compatibility. Include an explanation of parts on hand, knowledge of existing system, trained staff, and so on.

5. What information do you have on any competitive bids/quotes for these goods or services?

6. If the selection of this supplier is directed by the prime-sponsoring agency, by government statute, or time constraints that do not permit formal competition, please explain the circumstances.

7. If Purchasing agrees that your sole source request meets the criteria, what information do you have that can help us validate price reasonableness?

> Signature: _____ Title: _____   _____
>   MSO, equivalent or higher   Date
>
> Purchasing Division Concurrence:_____   _____
>   Buyer   Date

Figure 7-2. Sole Jobber Justification Form

Suppose that the service is custodial contracting. Ask the following questions:

- How many custodians will be on duty for how many hours per day?
- How will you monitor their work?
- Are they bonded?
- Who are their current and previous customers?
- Will they provide the cleaning supplies?
- Do they provide the materials safety data sheets for cleaning supplies used?
- Is the library held harmless for on-the-job injuries?
- Do the custodians wash windows or just empty wastebaskets?

Examples of Jobber and Sole Source Lists

Alpine School District. Approved sole source list. www.alpine.k12.ut.us/depts/media/budget/sole_source-list.html.

Socorro (TX) Independent School District. Sole source vendor list. http://departments.sisd.net/purchasing/pdfs/sole_source.pdf.

Yahoo! provides a links to jobbers. http://dir.yahoo.com/Business_and_Economy/Business_to_Business/Information/Library_Services/Book_Jobbers/.

Examples of Bid Postings

Boston. Bid WebSite. www.cityofboston.gov/purchasing/bid.asp.

Denton (TX). Bidding procedures and tabulations. www.cityofdenton.com/pages/howtobid.cfm.

Denton (TX). Requests for bids. www.cityofdenton.com/pages/biddernotify.cfm.

Examples of Specifications for Equipment

Bookmobile specifications: www.ccpls.com/Replacement%20Bid20Bookmobile.htm.

Specs for library telephone system: www.ci.larchmont.ny.us/departments/telrfp01.html.

Some Sources of Library Management Software

Library management software: www.allwonderssoftware.com/library.html.

Sources of library management software: http://www.capterra.com/library-automation-software.

Additional sources: http://acqweb.library.vanderbilt.edu/pubr/opac.html.

EQUIPMENT

You need to be just as specific when you solicit bids for equipment as when you solicit bids for materials or services. Frequently, you or the other librarians will not have the technical knowledge to prepare the specifications for a bookmobile, computer system, or new air conditioner. It is generally legal and permissible to use the specifications of an acceptable vendor's product, then state in the bid request that the specifications must meet or exceed those of that product.

SUMMARY

One of your responsibilities is to solicit bids for materials, services, and equipment. This involves soliciting information, quotations, and proposals. Although this requires careful, detailed work, if you are fair, informed, and impartial in your handling of bids and vendor relationships, you will be on the right path to purchasing an excellent product. Furthermore, your purchase will be based upon a well-constructed, written contract that protects the owners (the public), managers, and service providers or vendors.

ALTERNATIVE LIBRARY FUNDING

8 FUNDING SOURCES

OVERVIEW

Libraries have undertaken a wide range of alternative fundraising endeavors in recent years, and they have many means at their disposal for managing funding initiatives. Alternative funding initiatives have become a godsend in a time when libraries are undergoing budget cuts, closing branch libraries, reducing library programs and operating hours, and laying off staff. Because of economic constraints, it is important for you to begin exploring different funding models and strategies.

Fortunately, there is a wide array of funding sources that can help you to provide new and improved services. In this chapter, you will find out about seven sources:

- Library foundations
- Friends of the Library
- Volunteers
- Trusts and wills
- Endowments and restricted funds
- Gifts and donations
- Partnerships

You will also read about the importance of maintaining excellent donor relations and separate fund accounting.

Worth checking out . . .

"ALA's Report on Library Funding in the United States: 41 States Report Cuts."
www.ala.org/ala/news/libraryfunding/libraryfunding.htm.
"Public Library Peer Comparisons." http://nces.ed.gov/surveys/libraries/public.asp.

MOST COMMON SOURCES OF FUNDING

The "E.D. TAB: Public Libraries in the United States: Fiscal Year 2001" (http://nces.ed.gov/pubsearch/pubsinfo.asp?pubid=2003399), released in June 2003 by the National Center for Education Statistics, revealed the following sources of income for public libraries (see also figure 8-1):

- 77 percent of public libraries' total operating income of about $8.2 billion came from local sources,
- 13 percent from state sources,
- 1 percent from federal sources, and
- 9 percent from other sources, such as monetary gifts and donations, interest, library fines, and fees.

FOUNDATIONS, FRIENDS, AND BOARDS

Like many other libraries, you may have a library foundation, a friends organization (typically called Friends of the Library), and a library board. Each has a different function and different rights.

Foundations are legally formed entities, different from the friends organization. Foundations usually have a 501(c) (3) designation from the Internal Revenue Service. The 501(c) (3) status does not permit them to exercise political influence, but it does allow them to raise funds with a charitable-giving designation. The role of the foundation is to raise funds that are designated as charitable giving, and typically foundations ask for large charitable contributions, conduct fundraising drives, and solicit grants and partnerships that benefit from the foundation's 501(c) (3) status.

Friends of Libraries are generally formed for the purpose of supporting libraries and—if they do not have the 501(c) (3) charitable-giving designation from the IRS—lobbying to influence legislation that supports libraries. If they do have the 501(c) (3) status, by law they are not allowed to lobby. For this reason, friends groups often decide they do not want that status. It is helpful to have one support group that is politically active on behalf of the library.

The role of Friends of the Library is raising funds for the library, so that those funds can support improved library services. They might raise

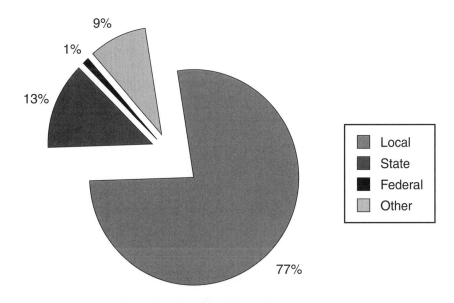

9%

1%

13%

Local
State
Federal
Other

77%

Figure 8-1. Sources of Income for Public Libraries

funds for specific projects (such as staff scholarships) and conduct fundraisers that promote the library while raising monies to cover their own expenses. Examples of friends' fundraisers are used bookstores, library gift shops, library holiday-ornament sales, and author tours, which help increase the library's visibility.

Library boards are appointed by a governing authority or elected by the voters. Library boards are advisory or administrative; they make or recommend policy rather than raising funds or public support. The library board works with the legislative authorities to improve the library's budgets and policies, but typically library boards do not conduct fundraising drives, and by law they are not allowed to influence legislation.

It is not unusual to find the same library supporters on the library board, Friends of the Library, and library foundation. It is very important that they remember which organization they are representing when lobbying, fundraising, or speaking before a city council.

FOUNDATIONS

The level of administration needed to manage funds will determine what venue a library will take to manage alternative funds, ranging from a simple savings account to a library endowment fund. More and more, libraries are forming foundations to manage alternative funds separate from tax revenues. Sometimes libraries, or a consortium of libraries, will opt to set up a foundation to manage specific funding for special programs. This section explores practical information and suggests resources on the benefits of a foundation, forming a foundation, and applying for tax-exempt status.

BENEFITS OF A LIBRARY FOUNDATION

Individual libraries have their own reasons for forming library foundations, but these are some of the more common reasons:

- Increased visibility for fundraising activities allows donors to easily contribute to library initiatives through this tax-exempt, public relations vehicle.
- This structure allows for a delineated separation of funds earmarked for foundation programs that might be managed by a volunteer group rather than by the library or city administration.
- There is an increased return on investment. The board that manages the foundation funds is usually different from the board managing the general library funds, and these funds can be invested more aggressively than those managed by the city or library boards.

Tax Forms and Publications for Nonprofits Available through the Internal Revenue Service

"Application of Exemption Form 1023." www.irs.gov/pub/irs-pdf/f1023.pdf.
"Charities and Nonprofits." www.irs.gov/charities/index.html.
Form PF 990. www.irs.gov/pub/irs-pdf/i990pf.pdf.
"Private Foundations." www.irs.gov/charities/charitable/article/0,,id=96114,00.html.
Publication 557. www.irs.gov/pub/irs-pdf/p557.pdf.
Publication 578. www.irs.gov/pub/irs-pdf/p578.pdf.

Worth checking out . . .

Clow, Faye. *Forming and Funding Public Library Foundations.* Chicago: Public Library Association, 1993.
Edie, J. A. *First Steps in Starting a Foundation,* 5th ed. Washington, DC: Council on Foundations, 2002.
Hopkins, B. *Legal Guide to Starting and Managing a Nonprofit Organization,* 2nd ed. New York: John Wiley & Sons, 1993.

FORMATION OF A LIBRARY FOUNDATION

There are government regulations that direct the formation of foundations and control their activities. Although the Internal Revenue Code (www.irs .gov/charities/index.html) governs the operations of foundations in the United States, each state has its own rules for the formation and maintenance of foundations. When establishing a library foundation, the library board and the foundation board should work with their city attorney, county treasurer, state tax-exempt registration department, and/or the district attorney's office to address legal and financial issues.

There are library foundations for all types of libraries: public, university, school, and private. Library community foundations are sometimes used to manage several library foundation funds.

FRIENDS OF THE LIBRARY

The main objective of the Friends of the Library is to assist the library in its fundraising and advocacy efforts. They volunteer and raise money, awareness, and political support for their public, academic, or school libraries.

OBJECTIVES AND PURPOSE OF A FRIENDS OF THE LIBRARY GROUP

Some of the reasons that libraries set up Friends of the Library are:

- to maintain an association of people interested in public libraries;
- to focus public attention on library services and facilities, and the needs of the community library system; and
- to foster gift giving and donations to the library, including reading materials, endowments, special collections, grants, and other volunteer support as required.

Figures 8-2 and 8-3 give advice on starting your own friends group and designing a fundraising campaign.

> **Outstanding Resources**
>
> Friends of Libraries U.S.A. (FOLUSA). www.folusa.com. FOLUSA is a membership organization of more than two thousand individuals and Friends of Libraries groups. Their mission is to motivate and support local friends groups across the country in their efforts to preserve and strengthen libraries.
> FOLUSA. "Fundraising Ideas." www.folusa.org/html/fundraising.html.

FOLUSA FACT SHEET 1:

How to Organize a Friends Group

   Every library needs Friends! Whether you are a community member or librarian—congratulations, by starting a Friends group you'll be giving an important gift to the community.

1. If you are a librarian, reach out to some of your most faithful and energetic volunteers or a few of your most devout patrons to start a small steering committee. If you are a library lover who wants to start a group, contact your librarian and share your plans. It is critical to the success of the group that the librarian and the Friends' steering committee work closely together.

2. The steering committee should reflect the community. Again, it should include the librarian and a small core of active volunteers and/or patrons. It is important to have access to an attorney, public relations and advertising talent, and high-profile leaders.

3. Determine the group's purpose and mission so that you can plan an organizational structure to accomplish them. This structure will include the types of standing committees you'll need to carry out your work.

4. Work on federal and state tax-exempt status with a lawyer's help so that when you collect dues they will be deductible. At the same time, work on developing the group's constitution and by-laws. Contact FOLUSA for materials that will provide you with sample by-laws and assistance for writing your constitution.

5. Determine what your dues structure will be. Consider a structure that will optimize both the number of members who will join and your ability to raise funds through dues. Starting with a low student or retired rate and increasing the dues incrementally for "higher" categories of giving should accomplish both objectives.

6. Once you have developed an organizational structure and have 501(c) (3) tax-exempt status, you will want to embark on a membership drive. This will probably include a direct mailing and a membership brochure to hand out at the library, doctor's offices, grocery stores, and other places where members might be recruited.

7. Design a professional-looking brochure for the membership drive. The brochure doesn't have to be expensive but it does have to look professional. Be sure that you include a space for new members to become active participants and volunteers in the organization. Follow up right away to involve those who want to volunteer!

8. Hold your first "all-member" meeting following the membership drive. This meeting should include a program component to attract a high attendance. At this program/meeting, elect officers and committee chairs to set and accomplish the group's goals.

9. Develop a long-range plan for your Friends group that includes participation from library staff so that your group's goals can stay in alignment with the library's vision and goals.

10. Join FOLUSA to get access to our special toolkit for members only on how to start and reenergize Friends groups and a host of other materials and advice to help you do what you do even better!

Figure 8-2. How to Organize a Friends of the Library Group

Source: FOLUSA, http://www.folusa.org/html/fact01.html.

FOLUSA FACT SHEET 2:

Fundraising

Friends often embark on fundraising campaigns for special library needs. It can be a small campaign to help purchase new equipment or to bring professional programming to the library, or it can be a major campaign to support library automation or even a new library.

If the campaign is for a significant amount of money, you should seriously consider consulting a professional fundraiser. While these experts won't go out and raise the money for you, they will help you design the campaign, select potential donors, help you make the case for the campaign, and teach you how to make "the ask." In the meantime, here are some tips on running a successful fundraising campaign.

1. If you are not already a tax-exempt 501(c) (3) organization, begin this process before embarking on a fundraising campaign. This will prevent you from having to pay taxes on the money you raise and it will allow donors to write the value of their gifts to you off their taxes. Check the Friends Zone on FOLUSA's website (www.folusa.org) for Toolkit#1, "Starting and Revitalizing Friends Groups," for information on what you'll need to get tax-exempt status. You will probably want to engage an attorney to help with the process.

2. There is always competition with other worthy projects. Consider the timing of your campaign. If there is another high-profile campaign already in progress, you might want to wait until it concludes.

3. Engage high-profile community leaders to "head" the campaign—this will help give your efforts higher status and more credibility. These leaders only need to lend their names; they don't have to do the work.

4. Develop a "Case Statement." This is the written articulation for why you are raising money. Present your case with facts, benefits, and reasons for giving. Be sure all volunteers have the Case Statement to share with potential donors.

5. Consider local foundations and corporations as potential donors.

6. Though you will want to include community-wide fundraising at the end of your campaign, begin with asking potential high-level donors in person. Two volunteers can visit a potential donor together. Be sure that the volunteers have a specific amount to ask for and are prepared to articulate the need (Case Statement).

7. Leadership gifts are important. Go after the biggest donors first. Send the right person(s) at the right time to the right prospect for the right amount.

8. After the potential large donors have been approached, take your campaign community-wide. Address all the community organizations you can such as women's clubs, veterans' organizations, civic clubs, church and synagogue groups, library groups, and PTAs.

9. Follow up with a community-wide event or initiative that will give everyone the opportunity to contribute.

10. Accept cash, checks, or pledges. Ninety percent of the people who make pledges honor them. In-kind gifts are appropriate, as are memorials and endowments.

11. Finally—DON'T FORGET TO SAY THANK YOU to both workers and donors!

Figure 8-3. Fundraising Advice for Friends of the Library

Source: http://www.folusa.org/html/fact02.html, folusa@folusa.org.

VOLUNTEERS

I don't know what your destiny will be, but one thing I do know. The only ones among you who will be really happy are those who have sought and found how to serve.

—Albert Schweitzer

WHY USE VOLUNTEERS?

Libraries do not always use volunteers as much as they might. However, there are good reasons for building a strong volunteer program.

1. Support comes from volunteers who donate time and effort.
2. Although volunteering may not be readily viewed as an alternative funding source, it is a fact that every organization has a finite amount of time, talent, and resources at its disposal.
3. Volunteers can extend the valuable resources of personnel time and talent in a library.

You should be proactive in seeking out individuals who will serve the needs of the institution and programs. A couple of well-placed volunteers can provide the library with hundreds of staff hours a year. Rarely does the library have enough staff.

At my previous library, one of my thrills was reading the number of volunteers (usually about seventy-five) and the number of hours they worked (usually about fifteen thousand per year) at the annual volunteer tea, and then announcing that they did the work of nine full-time employees. The volunteers made it possible for us to spend more money on professional librarians (40 percent of our staff) while they helped perform some of the jobs normally assigned to support staff.

Many volunteers are at the heart of capital campaigns and fundraising endeavors. The list of possible projects that volunteers undertake to raise funds for local libraries is as varied as the volunteers' imaginations.

Worth checking out . . .

Karp, Rachel. "Volunteers in Libraries."
   www.ala.org/ala/lama/lamapublications/smalllibspubs/volunteerslibraries.htm.
"Volunteer Program Benefits and Purposes."
   www.ala.org/ala/ourassociation/publishing/alaeditions/samplers/drigdum_volun.pdf.

VOLUNTEER RECOGNITION

There are two key ways to show your appreciation to volunteers:

1. First, find ways to thank them—often.
2. Second, give them the knowledge, support, and training they need to accomplish their tasks and goals.

Since there is no monetary compensation for volunteers (besides deductions allowed for expenses related to volunteering, e.g., mileage, fares, and tolls), the library must promote other benefits of volunteering. If you were to recruit volunteers with a list of "Reasons for Being a Library Volunteer," this is what you might include:

- A means to give of yourself, your time, and your talents to the community in which you live and work.
- Responsibility as a spokesperson and caretaker to one of the most powerful public resources in the community.
- Knowledge that your efforts often keep the library doors open for patrons of all ages when they might otherwise be closed.

There are many ways to recognize the gift of volunteers' time, talent, and resources:

- Recognize them publicly. (This can be as simple as a name in a newsletter or on a bulletin board.)
- Express your appreciation in writing as well as in person. Library staff should make a concerted effort to greet and thank volunteers at every opportunity, and the library administration should send timely thank-you notes.
- Acknowledge their importance to the library and their permanent place there. One way to do this is to give out permanent, individualized volunteer nametags and a volunteer manual or training guide.

One simple way to acknowledge volunteer efforts is to record and reward volunteer milestones in the number of hours served. Small tokens of appreciation and public recognition of these milestones are the least the library can do for a volunteer who has served one hundred, two hundred, three hundred, or more volunteer hours.

For our library's annual volunteer tea, we invited the mayor and city council members to take part in recognizing the library's volunteers. The mayor presented recognition gifts to each volunteer as the staff supervisor read the volunteer's name and the number of hours worked. Then the volunteers shook hands with each council member. As they were shaking hands with the mayor, we took their pictures with the council members in the background. A few days later, the mayor wrote a note to each volunteer with thanks for their efforts and enclosed the photo. This gesture meant more to the volunteers than their awards or the reception.

Source for volunteer recognition gifts: www.hospitalconnect.com/asdvs/marketplace/recognition.html.

Worth checking out . . .

"Metropolitan Library System Volunteer Brochure." www.mls.lib.ok.us/volunteer1.htm.

TRUSTS AND WILLS

Occasionally, someone will contact the library director about setting up a trust for the library or putting the library in his or her will. When that happens, urge the person to obtain legal advice so that the intent of the gift can be preserved.

A trust is a legal way to transfer an individual's assets to a beneficiary (the library). Those funds are then invested or managed for the benefit of the library. Sometimes the grantor will continue to donate funds to the trust over time while still living, or the trust may be set up so that the funds do not go to the library until the person dies. Trusts take various forms: bonds, stocks, land, life insurance, or real estate.

Trustees are responsible for managing funds in a trust, preserving original gift documents, and following restrictions outlined in the trust. The trustees are responsible for deciding upon the most profitable investment plan for the monies in the trust. If the library is the beneficiary of the trust, there may be restrictions that limit annual dispersions to the interest, or the library may be able to withdraw a specific percentage (say, 10 percent) of the principal each year for a specific project.

ENDOWMENTS AND RESTRICTED FUNDS

An endowment is a gift of money to an institution for a specific purpose. The monies are invested to create an endowment fund, a regular source of

---

Examples of Library Trusts

"Barret Trust Funds New Library." www.rhodes.edu/NewsCenter/NewsArchive/Paul-Barret-Jr-Trust-gives-35-Million-to-Fund-new-Library.cfm.

Cousins, Dale. "Library Trust Fund." Official site for Wake County Government, Wake County, North Carolina Libraries, Wake County Library Trust Fund. www.wakegov.com/county/libraries/about/libraryfund.htm.

"Paul Barret Jr. Trust Gives $35 Million to Fund New Library." *Rhodes Magazine* (April 30, 2001). www.rhodes.edu/NewsCenter/NewsArchive/Paul-Barret-Jr-Trust-gives-35-Million-to-Fund-new-Library.cfm.

Worth checking out . . .

Resources and sample policies for establishing library endowment funds, provided by the Outagamie Waupaca (WI) Library System: www.owls.lib.wi.us/info/links/endowments.htm.

Worth checking out . . .

Alexander, Johanna O. "Fundraising for the Evolving Academic Library: The Strategic Small Shop Advantage." *Journal of Academic Librarianship* 24, no. 2 (1998): 131–38. Contains approximately fifty references to library fundraising literature.

American Library Association. *Success Stories: How 15 Libraries Raised Money and Public Awareness.* Chicago: American Library Association, 1983. This booklet provides brief snapshots of the fundraising projects of the fifteen library nominees for the Gale Research Companies' first Financial Development Award, given in 1983. One project is from an academic library (Oakland University). The rest are from public libraries or library systems.

Atlas, Michael C. "Development in Academic Libraries: A Review of the Literature." *Journal of Academic Librarianship* 20, no. 2 (1994): 63–70. A comprehensive review of journal and monographic literature on library fundraising through 1993.

Burlingame, Dwight F., ed. *Library Fundraising Models for Success.* Chicago: American Library Association, 1995. This book provides seven case studies on fundraising, three of which describe fundraising programs in university libraries.

Corson-Finnerty, Adam, and Laura Blanchard. *Fundraising and Friend-Raising on the Web.* Chicago: American Library Association, 1998. The authors provide useful how-to information about using the Web to supplement development activities. Although such information is quickly dated, this is a thought-provoking source of good and practical information.

Dewey, Barbara I., ed. *Raising Money for Academic and Research Libraries.* New York: Neal-Schuman, 1991. Experienced development authors provide sound information on the process of library fundraising, from creating a fundraising plan to hiring a development officer.

Dolnick, Sandra, ed. *Fundraising for Nonprofit Institutions, Foundations in Library and Information Science.* Greenwich, CT: JAI Press, 1987. This book offers nine studies on fundraising in nonprofit organizations. Two cases discuss different aspects of preparing for public library fundraising, and one chapter focuses on fundraising for a research library.

Hayes, Sherman. "Fund Raising: A Brief Bibliography." In *Library Development: A Future Imperative,* edited by Dwight F. Burlingame. Special issue of *Journal of Library Administration* 12, no. 4 (1990): 135–52. Extensive bibliography of fundraising literature focused on the 1980s.

Hood, Joan M. "Past, Present, and Future of Library Development (Fund-Raising)." *Advances in Librarianship* 22 (1998): 123–39. This article is a selective review of some key literature on library fundraising of the 1980s and 1990s.

Lee, Hwa-Wei, and Gary A. Hunt. *Fundraising for the 1990s: The Challenge Ahead. A Practical Guide for Library Fundraising from Novice to Expert.* Canfield, Ohio: Genaway & Associates, 1992. This book contains two useful case studies: the campaign at the University of Kentucky to raise $20 million for a new library building, and the goals and activities of the Brandeis University Women's Committee, a key partner in library development.

Lee, Sul H. *Library Fundraising: Vital Margin for Excellence.* Ann Arbor, MI: Pierian Press, 1984. Though now dated, this was the first collection of essays that focused on the theoretical and philosophical approaches to library fundraising and development to appear in the library literature.

Martin, Susan K. "The Changing Role of the Library Director: Fundraising and the Academic Library." *Journal of Academic Librarianship* 24, no. 1 (1998): 3–10. A veteran director and library fundraiser describes the role and responsibilities of the director in library fundraising and offers sage advice about setting priorities and delegating responsibilities to accommodate competing demands.

————, ed. "A Special Issue on Development and Fund-Raising Initiatives." *Library Trends* 48, no. 3 (Winter 2000). This special issue of *Library Trends* offers excellent coverage of the principles and practices of library development. It looks at the distinctions between development activities in academic and public libraries, and infers some trends for the future.

Steele, Victoria, and Stephen D. Elder. *Becoming a Fundraiser: The Principles and Practice of Library Development*, 2nd ed. Chicago: American Library Association, 2000. This is the best general primer on fundraising for libraries. This second edition is essentially the same as the 1992 edition.

Wilkinson, Janet. "Fundraising for University Library Development: The Case of the London School of Economics." *New Review of Academic Librarianship* 4 (1998): 133–46. The author describes efforts from 1993 to 1998 to raise 12 million British pounds ($24 million) for an extensive renovation of the London School of Economics library building. British fundraising experiences are compared to North American academic libraries' experiences.

income to the library. The library director is usually responsible for managing the endowment's investment and the income, reviewing profit and loss statements on investments, and overseeing how the endowment income may be spent or reinvested. Often the income from these funds has restrictions on how it can be spent. Private universities have been using this source of alternative funding for years.

With a pure endowment, the corpus (original gift) cannot be used. Only its earned interest or capital gains can be used for projects. The quasi-endowment does not have such a stipulation and can be used as needed, within the stipulations of the endowment.

Michigan State University Libraries give supporters an opportunity to donate online at various levels, from "Adopting a Book" to providing an endowment. The donation form for their "Giving On-line" website is shown in figure 8-4.

GIFTS AND DONATIONS

Your library needs a written policy governing the receipt of gifts and donations, as well as a policy regarding the naming of collections, rooms, or buildings. If you have a written policy in place, you can avoid the personal embarrassment and emotion that can accompany a donation (especially when that gift is a memorial).

Be sure that you have discussed the gift policy with the library board and the community and that it has been officially adopted before you accept any gifts. This is so that you avoid the conflict that can occur when a donor dies, someone in the community wants to name a branch after a controversial figure, or an eager benefactor gives the library something it cannot afford to maintain.

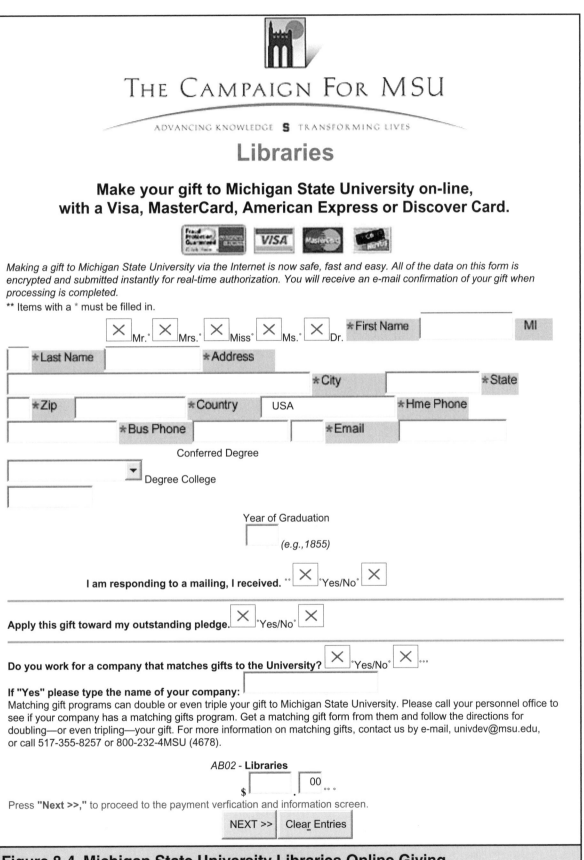

Figure 8-4. Michigan State University Libraries Online Giving

Soliciting Gifts

One way to solicit gifts is to use the library's home page to post an online form for donors to send contact information and contributions. The web page can also be an additional venue for publishing a quarterly fundraising newsletter, recognizing and thanking donors who allow their names to be publicized, and announcing milestones and the timeline of capital campaigns.

Before accepting a gift or writing a gifts policy, consider the following:

1. What conditions, or "attached strings," are acceptable to the library?
2. Does giving a collection, building, or land guarantee naming rights to the library or collection? What are the criteria for naming rights?
3. Is it the donor's intent that this be an unconditional gift? May the gift be used for any purpose, or is it a designated gift (e.g., for the building fund or for collection development for the genealogy collection)?
4. When will the gift be available for use? Does the library receive the gift before or after the donor's death? Is the gift an outright donation, or is it established as a trust?
5. What are the donors' expectations for the gift? (Does the donor realize that it may be circulated, put on reference, sold at the next Friends of the Library book sale, etc.?)
6. What level of gift may each governing body accept? Do gifts of a certain monetary level or gifts requiring ongoing funds for maintenance need to be approved by a higher governing board?

Figure 8-5 is a library gift policy from the Jackson County (OR) Library, and figure 8-6 is a policy on naming library facilities from the San Francisco Public Library. For information on starting a major donor program, see Appendix E.

ACKNOWLEDGING GIFTS AND DONATIONS

Donations to libraries are generally tax deductible as charitable contributions. Frequently donors will ask the library staff to appraise the gift, but most library staff are not qualified to make appraisals. Therefore, write the receipt so the donor can add the value of the donation.

The receipt can also include a quit-claim deed (see figure 8-7). With this form, the donor releases all claims to the gift. There is also a place for the donor to enter his or her claimed value of the donation. One copy of the receipt form is given to the donor; the other is kept with the gift so that it can be acknowledged. Gifts valued at $250 or more require a receipt in order to be used as a charitable contribution.

"Determining Fair Market Value" (IRS guidelines). www.irs.gov/pub/irs-pdf/p561.pdf.
"IRS Guidelines on Charitable Contributions." www.irs.gov/pub/irs-pdf/p526.pdf.

Gift Policy Statement

The Library Foundation is happy to discuss specific gifts and naming opportunities with donors. Please contact XXXX.

For branch gifts, JCLF will recognize all donors to Branch Enhancement campaigns on a special board located in the designated branch library. In addition, all donors to the new building campaign will be listed in a donor book in the Central Library in Medford.

JCLF may recognize individual, foundation, business, and public agency names on donor plaques. Logos will not be included.

Donors may make their contributions anonymously.

In the case of a donor wishing to make a memorial gift, contact JCLF to discuss suitable ways to provide for this opportunity.

The Jackson County Board of Commissioners will review all named spaces in advance of their designation.

At the conclusion of the new building campaign (determined by the date of dedication of each branch), JCLF will recognize all donors of $100 or more with an appropriate naming opportunity in a branch library of their choosing (unless the gift is anonymous).

The Library Foundation reserves the right to refuse contributions.

Figure 8-5. Gift Policy

SUBTLE (AND NOT-SO-SUBTLE) SOLICITING THAT WORKS

Some libraries leave memorial-donation forms in family rooms at funeral homes or put them on the circulation desk around Mother's Day, Father's Day, and Memorial Day for contributions in memory of a loved one. Dallas Public Library even has a Pet Memorial Fund at http://dallaslibrary.org/petfund.htm. Figure 8-8 is the donor form used by the Rathbun Free Memorial Library in Haddam, Connecticut.

San Francisco Public Library Commission Policy Manual

Library Facilities Naming Policy	Policy #601

Section: Facilities

Adopted: June 1996

Revised: June 2002

It is the policy of the San Francisco Public Library to name libraries according to geographic location and to identify each branch facility with the neighborhood where it is located or the neighborhood it primarily serves. This Policy enables anyone interested in finding a library to easily ascertain its location by its geographic or neighborhood name. This policy does not address the naming of rooms or other areas or features within branch libraries or within other library facilities.

It shall be the general policy of the San Francisco Public Library not to name any library facility for any person, living or deceased. However, in the rare instance where there are reasons so compelling that adding the name of a person to the geographic name of a specific branch library, or to another library facility, may be appropriate, it shall be the policy of the San Francisco Public Library not to name any library facility for any living person, or for any person deceased less than one year. This restriction permits the Library Commission to evaluate the lifetime contributions and accomplishments of a proposed honoree, and protects from making decisions in reaction to transitory or emotional considerations.

The Library Commission shall approve adding the name of a person to the geographic name of a specific branch library, or to another library facility, only where:

The proposed honoree is associated with a myriad of services and has dedicated a substantial amount of energy, time, resources, leadership, and/or volunteer service to improve and benefit the San Francisco Public Library system or the library facility in question. The depth and breadth of the contributions must be obvious and compelling and must reflect a dedication and beneficence to the San Francisco Public Library system or the library facility in question over a great span of time;

There must be a strong consensus among library users and, in the case of branch libraries, residents of the surrounding neighborhood to add the name of the proposed honoree to the library facility in question;

The proposed honoree should reflect the spirit of the San Francisco Public Library's mission of free and equal access to information for all;

The new name should avoid controversy and not carry the banner of a transitory cause, no matter how worthy, but rather reflect the tradition and stability of the Library as an institution, and it must be in the public interest to approve the proposed name.

In summary, adding the name of a person to a library facility is reserved for the rare individual whose dedication and service to the San Francisco Public Library system or the library facility in question is extraordinary, unique, and of the highest quality.

Figure 8-6. Library Facilities Naming Policy

**Procedures For Evaluating Proposals To Add The Name Of A Person
To The Geographic Name Of A Library Facility**

1. Any member of the Library Commission or member of the public may propose a name to be added to the geographic name of a specific branch library, or to another library facility, by submitting a request in writing to the Library Commission, or by making an oral request during public open time at any regularly scheduled meeting of the Library Commission. The proponents of the name addition must submit thorough and rigorous written research demonstrating that the proposed honoree meets the stringent criteria set forth in this Policy.

2. The President of the Library Commission, in his or her sole discretion, shall determine whether a proposal is sufficiently documented to warrant further consideration by the Library Commission. Where a proposal does not appear to meet the criteria of this Policy, or where the proposal lacks sufficient documentation to determine whether it satisfies the criteria, the President shall advise its proponents of the deficiencies and provide a reasonable opportunity for the proponents to supplement the request. The President shall keep the Library Commission advised as to the existence and status of pending naming requests.

3. The President of the Library Commission shall place any proposal that appears to meet the criteria set forth in this Policy on the Library Commission agenda for general discussion and public comment at one or more regular or special meetings of the Library Commission. Where the proposal involves a branch library, the President shall schedule a meeting in the branch library facility for which the name is proposed or elsewhere in the neighborhood served by such facility to obtain direct testimony from members of the public living in the neighborhood of the facility.

4. At any time after giving proponents of the name addition and the public an opportunity to be heard, after obtaining direct neighborhood testimony (in the case of branch library proposed name additions), and upon proper notice, the Library Commission shall call for a vote on the issue of whether the proposal meets the criteria set forth in this Policy and whether it is in the public interest to add the proposed name to the geographic name of a neighborhood branch library or to another library facility. The affirmative vote by a majority of the members of the Library Commission shall be required to approve the addition of a person's name to a library facility. In all cases involving branch libraries, the geographic name of the facility shall precede the honorific name.

5. The Library Commission shall, either at the time it approves the addition of an honorific name or in a subsequent meeting, designate the method of display of the name addition, which may be by exterior building signage, interior plaque, or any other means appropriate to the specific site. The party who proposed the name to be added to the geographic name of a branch library or other library facility shall bear all costs associated with adding the honorific name, including staff time and material expenses, unless the Commission finds it in the public interest to waive this requirement in whole or in part.

Figure 8-6. Library Facilities Naming Policy (*Continued*)

Source: Reprinted with the permission of San Francisco Public Library.

Anywhere Library

Thank you for your donation to the Anywhere Library. Your gift is acknowledged and received by this receipt and quit-claim deed, which may be used for income tax purposes.

THE DONOR, whose name and address is listed below:

Name:_____

Address:_____

City:_____ State:_____ Zip:_____

does hereby convey and quit claim to the following items that are donated to the Anywhere Library for the most appropriate use as determined by library staff.

Donated items:

Value for charitable contribution purposes (to be provided by donor):

$_____

The library does not appraise donated items or provide an estimation of value. The Donor may assign a value to the items. The library does qualify for charitable contributions according to the Internal Revenue Service regulations.

A copy of this quit-claim deed may be used for income tax contribution purposes.

Dated this _____ day of _____, 20____.

_____

Donor's Signature

_____

Library Staff Member Signature

Figure 8-7. Sample Quit-Claim Deed

DONOR RELATIONS

Potential major donors look for certain qualities in the library to which they are considering making a contribution:

- Good stewardship of funds
- Clear delineation of goals and objectives with credible leadership

---

Rathbun Free Memorial Library
Donation Form

This year the Friends and the Library Council joined forces in an attempt to make your life easier! If you have misplaced the Drive letter, feel free to print out this donation page for your convenience. This form may also be used for designating memorial gifts. Your contribution is tax-deductible to the extent provided by law.

Please print and mail this form with your donation to:

Joint Annual Drive 2003
Rathbun Memorial Library
P.O. Box G, 36 Main Street
East Haddam, CT 06423

My/Our donation to the library is

$_____

Please make your check payable to the Rathbun Memorial Library.

Name:

_____

Address:

_____

City: _____

State: _____ Zip Code: _____

Gifts may be made to the Library in honor or in memory of a person, to celebrate a family event, or to mark any special occasion.

This gift is in honor of/in memory of:_____

Please notify_____ of my gift.

Figure 8-8. Library Donation Form

Three Good Online Donor Sites

Clark Memorial Library (Carolina, RI): www.clarklib.org/support/dform.htm.

University of California, Santa Cruz: http://library.ucsc.edu/development/.

Villa Park (IL) Library: www.villapark.lib.il.us/library/contrib.htm.

- Enthusiastic support from administration and those requesting funds
- Ease of transaction and no additional tax burden
- Evidence of contributions by other community members and those requesting funds

Donors give to projects and causes that they perceive will be successful and that fill a need. Most donors want to be recognized, but they do not want a great amount of money to be spent on that recognition; they want the money to go to the cause for which they gave the funds. There are some things to keep in mind when you are soliciting funds.

- Potential donors appreciate the research that you have done to identify them as donors.

- Donors can always give less than you request, but they are unlikely to give more.

- Donors will want information about your organization and about how the organization intends to use the funds. See figure 8-9 for a "Donor Bill of Rights."

- Do not be embarrassed about asking for money. You are not asking for it for yourself; you are inviting the donor to participate in a cause for which you are personally contributing much time, money, and effort.

- If you, or others who are soliciting funds for your library's cause, have not given personal funds to the project, then you should not be asking others to contribute. It's a matter of commitment.

SEPARATION VERSUS COMMINGLING OF FUNDS

You must be absolutely meticulous in your accounting procedures when you are managing all library funds. The least a donor can expect from the caretakers or financial managers of the library, endowment, and foundation is accountability for every cent that is spent.

You need separate accounting records for grant funds, donor funds for specific projects, and foundation funds so that you can track them and have them audited separately. Do not commingle donated funds with tax funds or other monies from the governing entity. If you do, these funds may be eligible for reappropriation by the governing authority (not good headlines for donors to read).

When filing IRS nonprofit tax returns (IRS Form 990 at www.irs.gov/pub/irs-pdf/f990.pdf), you will need the carefully detailed documentation that the law requires. Other IRS tax information for charitable and nonprofit organizations can be found in "Compliance Guide for 503(c)(3) Tax-Exempt Organizations" at www.irs.gov/charities/charitable/index.html.

A Donor Bill of Rights

PHILANTHROPY is based on voluntary action for the common good. It is a tradition of giving and sharing that is primary to the quality of life. To assure that philanthropy merits the respect and trust of the general public, and that donors and prospective donors can have full confidence in the not-for-profit organizations and causes they are asked to support, we declare that all donors have these rights:

I.

To be informed of the organization's mission, of the way the organization intends to use donated resources, and of its capacity to use donations effectively for their intended purposes.

II.

To be informed of the identity of those serving on the organization's governing board, and to expect the board to exercise prudent judgement in its stewardship responsibilities.

III.

To have access to the organization's most recent financial statements.

IV.

To be assured their gifts will be used for the purposes for which they were given.

V.

To receive appropriate acknowledgment and recognition.

VI.

To be assured that information about their donations is handled with respect and with confidentiality to the extent provided by law.

VII.

To expect that all relationships with individuals representing organizations of interest to the donor will be professional in nature.

VIII.

To be informed whether those seeking donations are volunteers, employees of the organization, or hired solicitors.

IX.

To have the opportunity for their names to be deleted from mailing lists that an organization may intend to share.

X.

To feel free to ask questions when making a donation and to receive prompt, truthful, and forthright answers.

DEVELOPED BY

AMERICAN ASSOCIATION OF FUND RAISING COUNSEL (AAFRC)

ASSOCIATION FOR HEALTHCARE PHILANTHROPY (AHP)

COUCIL FOR ADVANCEMENT AND SUPPORT OF EDUCATION (CASE)

ASSOCIATION OF FUNDRAISING PROFESSIONALS (AFP)

ENDORSED BY

(IN FORMATION)

INDEPENDENT SECTOR

NATIONAL CATHOLIC DEVELOPMENT CONFERENCE (NCDC)

NATIONAL COMMITTEE ON PLANNED GIVING (NCPG)

COUNCIL FOR RESOURCE DEVELOPMENT (CRD)

UNITED WAY OF AMERICA

Figure 8-9. Donor Bill of Rights

One of my favorite partnership publications is by Dr. Glen E. Holt, retired director of St. Louis (MO) Public Library, *Public Library Partnerships: Mission-Driven Tools for 21st Century Success,* published by Bertelsmann Foundation Publishers in 1999.

PARTNERSHIPS

A growing trend in library projects is partnering and pooling resources with businesses and community leaders and organizations. Many libraries are looking for collaboration with nonlibrary partners to increase efficiency. Partnerships such as these enable the library to provide services or products that would not normally be accessible to library patrons. Printing services, genealogical workshops, community college seminars, coffee shops, and Internet wireless networking at the library are potential areas in which partnering can help the library to become more entrepreneurial.

The Public Library Funding Initiative Group's surveys (www.plfig.org/coopreport6-8.html) identified the following sources of "other" income:

1. Workshop fees and continuing education income
2. Shared automated system contract fees
3. WAN and automation-expense reimbursements
4. Associate fees and Internet reimbursement from associate members
5. Pass-through reimbursements, including member supplies and equipment (Pass-through reimbursements are funds that are spent by a member and reimbursed by the library, e.g., grant funds or tuition fees.)
6. Contracts for books-by-mail service
7. ISP (host services) income
8. Additional delivery services
9. Building rental to ISP host service
10. Acquisitions
11. Multitype contracts
12. Cataloging
13. Donations
14. Video income
15. Library for the blind
16. Interest
17. Universal service fund
18. Federal grants
19. Reserve fund
20. Consulting

Libraries around the country also participate in a broad range of cooperative programs with other libraries and the state library to ensure appropriate access to resources and services not available within their walls. This has gone beyond the traditional interlibrary loan and OCLC cataloging database. Partnering is a win-win opportunity in which both partners benefit from the relationship, such as the partnerships with bookstores discussed in the next section.

PARTNERING WITH BOOKSTORES

Bookstores and libraries make great partners and serve the same clientele. Steve Coffman of the County of Los Angeles Public Library proposed a fundraising model for libraries that is currently used by schools, public broadcasting and radio, museums, and zoos (www.infotoday.com/searcher/mar99/coffman.htm and www.infotoday.com/searcher/jan00/coffman.htm). Many libraries are implementing his suggestions for permitting patrons to purchase books from Amazon.com through the library's catalog as a public service and a fundraiser. The library catalogs have links to Amazon, Barnes & Noble, or other book sources, and the libraries receive a percentage of the orders placed through their catalogs. For example, see the Solano, Napa, and Partners Library Consortium website at www.snap.lib.ca.us/. Barnes & Noble and other bookstores frequently host special fundraising events for libraries. The Denton (TX) store held a pre–grand opening fundraiser for the Denton Public Library. Clearwater (FL) Public Library annually has a fundraising evening at Barnes & Noble.

SUMMARY

Donors are frequently looking for a place to make a contribution where it can do the greatest good and reach the greatest number of people in a community. The library serves the entire community (school district, university, etc.), is politically neutral, and reaches all age, religious, educational, and socioeconomic levels of the community. Raising private funds to support libraries is easier than most novice fundraisers anticipate. Part of the trick is to recognize and use all of the assistance that you can get: library foundations, Friends of the Library, and partnerships.

9 GRANTS FOR LIBRARIES

OVERVIEW

Grant: Funding, subsidy, or monetary aid from any government source, foundation, or corporation for a nonprofit organization, usually for a specific project, which requires formal reporting and evaluation.

This chapter introduces you to the fundamentals of grantsmanship. The steps highlighted in the following sections follow the general procedures for pursuing a grant: formulating an idea, identifying and tracking various types of funding sources, investigating funding agencies before writing a proposal, drafting the grant proposal content and consulting writing guides, referring to the compliance and submission checklist, submitting the grant, compiling a postaward report, and evaluating the project. Some say that grant writing is both an art and a science. This chapter tells you how you can get grants for libraries by relying on basic investigative and writing skills, and it demystifies the process for novice grant writers.

GRANTSMANSHIP: GERMINATION OF AN IDEA

The basics of grantsmanship are simple: Come up with an idea and match your project idea to a granting source. A grant is just a gift or donation from a private or public donor, usually in response to your application, in which you outline the project or program to be conducted if the grant is received. So you want to apply to a compatible donor.

The basic elements to every part of the process are

1. a well-thought-out approach to identifying funding sources, and
2. a simply defined project; clarity and meticulousness are of prime importance.

The key to finding funding is to match your project idea and needs with the mission of potential sponsors. There are two important requirements for

173

doing this successfully, and they are closely related to the two basic elements that were just named above.

- You must know the mission, goals, and restrictions of various funding agencies.
- You must have a well-formulated idea.

To align your project with a funding agency,

- you must initially mold your project characterization into an idea that you can easily communicate as the solution to a problem or need, and
- these problems or needs will have to align with the funder's goals for improving or addressing social issues.

If your project doesn't have some element of universal appeal, then it is unlikely to get funded.

GRANT-FUNDING SOURCES

There are many avenues to finding grant-funding sources. If you want to understand the grants environment, you need to understand the different types of funding bodies.

It is a good idea to identify the parent funding bodies for the grants that interest you so you can effectively research them. This chapter divides grants into two categories: *foundation grants* and *government grants*. Associating grants with their funding bodies will make it possible for you to understand the underlying mission of each funding agency, identify special requirements in each category, understand the reporting requirements associated with various types of categories, and explore the distinct tools you need to research the grants available in each category.

The key to successful grant seeking is gathering complete and accurate information on each potential funding source; this is the first step after formulating an idea for a project. The following items are suggestions for the preliminary information that you need to record and analyze as you begin to research potential funders:

- Name and type of potential funding source with information on specific programs
- Contact information
- Mission statement (if available)

- Funding periods
- Deadline for submission
- Proposal submission emphasis
- Restrictions
- Examples of previously funded grants with amounts awarded
- Researcher and date of research

As you identify potential matches, you will need to gather further information. One resource that you are likely to find particularly useful is the Foundation Center. The mission of the Foundation Center, according to their website, is "to strengthen the nonprofit sector by advancing knowledge about U.S. philanthropy" (http://fdncenter.org). The Foundation Center was founded in 1956, and it is a well-established source of information on philanthropy for grant seekers and other individuals and institutions needing information on foundation funding sources and resources. It operates five main libraries—in New York; Washington, D.C.; San Francisco; Cleveland, Ohio; and Atlanta, Georgia—and more than two hundred cooperating collections around the country. These libraries house a host of grantsmanship materials as well as a database and print directories for prospect research. It may be worth the nominal cost of a Foundation Center membership to join while you are researching grants.

One Foundation Center tool that will help you is the "prospect worksheet" (Figure 9-1). This prospect worksheet includes the following categories to be researched and evaluated for potential funding opportunities: basic contact information, financial data with funding periods, questions to consider when determining if the sponsor would be a good match, application information, and sources of data. It is generic enough to be used for all types of funding programs and is available online free of charge at the Foundation Center Web site.

For government funding, it would be helpful to add information identifying the legislation that made the grant program possible. This information helps you identify the purpose and mission of the program. Increasingly, grant writers are organizing their grant research in prospect-information databases. For example, you can use a standard contact database with additional fields that correlate to the information gathered in the foundation prospect worksheet.

> The Foundation Center publishes the Grant Guides series and FC Search, which is the Foundation Center's database on CD-ROM. These are available in all Foundation Center libraries and cooperating collections. FC Search contains profiles of more than 50,000 foundations and 200,000 grant descriptions for recently awarded grants. The Foundation Center Web site contains a wealth of information on foundation funding and is available at http://fdncenter.org.

> The Foundation Center maintains a useful tool for reviewing foundation funding trends: http://fdncenter.org/research/trends_analysis/index.html.
>
> The Center also provides a tutorial with more detailed characterizations of different types of foundations: http://fndcenter.org/learn/classroom/ft_tutorial/index.html.
>
> The Grantsmanship Center is another online and print source of information on foundation grants as well as some federal grant announcements: www.tgci.com.

Valuable Resources

Ranked list of the hundred largest U.S. grant-making foundations:
    http://fdncenter.org/research/trends_analysis/top100giving.html.
Websites of private foundations: http://fdncenter.org/funders/grantmaker/gws_priv/priv1.html.

Date	
Basic Information	
Name	
Address	
Contact Person	
Phone/Fax	
E-mail/Website	
Financial Data	
Total Assets	
Total Grants Paid	
Grant Ranges/Amount Needed	
Period of Funding/Project	

Is Funder a Good Match?	Funder	Your Organization
Subject Focus	1.	1.
(list in order of importance)	2.	2.
	3.	3.
Geographic Limits		
Type(s) of Support		
Population(s) Served		
Type(s) of Recipients		
People (officers, donors, trustees, staff)		

Application Information		
Does the Funder Have Printed Guidelines/Application Forms?		
Initial Approach (letter of inquiry, formal proposal)		
Deadline(s)		
Board Meeting Date(s)		

Sources of Above Information		
❏ 990-PF—Year:	❏ Requested	❏ Received
❏ Annual Report—Year:	❏ Requested	❏ Received
❏ Directories/Grant Indexes		
❏ Grantmaker Website		
Notes:		
Follow-up:		

Figure 9-1. Foundation Center Prospect Worksheet

FOUNDATION TYPES

There are four basic types of foundations:

- *Private foundation*: a nongovernmental organization with an endowment fund administered by a board of trustees
- *Corporate foundation*: a company-sponsored foundation in which funding is the product of donations of a for-profit business
- *Operating foundation*: a nongovernmental, charity institution whose sole purpose is to administer grants within its own organization for projects that it sponsors
- *Community foundation*: a community-based foundation that makes grants in a specific community or geographic region

According to Mark Guyer (author of *A Concise Guide to Getting Grants for Nonprofit Organizations* [New York: Kroshka Books, 2002]), the following sources are most likely to give you a grant (in order of likelihood):

1. Local foundations
2. Major corporations headquartered in your area
3. State and local government
4. Major corporations with employees or much of their sales in your area
5. Major foundations not located near your area
6. Federal government

Your best odds for getting funding are usually at the local level.

FOUNDATION GRANTS FOR LIBRARIES

The Foundation Center provides a classification system for types of grants (http://fdncenter.org/research/grants_class/index.html) that facilitates searching their database. The library listings are under the education taxonomy, as shown in figure 9-2.

Current Term	LIBRARIES/LIBRARY SCIENCE (B70)
Scope Note	Facilities that house a collection of materials including books, manuscripts, journals, government documents, and nonprint formats such as paintings, musical recordings, videotapes, films, and data files on magnetic tape that are organized to provide physical, bibliographic, and intellectual access to a targeted group of people and that generally make available staff to provide services and programs related to the information needs of the targeted group. The primary service of libraries is the circulation of books and other materials for reading, study, and reference.
Broader Term	EDUCATIONAL INSTITUTIONS AND RELATED ACTIVITIES (B)
Narrower Term	ACADEMIC/RESEARCH LIBRARIES(B73)
	ARCHIVES (B77) LAW LIBRARIES (B75) MEDICAL LIBRARIES (B74) PUBLIC LIBRARIES (B71) SCHOOL LIBRARIES (B72) SPECIAL LIBRARIES (B76)

Figure 9-2. Foundation Center Classification System for Libraries

Online Sources of Foundation Funding

America's Charities: www.charities.org.

Chronicle of Philanthropy: http://philanthropy.com.

4 Non-Profits.com: http://4nonprofits.4anything.com.

Funders Online. "Search Europe's Online Philanthropic Community." www.fundersonline.org/grantseekers/.

Fundsnet Services: www.fundsnetservices.com.

Internet Nonprofit Center: www.nonprofits.org.

Non-Profit Resource Center of Texas: www.nprc.org.

School Grants: www.schoolgrants.org.

SRA International's Foundation List: www.srainternational.org/newweb/default.cfm.

Comparisons of Foundation, Corporate, and Government Grants

Foundation Grants: Pros	Foundation Grants: Cons
1. Once funded, the second funding becomes much easier.	1. Competition is very high for foundation dollars.
2. Foundations are often tailored to specific giving.	2. The time invested in proposal preparation may have a low payback.
3. Local foundations can be very supportive of local organizations.	3. It is very time consuming to seek out foundations that match your agency's needs.
Corporations: Pros	**Corporations: Cons**
1. Potential for monies is high.	1. It requires a significant amount of time to make contacts.
2. Local small corporations can be big supporters.	2. May require tailoring the proposal to the potential grant provider.
3. Corporations are usually seeking tax breaks.	3. You may need to establish a nonprofit foundation to receive donations.
4. Programs that enhance images are particularly attractive.	
5. Small corporations can be major givers.	
Federal and State Government: Pros	**Federal and State Government: Cons**
1. A large amount of funds is available.	1. Competition is very high for grant dollars.
2. They have a wide variety of funding areas.	2. Extensive detail is expected in the application process.
3. Multiyear funding is possible.	3. It entails much red tape.
4. Once funded, the second funding becomes much easier.	4. The process is very political.

Source: The chart is from coursework notes from the University of North Texas Fall 2004 COMS 5610.900 Proposal Writing and Grant Administration and BIOL 6150.001 Scientific Teaching, Research, and Graftmanship.

GOVERNMENT SOURCES

There are three levels of government grants: federal, state, and local. The scope of material on government grants is vast. The main focus of this chapter is an overview of federal government grants because state and local grants differ for each geographical entity. There are also international grants, which are beyond the scope of this text.

> If you are interested in international funding, you might check the sources listed in Deborah Kluge's blog, ProposalWriter.com (www.proposalwriter.com/intgtrants.htm).

GENERAL ADVICE FOR SEEKING STATE AND LOCAL FUNDING

Although the specifics for state and local funding vary, there are some general considerations that are applicable in all geographic locations.

1. Find out where local and state opportunities are announced.
2. Garner as much support as you can at the local and state levels.
3. Restrict your funding requests to the often reduced funds available at these levels.

Each state usually has a compilation of its funding opportunities. In Texas, the *Texas State Comptroller of Public Accounts' Grant Directory* compiles information from various Texas state agencies as well as from the *Catalog of Federal Domestic Assistance (CFDA)* to provide key information about federal and state grants and loans that are processed at the state level. The *Texas State Grant Directory* lists the types of grants available, technical assistance programs that benefit local governments, and contacts for local chambers of commerce. There are also state agency publications and newsletters, which are good primary sources of information on state grants. Although the funding pool is often smaller at the local and state levels, this sometimes makes grant opportunities somewhat less competitive. It would be in your library's best interest to investigate these opportunities.

FEDERAL GRANTS

Federal grants can be "direct" or "pass-through." *Direct grants* are awarded directly from the federal government, while *pass-through* grants are awarded to states or districts, which, in turn, assign the grants to projects. Detailed information about existing federal programs can be found in the *Catalog of Federal Domestic Assistance (CFDA)* at http://12.46.245.173/cfda/cfda.html and in the *Federal Register* at www.gpoaccess.gov/fr/index.html.

The *CFDA* is published by the General Services Administration (GSA), a department of the U.S. federal government. It is a government-wide compendium of federal programs, projects, service, and activities to assist the public. Program information is cross-referenced by five indexes:

- functional classification
- subject
- applicant

Marc Green has written a great article listing state and local print resources, "Finding Local Funding Sources: A Guide to State Foundations Directories," *Grantsmanship Center Magazine* (Fall 2001), www.tgci.com/magazine/01fall/statedirs.asp.

- deadlines, and
- authorizing legislation.

IMLS Grants

The Institute for Museum and Library Services (IMLS) provides grants for museums and libraries for projects as well as for research. You will find its grant announcements and application forms online at www.imls.gov.

There is also an online project-planning tutorial for each grant type (http://e-services.imls.gov/project_planning/) to enable librarians to plan projects and submit applications to IMLS grants online. Before developing a proposal to submit to IMLS, peruse the tutorial and follow all instructions to improve your chances of creating an acceptable grant proposal.

IMLS is especially good at helping libraries provide outcome-based evaluation. You will find several online tools for developing an evaluation plan at www.imls.gov/grants/current/crnt_obe.htm. Outcome-based evaluation is discussed in greater detail later in this chapter.

To view IMLS grants and awards, go to www.imls.gov/grants/index.htm. This site provides a list with descriptions of all previously funded projects that have been awarded by IMLS.

> The GSA's website for the *Catalog of Domestic Federal Assistance (CFDA)* at www.cfda.gov is the primary means of disseminating the catalog. The purpose of the *CFDA* is to "assist users in identifying programs that meet specific objectives of the potential applicant, and to obtain general information on Federal assistance programs" ("*CFDA* Introduction," http://12.46.245.173/CFDA/pdf/whole.pdf).
>
> The Federal Register is a daily publication of the U.S. Government that announces grant opportunities. You can search by date range for the most current federal grants available. The U.S. House of Representatives also publishes *Notices of Funding Availability from the Federal Register* at www.house.gov/ffr/federal_funding_reports.shtml.

PRE-PROPOSAL INVESTIGATIONS

In their book *Demystifying Grant Seeking: What You Really Need to Do to Get Grants,* published as part of the Jossey-Bass Nonprofit and Public

---

Other Resources for Discovering Federal Grants for Libraries

Federal Grants: http://fedgrants.gov/Applicants.
FirstGov for Non-Profits: http://firstgov.gov/Business/Nonprofit.shtml.
Grants.Gov: http://grants.gov.
Library of Congress Gateway to Federal Agencies: http://lcweb.loc.gov/global/executive/fed.html.
National Archives and Records Administration: www.archives.gov.
National Historic Records and Publications Commission: www.archives.gov/grants/index.html.
National Library of Medicine: www.nlm.nih.gov/ep/extramural.html.
National Science Foundation: www.nsf.gov.
Public Administrator's Grants Network: www.grantspy.com/index.php.
U.S. Health and Human Services Grants and Contracts Office: www.acf.dhhs.gov/grants.html.
U.S. House of Representatives Federal Funds Express: www.house.gov/ffr/resources_all.shtml.

Management Series (2001), authors Larissa and Martin Brown outline a five-step grant-seeking cycle:

1. Learn about your organization, community, and potential funders.
2. Match your request to a funder.
3. Invite a funder to invest in your organization.
4. Follow up with your organization and your funder.
5. Evaluate your results, methods, and opportunities.

The first and second steps are interdependent. "Learn" about your library program's needs and goals as well as the mission and goals of funding agencies. You have to match these two for compatibility. You can do this by investigating the nature of the grants awarded by the granting agency and verifying that your idea is not duplicated but is within the realm of those supported by the grant funder's mission. There are several resources that will help with the investigation, not the least of which is the funding agency's website.

The third step highlights the aspect of grantsmanship that many forget amidst the piles of forms and seemingly endless paperwork. Your proposal is an invitation to have a funder participate in your project's endeavor.

The fourth step is the follow-up process. The formal invitation is your proposal, but the interpersonal relationship that precludes your submission

---

Bibliography of Library Funding Information

The Big Book of Library Grant Money, 2002–03. Prepared by the Taft Group for the American Library Association. Chicago: ALA, 2002.

Corry, Emmett. *Grants for Libraries: A Guide to Public and Private Funding Programs and Proposal Writing Techniques.* Littleton, CO: Libraries Unlimited, 1986.

Costabile, Mary R., and Frederick D. King. *Federal Grants and Services for Libraries: A Guide to Selected Programs.* Washington, DC: American Library Association Washington Office, 1993.

Foundation Center. *The Foundation 1000: In-Depth Profile of the 1000 Largest U.S. Foundations.* New York: Foundation Center, annual. For purchasing information, see www.fdncenter.org/marketplace/catalog/product_directory.jhtml?id+prod10015.

———. *Grants for Libraries and Information Services.* New York: Foundation Center, annual (latest version December 1, 2004).

———. *National Data Book of Foundations.* New York: Foundation Center, annual (published since 1989).

International Communications Industries Association. *Foundation Grants Guide for Schools, Museums, and Libraries.* Fairfax, VA: ICIA, 1984 (o.p.).

Smith, Amy Sherman, and Matthew D. Lehrer. *Legacies for Libraries: A Practical Guide to Planned Giving.* Chicago: American Library Association, 2000.

Wallen, Denise, and Karen Cantrell, eds. *Funding for Museums, Archives, and Special Collections.* Phoenix, AZ: Oryx Press, 1988.

is part of what the Browns define as the follow-up. A letter of inquiry, a phone call to agency contacts, or other personal investigation into the support potential and funding inclinations of a prospect may be warranted before a proposal is submitted. You must be prepared to discuss your project, market your idea, and highlight the benefits and outcomes expected. Although some large funding bodies discourage these inquiries, other agencies are more receptive to them. Through networking or general research (*Foundation Directory, Annual Registry of Grants*, and/or corporate reports), you should be able to obtain the name of the principal officer in charge of grant solicitations as well as the correct address and phone numbers.

A personal contact should only be initiated after you have done some investigation. Many foundations require that you write or call to receive grant guidelines and application forms. The typical inquiry letter should include the name of the personal contact with appropriate title and address; your name, address, and phone number on letterhead; a very brief description of the project plan (one or two paragraphs); a profile of yourself and your library; and a request for a grant kit, all in a page or less. There are many follow-ups, formal and informal, both before and after a grant proposal is submitted. One of the best follow-ups is to thank the representatives from the funding agency by phone, letter, or e-mail for their time and assistance, whether or not you are being funded.

If you are funded, the recognition will be much more formal, and guidelines for crediting the funding body are usually detailed in the grant compliance guidelines. Other formal follow-ups are geared at keeping those within the library appraised of the status of your proposal.

The fifth step, evaluation, is part of the formal reporting you will do if the grant is funded. Formal reports integrate the interpersonal aspect of the "follow-up" process with the evaluation component. The formal evaluation is an integral part of the funding process and is discussed in great detail later in this chapter.

GRANT WRITING

By the time you reach the grant-writing stage, you have already defined your project, including its mission, goals, and objectives, and identified funding sources that are sympathetic to the purpose of your project. A potential funding body will state its funding priorities and preferences in its submission guidelines. Before you begin drafting your proposal, it is important to be clear on these points as well as the upper and lower limits of available funding and any other restrictions (e.g., submission deadlines, eligibility restrictions, budget formats, and contacts). These preparatory steps are critical to the next phases of the grant-writing process. Grant-funding sources will tell you exactly what they are looking for in a grant. (A good, simple example is Ben and Jerry's guidelines: www.benjerry.com/foundation/guide-lines.html). Provide your future beneficiary with a proposal that meets their funding wishes.

WHAT'S IN A GRANT PROPOSAL?

Clear concise language, a complete submission that follows agency guide-lines, and a realistic funding request are the critical factors that determine the success of the proposal. The sidebar "What's in a Grant Proposal?" lists the components of a typical grant submission; be sure to check for the variations that are specified in the funding body's grant submission guide-lines. Proper pagination and section labeling are important for those re-viewing your submission. It is usually appropriate to include a cover letter that includes a one-sentence project narrative and your complete contact

---

What's in a Grant Proposal?

1. *Title page, abstract, and table of contents.* The abstract is a summary of the proposal; it includes the project's purpose, which is aligned with the funder's mission, and any other critical informa-tion needed upfront.

2. *Application form(s).* These are provided by the funding source. Remember, neatness and completeness count when filling out these forms. Don't forget to sign the documents!

3. *Project description.* Here is where you tell what you plan to do and provide an overview of how it will be done. This is not at a task-list level. Include the project mission statement, goals, and objectives.

4. *Need/problem statement.* Explain the impact and significance of the project, and why it's needed. The problem statement should be allied with your institution's vision statement and the mission of the funding body. Provide statistics, quote authorities on the issue, and give other supporting data.

5. *Timeline.* You will need to provide both the duration of the project and the amount of time actually to be spent on the project. For personnel, you will need to outline the amount of effort (either percentage of time the staff member will allocate to the project

or number of hours dedicated by key personnel).

6. *Methodology.* You may include a narrative of the work plan, action steps, and outcome.

7. *Budget.* List all expenses and resources that will be needed for the project. Follow the budget guidelines of the funding agency.

8. *Explanation of budget and resources.* Write a narrative description of each line item in your budget and the resources at your disposal.

9. *Key personnel.* Explain who will work on this project and their qualifications. Include roles or major duties as well as résumés or vitae for project personnel.

10. *Outcome evaluation and reporting.* Validate your methods; explain how you will measure the out-come and disseminate the results to stakeholders.

11. *Appendices.* Other documents are sometimes included (letters of recommendation or other statements of support, contact information for project sponsors or stakeholders, funding-matching viability, resource availability, service statistics, letters of commitment from partners, audits, IRS tax information, etc.). These are supplemental materials that support your proposal.

information. The funding agency will find this useful if they have any questions about your submission.

Remember that neatness and completeness count, and this is one case in which the old adage "better late than never" doesn't count. If you miss the submission deadline, it will be as if you had never submitted a proposal at all. Late submissions do not get funded.

GRANT COMPLIANCE

If you accept a grant, you also accept the obligation to comply with many regulatory areas. A legal contract ensues between your institution/personnel and the funding agency.

Certain government compliance approvals must be obtained before a grant proposal is accepted by a funding agency, such as human participants, animal research, nondelinquency on federal debt, and so on. Each funding agency provides detailed guidelines of the specific terms and conditions of their grants as well as some of the ways in which they measure your compliance with them.

The *Federal Grants Management Handbook* (www.thompson.com/libraries/grantmanage/gran/) is a comprehensive guide to all of the steps needed to ensure compliance with all governmental and administrative requirements for federal grants. It covers the entire process from submitting proposals to grant closeout. You will also find all of the primary source documents that you need, such as circulars from the Federal Office of Management and Budget (OMB), U.S. Treasury regulations, lobbying restrictions, nondiscrimination, and more. You will also find helpful tools such as checklists and sample forms.

Insuring compliance to administrative requirements of grants is a precursor to ensuring that your project's evaluation will be successful. Adhering to basic obligations outlined in the grants description and in resources

Worth checking out . . .

"Developing a Grant Proposal." *Catalog of Federal Domestic Assistance.* http://1246.245173/pls/portal30/CATALOG.GRANT_PROPOSAL_DYN.show.

"Sample School Grant Proposal—Library and Literacy."
www.schoolgrants.org/Samples/2003_Library&Literacy.pdf.

"School Grants Proposal to Ronald McDonald Foundation."
www.schoolgrants.org/Samples/RonaldMcDonaldGrant.pdf.

Many funding bodies are going completely online to streamline their grant-submission process. A bibliography of sources for grant writing is found at the end of the chapter.

listed above, although not always directly stated in the evaluation plan, is an absolute necessity for successful grant evaluation. Periodically, funding bodies will conduct grant compliance and financial audits to ensure that agencies are adhering to these requirements.

GRANT REPORTING

Grantees are required to develop and implement a systematic process for assessing their project's progress. Funding agencies usually provide guidelines for reporting requirements. The agencies are interested in monitoring progress and ensuring that the outcome set forth in the proposal is produced. There are two veins of grant reporting: (1) accountability to the funding agency, and (2) dissemination of findings.

Accountability is achieved through

- open, timely communications;
- maintenance of proper financial records;
- transparent methodology (tasking and activities); and
- timely evaluation of outcome.

Maintaining open communications requires creating and maintaining a personal relationship with your agency contact. They should feel they are fellow cohorts on the project. It goes without saying that you need to be approachable, honest, and forthright in all communications. Your proposal is your initial contract, and you are held accountable to the letter for items written in the proposal and any documented requirements of the funding body.

You should never deviate from the budget or methods without asking permission from the funding agency. You must keep your contact well informed of your project status and your successes or inevitable glitches. This is much easier when the communication has been open from the start. Follow these basic suggestions to maintain a good relationship with your funding agency:

- Document, sign, and date everything (don't forget to add your title, project, and grant ID number on your correspondence).
- Clarify any questions on the grant limitations with your contact.
- Treat the proposal as a legal document.
- Be meticulous and timely in your financial records, reporting, and final evaluations.

OUTCOME-BASED EVALUATION

Most grants now require some form of outcome-based evaluation. Granting agencies want to know that their monies made a difference, that they changed the circumstances for the people who benefited from the grant funding.

Evaluation of a library grant is not based on meticulous record keeping and financial data alone. Accounting for where and how funds were spent is just a small part of the equation for grant reporting. This is especially true of federal grants because "performance-based" evaluation is now mandated as a result of the passage of the Government Performance and Results Act (GPRA) of 1993 (see www.whitehouse.gov/omb/mgmt-gpra/print/gplaw2m.html#h1). This act is Public Law no. 103-62, and the official title as amended by the U.S. Senate is "An Act to provide for the establishment of performance-based budgeting and outcome-based evaluation in the Federal Government and for other purposes."

This law, responding to government officials and citizens' increasing demands for accountability for how public funds are being allocated, requires every government agency to establish and report measurable performance goals annually for each of its programs. Using performance-based evaluation of specific agency and program objectives, Congress is able to monitor each agency's level of achievement in reaching their published goals. Thus, funding agencies are requiring that grant recipients clearly state their program objectives and goals in measurable terms and report the impact of their programs.

With outcome-evaluation measures, libraries can demonstrate in a convincing way that they are using the grant money well, and these measures can help provide a compelling picture of the success of their services and projects. The ultimate question that outcome-based evaluation answers is, *How has this project, service, or program made a difference?* The outcome-evaluation model has four basic components that must be measured and monitored to answer this question:

- *Inputs:* resources used for a project
- *Activities:* project tasks and work
- *Deliverables:* accomplishments and services of the project
- *Outcome:* the benefits that the participants in the project experience

The outcome-based evaluation model is pretty straightforward, but you may find measuring each of these elements difficult. Also, you will have to think through carefully and document the defining indicators that correlate the "outcomes" to the project "inputs," "activities," and "deliverables." This is the purpose of an evaluation plan.

The evaluation plan and outcome measures should be linked directly to your project proposal's goals and objectives. You should develop your evaluation plan as a tool to measure how successful your project is in achieving these goals and objectives. The Institute for Museum and Library Services has a motto that represents the basic questions your evaluation plan and reports should answer: (1) "We wanted to do what?" (2) "We did what?" and (3) "So what?" ("Measuring Program Outcomes: Outcome-Based Evaluation for National Leadership Grants," a training workshop sponsored by the Institute of Museum and Library Services in the spring of 2002). These are the fundamental questions that funders need to have answered, and the evaluation plan is the tool that will answer them. Developing an effective evaluation plan will permit you to achieve reporting and compliance accountability, and it will also enable you to demonstrate the success of your project.

IMLS defines an outcome-based evaluation approach as a:

> set of principles and processes to provide information about the degree to which a project has met its goals in terms of creating benefits for individuals in the form of knowledge, skill, attitude, behavior, status, or life condition. ("IMLS Outcomes Based Evaluation Glossary of Project Planning Terms," www.imls.gov/grants/current/log_glossary.htm.)

Outcomes are often realized beyond the time boundaries of the project, but there should still be some specific measurable results of the project funded by the grant. For this reason, you will want a plan in place to collect and analyze project data.

Evaluation also entails fulfilling all requirements for *reporting* the project's performance and achievements as well as making recommendations for the future to the granting source and other individuals with a vested interest in the outcome of the project. You will have to submit periodic reports as well as the detailed final evaluation report that the leaders of the project submit. In the final report, you will need to describe the process of gathering and analyzing data that relate to the goals and objectives of the project (e.g., tools used, methodology, and specifics on evaluation for each objective and goal) and outline how the results and accomplishments will be disseminated or used to improve the project in the future.

Worth checking out . . .

Institute of Museum and Library Services, "Perspectives on Outcome Based Evaluation for Libraries and Museums," www.imls.gov/pubs/pdf/pubobe.pdf.

One consideration of the methodology is whether the project staff or outside experts will do the evaluation. You will need to establish procedures and schedules for gathering, analyzing, and reporting data before the project is underway. In fact, in order for the evaluation plan to be most effective, you should begin to think about it from the inception of the project.

SUMMARY

As stated at the beginning of this chapter, the basics concepts underlying all successful grant applications are simple: Come up with an idea and match your project idea to a granting source. Be sure that you can explain your project succinctly and that you have done your homework and investigated funding agencies well so that you can identify an agency that is likely to fund your project. Then follow the process described in this chapter carefully and completely, and don't forget the personal side of grantsmanship: Develop a good relationship with your contact person and follow his or her guidelines—from submission of your proposal through evaluation—to the letter.

Sources on Evaluation

Institute of Museum and Library Services. "Perspectives on Outcome Based Evaluation for Libraries and Museums." www.imls.gov/pubs/pdf/pubobe.pdf.

Project STAR (Support and Training for Assessing Results). San Mateo, CA: Project Star, 1999. Material on evaluation is available at www.projectstar.org/star/Library/Toolkit/evalplan.pdf. This material is primarily online, but other formats are available upon request from Project STAR, 480 E. 4th Ave., Unit A, San Mateo, CA 94401-3349, 1-800-548-3656, www.projectstar.org.

United Way of America. *Measuring Program Outcomes: A Practical Approach*. Alexandria, VA: United Way of America, 1996. To order, contact Sales Service/America at 800-772-0008 (toll-free in the United States) or 703-212-6300, and request Item no. 0989 ($5 plus shipping and handling).

Verzuh, Eric. *The Fast Forward MBA in Project Management*. New York: Wiley & Sons, 1999.

W. K. Kellogg Foundation Evaluation Handbook. January 1998. www.wkkf.org/Pubs/Tools/Evaluation/Pub770.pdf.

SUGGESTED REFERENCES FOR WRITING PROPOSALS

PROPOSAL WRITING MANUALS AND GUIDES

Funding Agency Manuals and Guides

Corporation for Public Broadcasting. *Basic Elements of Grant Writing.* www.cpb.org/grants/grantwriting.html.
Environmental Protection Agency. *EPA Grant-Writing Tutorial.* www.epa.gov/seahome/grants/src/grant.htm.
National Cancer Institute (NCI). *Quick Guide for Grant Applications.* http://deainfo.nci.nih.gov/EXTRA/EXTDOCS/gntapp.htm.
National Institute of Allergy and Infectious Diseases (NIAID). *All about Grants* (including "How to Plan a Grant Applications" and "How to Write a Grant Application"). www.niaid.nih.gov/ncn/grants/default.htm.
National Institute of Neurological Disorders and Stroke (NINDS). "Common Mistakes in NIH Applications." www.ninds.nih.gov/funding/grantwriting_mistakes.htm.
National Institutes of Health. "Grant Writing Tips Sheets." http://grants.nih.gov/grants/grant_tips.htm.
National Science Foundation, Division of Undergraduate Education. *A Guide for Proposal Writing.* www.nsf.gov/pubsys/ods/getpub.cfm?nsf04016.
Social Science Research Council. "The Art of Writing Proposals." www.ssrc.org/fellowships/art_of_writing_proposals.page.

GENERAL MANUALS AND GUIDES

Albert Einstein College of Medicine, Office of Grant Support. *Grantsmanship Tutorial.* www.aecom.yu.edu/ogs/Guide/Guide.htm.
Eastern Michigan University, Office of Research Development. *GRADORD Handbook for Proposal Writers and Project Directors.* www.gradord.emich.edu/_pages_ord/ordpubs/ordpubs_subdir/handbook/o_handbook.html.
Foundation Center. *A Proposal Writing Short Course.* http://fdncenter.org/learn/shortcourse/prop1.html.
Georgia Perimeter College (E. Brown's website). *Proposal Writing: Stages and Strategies with Examples.* www.gpc.edu/~ebrown/infobr3.htm.

Kraicer, Jacob. *The Art of Grantsmanship.*
www.utoronto.ca/cip/sa_ArtGt.pdf.

Levine, S. Joseph. *Guide for Writing a Funding Proposal.*
www.learnerassociates.net/proposal/.

Newman, Rhoda. *Grant Proposal Development (90-430 C).*
www.lib.msu.edu/harris23/grants/crsrpt.htm. Originally written
as a Congressional Research Service Report for Congress,
August 30, 1990, it is now a resource for funding sources
maintained by John Harrison on the Michigan State Libraries
Web site.

Racey, Janet S. *Fundamentals of Grantsmanship.*
http://healthlinks.washington.edu/rfs/gw/fundamentals.html.

The Regional Alliance Hub for Mathematics and Science Education
Reform. *TERC Grant Writing Guide.*
http://ra.terc.edu/publications/TERC_pubs/TERCGrantManual/
TOC.html.

Reid, Alice N. T. (instructor of English, Delaware Technical and
Community College, Wilmington Campus [areid@hopi.dtcc.edu].
A Practical Guide for Writing Proposals.
http://members.dca.net/areid/proposal.htm.

Roanoke College. "Proposal Tips."
www.roanoke.edu/grants/newgrants/proposal.htm.

Stephen F. Austin State University, Office of Research and Sponsored
Programs. *Proposal Writing Handbook.*
www.sfasu.edu/orsp/handbook.htm.

University of Michigan, Division of Research Development and
Administration. *Proposal Writer's Guide.*
www.research.umich.edu/proposals/PWG/pwgcontents.html.

University of Montana, Office of the Vice President Research and
Development. *ORSP Proposer's Guide.*
www.umt.edu/research/propgd.htm.

University of Nebraska–Lincoln. *Writing from the Winner's Circle.*
www.unl.edu/nepscor/newpages/noframes/pubs/winners/writing.
html.

University of Pittsburgh, Office of Research. *Proposal Writing Guide.*
www.pitt.edu/~offres/propwriting.html.

University of Southern California, Department of Contracts & Grants.
General Proposal Guidelines.
www.usc.edu/dept/contracts/gg.html.

PROFESSIONAL PROPOSAL WRITERS/CONSULTANTS

Grant, Andrew (andrew@grantservices.com). "Proposal Writing."
www.grantservices.com/serv02.htm.
Kendrick, Jim (kendrick@p2c2group.com). "Proposals, Plans &
Competitive Communication P2C2 Group."
http://users.erols.com/p2c2/.
Kluge, Deborah (dkluge@comcast.net). "ProposalWriter.com."
www.proposalwriter.com.
Len Duffy and Associates (customersupport@lenduffy.com). "Our
Proposal Process." www.lenduffy.com/proposal.html.

PROPOSAL WRITING COURSES AND WORKSHOPS

CBR Community Building Resources. "Aim High, Do It! Proposal
Writing." www.cbr-aimhigh.com/workshops/do_it/
proposal_ws.htm.
Foundation Center. "Proposal Writing Seminar,"
http://fdncenter.org/marketplace/catalog/subcategory_training.
jhtml?id=cat30003&navCount=2&navAction=push.
Grantsmanship Center. "Grant Proposal Writing."
www.tgci.com/training/proposal.htm.

BIBLIOGRAPHIES OF BOOKS/RESOURCES ON PROPOSAL WRITING

Michigan State University Library. *Grantsmanship Techniques.*
www.lib.msu.edu/harris23/grants/4fc_a.htm.
State Library of Ohio, World Wide Web Information Network. *Grants
and Grantsmanship: Selected Publications*, update February
2004. http://winslo.state.oh.us/services/reference/bibgrant.html.
University of Wisconsin–Madison, Grants Information Center. *Proposal
Writing: Internet Resources.*
http://grants.library.wisc.edu/organizations/proposalwebsites.html.
———. *Proposal Writing: Resources in Print.*
http://grants.library.wisc.edu/organizations/proposalbooks.html.

WRITING AIDS

Merriam-Webster Online. *Collegiate Dictionary* and *Collegiate
Thesaurus.* www.m-w.com/netdict.htm.
Writing-World.com. *Grammar.* www.writing-world.com/links/grammar.
shtml.

Roget's Internet Thesaurus. http://thesaurus.reference.com.

Strunk, William. *The Elements of Style*. Columbia University,
  Academic Information Systems (AcIS), Bartleby Library.
  www.bartleby.com/141/index.html.
WorldWideWeb. "Acronym and Abbreviation Server." www.ucc.ie/
  cgi-bin/acronym/.

Source: University of Pittsburgh Office of Research, June 10, 1997, revised February
17, 2004, www.pitt.edu/~offres/proposal/propwriting/websites.html.

APPENDIXES

APPENDIX A: SAMPLE LIBRARY ACCOUNTING MANUAL

The value of an accounting procedures manual for financial accountability and open communication of financial plans was discussed in Chapter 2. The following can be used as an outline for documenting financial management procedures and the financial plans and regulations behind the procedures. It is essential that this document be aligned with the community needs analysis, the institutional mission, library financial management goals, regulations regarding fiscal responsibilities, and established financial management practices and standards.

Purpose
Scope of Document (list any exclusions)
Financial Communication and Governance
Financial Organizational Chart
    Lines of Communication and Publicity Requirements
    Designation of Authority Levels
Accountability and Responsibility
    Overview of Library Director's Responsibilities
    Department Supervisors' Submission Requirements
      and Responsibilities
    Outsourced Accountant Responsibilities
      Library Board and Treasurer/Auditor
        Responsibilities
    Administrative Staff Responsibilities
    Grant and Special Funds Reporting and Governance
Guidelines for Library Director's Role in Library Financial
    Management and the Budget Process
    Ethical Responsibilities of Financial Management—
      Leadership and Vision
    Library Director as Budget Champion and
      Spokesperson
    Management Commitment to Accounting Policies and
      Procedures
Financial Processes and Accounting Controls
    Budget Development Process
    Budget Cycle and Timeline
    Budget Types Required and Accounting Objectives
    Guidelines and Approval Process

Annual Outcomes Review
Internal Audit Procedures
External Audit Requirements
Files and Records Management
Chart of Accounts
Management Reporting and Documentation
Guidelines
Documentation
Control of Financial Documents
Control of Related Records (e.g., contracts)
Accounting Transactions
Records Retention Policy
Management Reports
Financial Statements
Revenue and Asset Control
Revenue
Local Sources, Formulas, Referenda, and
Assumptions
State and Federal Sources, Formulas, and
Legislation
Grants
Donations and Gifts
Fees and Fines
Library Inventory Process
Inventory Control Software for Circulated Items
Inventory Reports of Missing and Damaged Items
Fixed-Asset Control
Fixed-Asset Depreciation
Cash and Cash Accounts
Petty Cash (cash receipts and deposits)
Check-Signing Authority and Bank Account
Reconciliation
Handle Patron Fines/Fees and Bounced Checks
Expenditures and Liabilities
Overview of Expenditures
Accounts Payable and Cash Disbursements
Collection Development Purchasing Policy
Departmental Purchasing Policies
Leasing
Vendor Selection Project
Project RFP Development and Approval Process
Facilities, Utilities, and Resource Maintenance
and Management
Insurance
Security and Safety Overview
Physical Security

APPENDIX B: SAMPLE LIBRARY ANNUAL REPORT FORM

<table>
<tr><td colspan="3">Texas Academic Libraries Survey
(Fiscal Year——)</td></tr>
<tr>
<td colspan="2">Return to:
Texas State Library and Archives Commission
Library Development Division
Box 12927
Austin, TX 78711-2927</td>
<td rowspan="2">Directory Information. Please Update</td>
</tr>
<tr>
<td colspan="2">If there are any questions, contact:
Kathleen Walls
Texas State Library and Archives Commission
512-463-5532
kathleen.walls@tsl.state.tx.us
DUE: FEBRUARY 1</td>
</tr>
<tr>
<td>1. Library contact for this survey</td>
<td>2. Title</td>
<td>3. Telephone (area code, number, ext.)</td>
</tr>
</table>

SCOPE OF REPORT

Are law library statistics included?

☐ Yes ☐ No ☐ We do not have a Law Library.

Are medical library statistics included?

☐ Yes ☐ No ☐ We do not have a Medical Library.

Are media services (audiovisual services) statistics included?

☐ Yes ☐ No ☐ We are not responsible for Media Services.

PART A—NUMBER OF PUBLIC SERVICE OUTLETS, FISCAL YEAR		
Line no.	Item	Number
01	Branch and independent libraries (exclude main or central library)	

PART B—LIBRARY STAFF, FALL (Current Year) Exclude Maintenance and Custodial Staff (Report data to two decimals)		
Line no.	Librarians and other professional staff	Number of FTEs
02	Librarians	
03	Other professionals	
04	Total librarians and other professional staff (sum lines 02 and 03)	
05	All other paid staff (except student assistants)	
06	Contributed services staff	
07	Student assistants	
08	Total full-time equivalent (FTE) staff (sum lines 04 through 07)	
PART C—LIBRARY EXPENDITURES, FISCAL YEAR Note: Do not report the same expenditures more than once		
Line no.	Category	Amount (whole dollars only)
	Salaries and wages:	
09	Librarians and other professional staff	$
10	All other paid staff (except student assistants)	$
11	Student assistants	$
	Information resources	
	Books, serial backfiles, and other materials	$
12	Paper and microform	$
13	Electronic	$
	Current serial subscriptions and search services	
14	Paper and microform	$
15	Electronic	$
16	Audiovisual materials	$
17	Document delivery/interlibrary loan	$
18	Preservation	$
19	Other materials	$

	Operating expenditures:	
20	Furniture and equipment (exclude computer equipment)	$
21	Computer hardware and software (exclude maintenance)	$
22	Bibliographic utilities, networks, and consortia	$
23	All other operating expenditures	$
24	Total expenditures (sum of lines 09 through 23)	$
25	Employee fringe benefits (if paid from the library budget)	$

PART D—LIBRARY COLLECTIONS, FISCAL YEAR

Line no.	Category	Added during the fiscal year (1)	Held at the end of the fiscal year (2)
	Book, serial backfiles, and other materials (include government document)		
26	Paper—volumes		
27	Paper—titles		
28	Microform—units		
29	Electronic—titles		
	Current serial subscriptions:		
30	Number of paper and microform subscriptions		
31	Number of electronic subscriptions		
32	Audiovisual materials—units		

PART E—LIBRARY SERVICES, FISCAL YEAR

Line no.	Category	Number
	Document delivery/interlibrary loans provided to other libraries:	
33	Returnable	
34	Nonreturnable	
35	Total provided (sum lines 33 and 34)	
	Document delivery/interlibrary loans received from other libraries or commercial services:	
36	Returnable	
37	Nonreturnable	

38	Total received (sum lines 36 and 37)	
	Circulation transactions	
39	General collection	
40	Reserve collection	
	Information service to groups	
41	Number of presentations	
42	Total attendance at all presentations	

PART F—LIBRARY SERVICES, TYPICAL WEEK, FALL		
Line no.	Category	Number in a typical week
43	Hours open in a typical week	
44	Gate count in a typical week	
45	Reference transactions in a typical week	

PART G—ELECTRONIC SERVICES

This section requests information about the availability of electronic services in the library and elsewhere, on-campus and off-campus access by your primary clientele and other users. Please respond to each item by marking an (X) in the appropriate column.

Line no.	Category	Mark (X) in appropriate column							
		Access from				Access off campus by			
		Within library (1)		Elsewhere on campus (2)		Primary clientele (3)		Others (4)	
	Does the library or parent institution make available the following services:	Yes	No	Yes	No	Yes	No	Yes	No
46	An electronic catalog that includes the library's holdings								
47	Electronic indexes and reference tools								
48	Electronic full-text periodicals								
49	Electronic full-text reserves								
50	Electronic files other than the catalog (e.g., finding aids, indices, or manuscripts) created by the staff								

51	Internet access								
52	Library reference service by e-mail								
53	Capacity to place interlibrary loan/document delivery requests electronically								
54	Technology to assist patrons with disabilities (e.g., TDD or specially equipped work stations)								
55	Instruction by library staff on use of Internet resources								
56	Electronic document delivery by the library to patron's account/address								
57	Video/desktop conferencing by or for the library								
58	Satellite broadcasting by or for the library								
	Category						Access from within library		
	Does your library provide the following services?						Yes	No	
59	Computers not dedicated to library functions for patron use inside library								
60	Computer software for patron use inside the library (e.g., word processing, spreadsheet, or custom applications)								
61	Scanning equipment for patron use in the library								
62	Services to your institution's distance education students (If your institution does not have distance education students, please check here. ☐)								

Remarks section: Please enter any remarks you may have in this section. By entering any explanations here, you may eliminate the need for telephone contact at a later date.

PART H—INSTITUTIONAL CHARACTERISTICS (First Semester)		
Line no.	Category	Number
63	Students, undergraduate—total full time	
64	—Total FTE of part time	
65	—Total FTE enrollment (if this figure is supplied, ignore lines 71–72)	
66	—Total headcount	
67	Graduate—total full time	
68	—Total FTE of part time	
69	—Total FTE enrollment (if this figure is supplied, ignore lines 67 and 68)	
70	—Total headcount	
71	Faculty, instructional—total full time	
72	—Total FTE of part-time	
73	Total FTE instructional faculty (if this figure is supplied, ignore lines 71 and 72)	
74	—Total headcount	
PART I—PROFESSIONAL SALARIES (CURRENT YEAR) (First Semester)		
75	Director	$
76	Average professional salary excluding director	$
77	Beginning professional salary (entry-level professionals without experience)	$

APPENDIX C: SAMPLE RFP FOR BUILDING CONSULTANT

REQUEST FOR PROPOSAL LIBRARY SERVICES AND DEVELOPMENT CONSULTANT

EXECUTIVE SUMMARY

Due to the community's use and support of library services, the Westmoreland County Federated Library System (WCFLS) looks forward to a very bright future—one filled with growth and the promise of serving greater numbers of people. To assure that the challenge of growth is met, WCFLS must plan its future proactively, taking a holistic view of the county, its communities' growth patterns, library service, and funding needs.

It also needs to educate the community and its key stakeholders (key funders, community opinion leaders, political and municipal officials, etc.) about library service and financial needs, rather than responding to service requests reactively.

Using an LSTA grant of $30,000, the Westmoreland County Federated Library System seeks to engage a library consultant to:

1. Develop a needs assessment that examines the library system's library service-priority needs covering the next ten-year period;

2. identify the resources required to address the library system's long-term needs and evaluate current public and private development activities; and

3. recommend an ongoing process to educate the library system's key stakeholders (key funders, community opinion leaders, political and municipal officials, etc.), both externally and internally, about the community's long-term library service needs.

This project is needed because:

1. The diversity of needs and inequity in the availability of public library service within Westmoreland County demands coordinated and cooperative efforts;

2. of the nine third-class counties in Pennsylvania, Westmoreland libraries receive the least amount of county funding, and the library system's concern with the level of funding necessitates research;

3. in prioritizing its core service roles, the library system needs to determine and obtain the financial resources required to effectively meet current and future needs; and

4. to generate support for library services, WCFLS must educate stakeholders (key funders, community opinion leaders, political and municipal officials, etc.) about the community's need for library services.

The final report will:

- Determine the community's library service priorities covering the next ten-year period;

- provide service alternatives and recommend the best options available for service improvements;

- recommend service roles for existing and proposed service points;

- identify any potential obstacles to addressing the needs, and recommend strategies for overcoming same;

- identify the financial resources required to implement the report's recommendations;

- evaluate the library system's current public and private development activities, and recommend improvements; and

- recommend an ongoing process for educating the library system's key external and internal stakeholders about the community's library service and financial needs.

TIMELINE

Date	Milestone/Activity
August 29, 2003	RFP Issued
October 10, 2003	Questions regarding RFP due
October 24, 2003	Proposals due

October 27–November 7, 2003	Interviews with selected consultants
November 17, 2003	Contract awarded
December 19, 2003	First progress report due from consultant
January 28, 2004	Complete any request for data from WCFLS staff
January 28, 2004	Second progress report due from consultant
February 27, 2004	Third progress report due from consultant
March 24, 2004	Fourth progress report due from consultant
April 2, 2004	Complete data collection, focus groups, stakeholder interviews, and so on
April 16, 2004	Preliminary draft report due from consultant
May 14, 2004	Revised draft report due from consultant
May 26, 2004	Final draft report due (includes presentation to WCFLS Board)

The deadline for proposal submission is October 24, 2003. A complete copy of the request for proposal is available by sending an e-mail to wcfls@monpldc.org.

Source: Reprinted by permission of the Westmoreland County Federated Library System (WCFLS), Monessen, PA 15062.

APPENDIX D: SAMPLE LEASE AGREEMENT

THIS AGREEMENT TO LEASE EQUIPMENT ("Lease") is made and effective
_____ [Date], by and between
_____ [Lessor], ("Lessor")
and _____ [Lessee],
("Lessee").

Lessor desires to lease to Lessee, and Lessee desires to lease from Lessor, certain tangible personal property.

NOW, THEREFORE, in consideration of the mutual covenants and promises hereinafter set forth, the parties hereto agree as follows:

1. *Lease*

Lessor hereby leases to Lessee, and Lessee hereby leases from Lessor, the following described equipment (the "Equipment"): [Equipment]

2. *Term*

The term of this Lease shall commence on _____ [Start Date] and shall expire _____ [Lease Length] months thereafter.

3. *Shipping*

Lessee shall be responsible for shipping the Equipment to Lessee's premises.

4. *Rent and Deposit*

A. The monthly rent for the Equipment shall be paid in advance in installments of _____ **[Installment Amount]** each month, beginning on
_____ **[Date of First Payment]** and on the first day of each succeeding month throughout the term hereof, at **[Address for Payments]**, or at such other place as Lessor may designate from time to time. Any installment payment not made by the tenth (10th) day of the month shall be considered overdue and in addition to Lessor's other remedies, Lessor may levy a late payment charge equal to one percent (1%) per month on any overdue amount. Rent for any partial month shall be prorated.

B. Lessee shall pay a deposit in the following amount prior to taking possession of the Equipment: _____ **[Deposit Amount]**. The deposit will be refunded to Lessee promptly following Lessee's performance of all obligations in this Lease.

5. *Use*

Lessee shall use the Equipment in a careful and proper manner and shall comply with and conform to all national, state, municipal, police, and other laws, ordinances, and regulations in any way relating to the possession, use, or maintenance of the Equipment.

_____
_____
_____
_____

[Other Restrictions]

6. *Right to Lease*
LESSOR WARRANTS THAT LESSOR HAS THE RIGHT TO LEASE THE EQUIPMENT, AS PROVIDED IN THIS LEASE.

7. *Repairs*
Lessee, at its own cost and expense, shall keep the Equipment in good repair, condition, and working order and shall furnish any and all parts, mechanisms, and devices required to keep the Equipment in good mechanical working order.

8. *Loss and Damage*

A. Lessee hereby assumes and shall bear the entire risk of loss and damage to the Equipment from any and every cause whatsoever. No loss or damage to the Equipment or any part thereof shall impair any obligation of Lessee under this Lease, which shall continue in full force and effect through the term of the Lease.

B. In the event of loss or damage of any kind whatever to the Equipment, Lessee shall, at Lessor's option:

(i) Place the same in good repair, condition, and working order; or
(ii) Replace the same with like equipment in good repair, condition, and working order; or
(iii) Pay to Lessor the replacement cost of the Equipment.

9. *Surrender*
Upon the expiration or earlier termination of this Lease, Lessee shall return the Equipment to Lessor in good repair, condition, and working order, ordinary wear and tear resulting from proper use thereof alone excepted, by delivering the Equipment at Lessee's cost and expense to such place as Lessor shall specify within the city or county in which the same was delivered to Lessee.

10. *Insurance*
Lessee shall procure and continuously maintain and pay for:
A. All risk insurance against loss of and damage to the Equipment for not less than the full replacement value of the Equipment, naming Lessor as loss payee; and,
B. Combined public liability and property damage insurance with limits as approved by Lessor, naming Lessor as additionally named insured and a loss payee.

   The insurance shall be in such form and with such company or companies as shall be reasonably acceptable to Lessor; shall provide at least thirty (30) days advance written notice to Lessor of any cancellation, change, or modification; and shall provide primary coverage for the protection of Lessee and Lessor without regard to any other coverage carried by Lessee or Lessor protecting against similar risks. Lessee shall provide Lessor with an original policy or certificate evidencing such insurance. Lessee hereby appoints Lessor as Lessee's attorney in fact with power and authority to do all things, including, but not limited to, making claims, receiving payments and endorsing documents, checks, or drafts necessary or advisable to secure payments due under any policy of insurance required under this Agreement.

11. *Taxes*
Lessee shall keep the Equipment free and clear of all levies, liens, and encumbrances. Lessee, or Lessor at Lessee's expense, shall report, pay, and discharge when due all license and registration fees, assessments, sales, use and property taxes, gross receipts, taxes arising out of receipts from use or operation of the Equipment, and other taxes, fees, and governmental charges similar or dissimilar to the foregoing, together with any penalties or interest thereon, imposed by any state, federal, or local government or any agency, or department thereof, upon the Equipment or the purchase, use, operation, or leasing of the Equipment or otherwise in any manner with respect thereto and whether or not the same shall be assessed against or in the name of Lessor or Lessee. However, Lessee shall not be required to pay or discharge any such tax or assessment so long as it shall, in good faith and by appropriate legal proceedings, contest the validity thereof in any reasonable manner that will not affect or endanger the title and interest of Lessor to the Equipment; provided, Lessee shall reimburse Lessor for any damages or expenses resulting from such failure to pay or discharge.

12. *Lessor's Payment*
In case of failure of Lessee to procure or maintain said insurance or to pay fees, assessments, charges, and taxes, all as specified in this Lease, Lessor shall have the right, but shall not be obligated, to effect such insurance, or pay said fees, assignments, charges, and taxes, as the case may be. In that event, the cost thereof shall be repayable to Lessor with the next installment of rent, and failure to repay the same shall carry with it the same consequences, including interest at ten percent (10%) per annum, as failure to pay any installment of rent.

13. *Indemnity*
Lessee shall indemnify Lessor against, and hold Lessor harmless from, any and all claims, actions, suits, proceedings, costs, expenses, damages, and liabilities, including reasonable attorney's fees and costs, arising out of, connected with, or resulting from Lessee's use of the Equipment, including without limitation the manufacture, selection, delivery, possession, use, operation, or return of the Equipment.

14. *Default*
If Lessee fails to pay any rent or other amount herein provided within ten (10) days after the same is due and payable, or if Lessee fails to observe, keep, or perform any other provision of this Lease required to be observed, kept, or performed by Lessee, Lessor shall have the right to exercise any one or more of the following remedies:

A. To declare the entire amount of rent hereunder immediately due and payable without notice or demand to Lessee.

B. To sue for and recover all rents, and other payments, then accrued or thereafter accruing.

C. To take possession of the Equipment, without demand or notice, wherever same may be located, without any court order or other process of law. Lessee hereby waives any and all damages occasioned by such taking of possession.

D. To terminate this Lease.

E. To pursue any other remedy at law or in equity.

Notwithstanding any repossession or any other action that Lessor may take, Lessee shall be and remain liable for the full performance of all obligations on the part of the Lessee to be performed under this Lease. All of Lessor's remedies are cumulative, and may be exercised concurrently or separately.

15. *Bankruptcy*

Neither this Lease nor any interest therein is assignable or transferable by operation of law. If any proceeding under the Bankruptcy Act, as amended, is commenced by or against the Lessee, or if the Lessee is adjudged insolvent, or if Lessee makes any assignment for the benefit of his creditors, or if a writ of attachment or execution is levied on the Equipment and is not released or satisfied within ten (10) days thereafter, or if a receiver is appointed in any proceeding or action to which the Lessee is a party with authority to take possession or control of the Equipment, Lessor shall have and may exercise any one or more of the remedies set forth in Section 14 hereof; and this Lease shall, at the option of the Lessor, without notice, immediately terminate and shall not be treated as an asset of Lessee after the exercise of said option.

16. *Ownership*

The Equipment is, and shall at all times be and remain, the sole and exclusive property of Lessor; and the Lessee shall have no right, title, or interest therein or thereto except as expressly set forth in this Lease.

17. Additional Document

If Lessor shall so request, Lessee shall execute and deliver to Lessor such documents as Lessor shall deem necessary or desirable for purposes of recording or filing to protect the interest of Lessor in the Equipment including, but not limited to, a UCC financing statement.

18. *Entire Agreement*

This instrument constitutes the entire agreement between the parties on the subject matter hereof and it shall not be amended, altered, or changed except by a further writing signed by the parties hereto.

19. *Notices*

Service of all notices under this Agreement shall be sufficient if given personally or mailed certified, return receipt requested, postage prepaid, at the address hereinafter set forth, or to such address as such party may provide in writing from time to time.

If to Lessor:

_____

[Lessor]_____

_____

[Lessor's Address]

If to Lessee:

_____

[Lessee]

_____

_____

[Lessee's Address]

20. *Assignment*
Lessee shall not assign this Lease or its interest in the Equipment without the prior written consent of Lessor.

21. *Headings*
Headings used in this Lease are provided for convenience only and shall not be used to construe meaning or intent.

22. *Governing Law*
This Lease shall be construed and enforced according to laws of the State of Texas.

WITNESS THE SIGNATURES OF THE PARTIES TO THIS AGREEMENT TO LEASE EQUIPMENT:

LESSOR:

Sign: _____

Print: _____ Date: _____

LESSOR:

Sign: _____

Print: _____ Date: _____

LESSEE:

Sign: _____

Print: _____ Date: _____

LESSEE:

Sign: _____

Print: _____ Date: _____

Source: Reprinted with permission of Steven Gilbert Companies, http://www.sgilbertcompaniesinc.com/sgci/leaseagm.html.

APPENDIX E: STARTING A MAJOR DONOR PROGRAM

PAT MUNOZ

Many years ago, when I was the membership director at American Rivers, our new president instructed me to begin listing all those members who had given $100 or more to the organization in the newsletter and annual report. I was a bit skeptical, but followed his instructions and in addition to recognizing them in this manner, began a special program to ask them to increase their giving with a personal letter, and sent them special updates. The results were impressive; Within two years, our base of $100 donors nearly tripled and a number of them increased their giving to the $1,000 level. This experience convinced me that most groups, regardless of their size, can benefit from instituting a special program to recognize and build the loyalty of their larger donors.

Since those days, I've learned a lot about major donor programs, all of which has only reinforced my conviction that they should be a part of every grassroots group's fundraising repertoire. In this appendix, I hope I can provide you with enough information to allow you to launch a major donor program of your own.

WHAT IS A MAJOR DONOR PROGRAM, AND WHY START ONE?

Major donors are individuals who make gifts to your organization at or above a certain threshold level. The minimum gift that qualifies a person as a major donor should be defined by each organization, depending on the wealth of the community in which it operates. For most grassroots river groups, a gift of $100 or more is a large gift, so for the purposes of this appendix, I will use $100 as the entry-level gift for a major gift program. The ultimate goal is, of course, to get donors to make larger gifts of four, and even five, figures.

A major donor program is a systematic way to encourage a particular set of your members who have the potential to make major gifts to increase their giving to your organization over time. The reason for starting a major donor program, simply stated, is that if you recognize and thank your members personally, and get them involved in some way in your organization, they will contribute significantly more money. Why do religious organizations receive approximately half of all the individual charity in the United States? There are many reasons, of course, but one that looms large is that they treat all of their members as potential major donors. Pastors usually shake hands with and address by name every member of their congregation, and they give their parishioners many chances to get involved in church activities through committees, boards, special events, and so on.

Most nonprofit organizations cannot have the direct personal contact with all their members that churches do, but we can try to identify those members who have the greatest potential to make large gifts and institute a formal program to recognize and involve these people in our organizations.

IDENTIFYING MAJOR DONORS

In an ideal world, you, like religious institutions, would treat all your members as potential major donors. But when staffs are small and time is limited, you can only have direct personal contact with a small percentage of your members. Indeed, many organizations derive as much as 60 percent of their individual member revenues from 10 percent of their donors. Your first job, then, is to identify that 10 to 20 percent of your members that you think has the potential to become larger contributors over time. A good place to start is by looking at all your members who have made a one-time gift of $50 or more as potential major donor prospects (unless you have some personal knowledge of the person that makes you think otherwise).

THE NEXT STEP

Once you have identified a list of potential major donors, and coded them in some way that allows you to do special mailings to them and to exclude them from the regular membership renewal mailings, you are ready to begin the process of building donor loyalty. If your list is sizable, this is probably best done by mail or by phone. One easy way to make these prospects feel appreciated is to send them an annual report with a note from the director, a copy of a recent news article, or a special bulletin on one of your projects. You may want to call your best prospects and give them some good news, or ask them to get involved in some specific way. One rule of thumb is that you should try to have at least four meaningful contacts a year with these prospects.

After an appropriate period of cultivation, you are ready to ask your prospects to increase their gift to $100 or more and become "major donors." This is best done in person, because people are more likely to give and almost always give more in response to a face-to-face request. However, if you have many prospects, you may be forced to rate them according to what you think they are capable of giving and tailor your solicitation method to that rating, asking the best prospects in person, and soliciting the others by telephone or by letter.

The amount you ask each prospect for will be based on a number of factors, including their past giving, their level of involvement in the organization, their giving record with other groups (if that is available), and your research on their financial capacity. There will always be prospects you cannot reach to set up a meeting, or who cannot meet with you; in these cases, try making the request by letter, and then following up with a phone call after a week or so in which you offer to clarify anything the prospect wishes to discuss.

Letter requests to major donor prospects should always be personalized. You may be able to use the text of a letter you have sent to your regular members as a special appeal, or even a new member solicitation, but you should also include information on the benefits of becoming a "River Guardian" (or whatever name you chose to give your donors) and how important these donors are to you. You should also make reference to their prior giving history in some way:

> "Last year you made a generous $50 gift to Friends of the Sandy," and specifically cite the amount you would like them to give.
>
> Or: "We hope you will consider joining our River Guardian program this year by increasing your gift to $100. Your gift will be used specifically for our campaign to stop mining along the Sandy River."

THANKING DONORS

Thanking major donors swiftly and personally is absolutely vital. Nothing cements donor loyalty more than a prompt, heartfelt thank-you. Thank-yous should go out immediately, or at most within two days. When a contributor sends you money, he or she is more interested in your organization at that moment than at any other time; by responding swiftly, you reinforce that interest, raising it to a higher level than ever before.

Thank-you letters or notes should usually be signed by the director of the organization. Keep thank-yous short and sweet, and as personal as possible. Avoid precooked-sounding phrases such as "It is contributions such as yours. . . ." Use plain, straightforward English to tell the contributor how much you appreciate his or her gift and what it will be used for. If possible, send something along with the thank-you, such as a recent news clipping or the latest summary of activities. Be sure to acknowledge any past contacts with the donor, or any relationship the donor has with the organization or its board, staff, or volunteers.

Many people give hoping to please a friend or relative connected with your organization. When this happens, it is important to indicate that the friend or relative will be told about the gift, particularly if they solicited the contribution in the first place. Remarkable as it may seem, this is seldom done, yet it can be as simple as showing a "cc."

DONOR CLUBS

One of the best techniques for getting people to become major donors, and then to upgrade their gifts year after year, is to create donor clubs with special names and special benefits attached to the various giving levels. Groups can opt for the standard names, such as sustainers, patrons, founders, and so on, or seek more creative names related to the geographic location or other peculiarities of the group involved. A simple structure for a major donor program might look as follows:

Sustainer: $100
Steward: $250
Patron: $500
Guardian: $1,000
Protector: $5,000
Founder: $10,000

Once these levels have been established and used successfully for an appropriate time (and adjusted, where appropriate), they should be incorporated into all the literature and brochures of the organization and communicated frequently to the membership. If an ongoing effort is made to educate and encourage members about opportunities to upgrade, they will often spontaneously increase their giving to one of these higher levels.

DONOR BENEFITS/PREMIUMS

Benefits can be used effectively to encourage donors to upgrade their gifts. For river groups, such benefits (related whenever possible to the mission of the organization) might include special reports from the director, invitations to special events, recognition in the annual report, maps, T-shirts, hats, posters, calendars, books, and river trips. I would offer the following advice to small groups undertaking major donor programs:

Don't let the lack of benefits/premiums stand in the way of your starting a major donor program. In my experience, benefits are not the real motivation for making higher gifts—your relationship with the donor and the donor's perception that the organization is doing important work comprise the most important motivator. So start simple; you can always add premiums later as your program becomes more sophisticated.

If you choose to use an item as a premium for one of your giving levels, keep the value of the item at no more than 10 percent of the gift, including packaging, postage, and handling.

If you do decide to offer premiums such as maps or calendars, be sure you can send them out quickly and easily; donors are turned off by organizations that promise to send them something, then fail to do so within a reasonable time.

DONOR RECOGNITION

One of the best ways to encourage higher gifts is through recognition. For most people, recognition is a powerful incentive for maintaining, and even increasing, their giving. One way to recognize major donors is to list them in your newsletter and annual report. In the newsletter, you can list new contributors since the last issue; in the annual report, you should list all the donors for the year in question. When compiling such lists, be sure to spell names correctly, include all qualified contributors who wish to be recognized, and omit any donors who ask to remain anonymous.

Another way to recognize really large gifts is to thank the donor publicly at the annual meeting or some other event. This kind of recognition has two benefits: It pleases the donor, and it encourages other potential donors to give similar gifts.

DONOR RECORDS

In order to recognize donors, personalize thank-yous, target solicitations, and record giving histories and other personal information, it is essential to keep good donor records. I recommend opening a folder on each individual who gives $100 or more and keeping copies of all correspondence with the donor in this file. It is also important to make a written record of any significant information exchanged during personal visits or phone calls with the donor, and place it in the donor's file. Finally, it is essential to have a good software program that can record individual gift amounts, dates, and sources and allow you to analyze and segment your membership by giving patterns and other criteria. For more information on membership software, see "A Guide to Membership Software," by Blake Andrews, published in *River Voices* (Winter 1994).

If your group plans on being around for the long haul, you can increase your income substantially over time by instituting a major donor program, and at the same time reap additional benefits from greater member involvement and commitment. A major donor program takes time, energy, and courage, but will pay off for your organization in the long run. Don't neglect this important strategy!

BASIC REQUIREMENTS FOR A MAJOR DONOR PROGRAM

To undertake a major donor program, your organization needs:

A clear mission statement and history of accomplishments. Before individuals make large gifts to an organization, they need to understand clearly what the organizational purpose is.

A committed base of members. In some cases, major donors can be recruited from outside the member base of an organization, but the best source of major donor prospects is those individuals who have joined the organization and have an established commitment to its work.

Opportunities to involve individuals in the work of the organization. Most four- and five-figure gifts to nonprofits come from individuals who serve on committees or boards or who are involved in some meaningful way in the work of the organization.

Staff, board, or volunteers who are willing to ask for gifts in person. Asking for money in person is at least twice as effective as asking by telephone, and almost always results in larger gifts.

A system that allows you to record, retrieve, and analyze information about individuals, including their giving history.

Pat Munoz is a watershed program manager at River Network. Reprinted with permission from River Network, "helping people to understand, protect, and restore rivers and their watersheds," www.rivernetwork.org.

INDEX

ABOUT THE AUTHORS

Arlita Hallam is associate dean of the School of Library and Information Sciences at the University of North Texas in Denton. She has developed, and currently teaches, courses in library management, financial and human resources management, and library buildings. Her previous experience includes positions as university librarian at a private university in Nairobi, Kenya; quality of life administrator for the City of Clearwater, Florida; and director of five public library systems in Illinois, Florida, and Texas. Hallam has a B.S. in English from Illinois State University in Normal; an M.S. in library science from University of Illinois at Urbana-Champaign; and a Ph.D. in public administration from the University of Texas at Arlington.

Teresa R. Dalston is currently completing her Ph.D. in information science at the University of North Texas. Dalston is a freelance writer and courseware developer. She also teaches as an adjunct professor at the University of North Texas. She has worked for the National Information Standards Organization, for the National Biological Information Infrastructure Program, and in industry as an applications engineer, web master, project coordinator, researcher, and technical writer. Her goal is to complete her Ph.D. coursework and defense before her son graduates from high school next year and complete her dissertation before her twin daughters graduate two years later.